Church and Society in Documents 100–600 A.D.

edited by

Alan L. Hayes

Canadian Scholars' Press Inc.   Toronto   1995

Church and Society in Documents: 100–600 A.D.

First published in 1995 by
Canadian Scholars' Press Inc.
180 Bloor Street West, Ste. 801
Toronto, Ontario M5S 2V6

Canadian Cataloguing in Publication Data

Main entry under title:

Church and society in documents: 100–600 A.D.

ISBN 1-55130-083-4

1. Church history – Primitive and early church,
ca. 30–600 – Sources.   2. Church and the world –
History – Sources.   I. Hayes, Alan Lauffer.

BR160.A2C58   1995   270.1 C95-931898-4

Page layout by Brad Horning

Printed and bound in Canada

To Margaret Hayes Parsons
My Mother

Table of Contents

Introduction ....: vii

Chapter 1
   The Pliny-Trajan Correspondence 1

Chapter 2
   Didaché 7
   Ignatius, *To the Ephesians* 19

Chapter 3
   Gospel of Thomas 27

Chapter 4
   Justin, *Second Apology* 45

Chapter 5
   Martyrdom of Perpetua 59

Chapter 6
   Hippolytus? *Apostolic Tradition?* 73

Chapter 7
   Origen, "First Homily on the Song of Songs" 97

Chapter 8
Cyprian, *Treatise to Demetrianus* 115

Chapter 9
Acts of the Council of Nicea 135

Chapter 10
Gregory Nazianzen, *Letters 101, 102, 202*
(Against the Apollinarians) 147

Chapter 11
Ambrose, *Letters 20, 21* 165

Chapter 12
John Chrysostom, *Homilies on the Gospel of St. John, 62* 181

Chapter 13
Paulinus of Nola, *Letter 29* 197

Chapter 14
Augustine of Hippo, *Letter 211 ("The Rule")* 215

Chapter 15
Patrick, *Confession* 229

Chapter 16
Pope Leo I, *"The Tome"* 247

Chapter 17
Antonius, *The Life and Daily Mode of Living of
Blessed Simeon the Stylite* 259

Chapter 18
The Penitential of Columbanus 273

Introduction

This book has grown out of an introductory course which I teach at the Toronto School of Theology in the history of Christianity to the year 600. When I first began teaching it, something over twenty years ago now, I began looking for early Christian documents which would fire my students' interest in that seminal era, prompt the kinds of questions of interpretation that would lead them naturally into the art of historiographical criticism, and give substance and colour to crucial historical events and personalities. If a document worked well in seminar discussions I continued to use it, and if it did not, I replaced it. The result is the selection that is offered here.

Out of the thousands of documents that I might have chosen, I have selected nineteen. Several criteria have guided my selection.

First, the documents included here really are primary sources, witnesses *in* the first six centuries *concerning* the first six centuries. They are not later traditions, paraphrases, or summaries. In them, students can read the very words of early Christians, in translation.

Second, these documents are as complete as we have them. They are not excerpts of larger documents. I have thought that documents which were written as a whole should be interpreted as a whole. A problem with excerpts is that it is the one who does the excerpting, not the student, who decides what is important in the document. An unabridged document gives the student better scope for practicing historiographical criticism.

Third, these documents are reasonably short, most of them between ten and twenty pages. Even a student who is taking a heavy load of other courses simultaneously can find time to read one of these documents each week for a term, and re-read it, and reflect on it, and perhaps even write a short essay about it.

Fourth, together these documents illustrate the diversity of early Christian literature, with its many genres, its many cultural settings, its many purposes and functions, and its many theological tendencies. More advanced students might well choose to concentrate on a specific institutional structure, pattern of devotional practice, doctrinal principle, or genre, but I have thought that in a survey course students should have an overview of the larger landscape.

Fifth, the documents open a few windows onto the ordinary life of ordinary Christian communities. In former years a function of a book of Church historical documents was usually to explain how modern denominational doctrine, worship, and institutional structures came to be. I have been more interested in the fascinating complexity of early Christian community. True, the documents we have were written by the educated, not the common, and preserved for their ecclesiastical importance, not for their historical value, but these constraints, though limiting, are not quite fatal.

Sixth, the documents show a few of the many ways in which Church and society interacted. In Pliny's letter we see clues to why a Roman governor might feel obliged to persecute Christians; in Perpetua's diary we see why a Christian might have felt joy in being persecuted. Justin, in his *Apology*, attempts to reconcile his faith with the best in paganism; Cyprian, in his treatise, prefers to dissociate them. In the *Didaché*, the letter of Ignatius, the work known as the *Apostolic Tradition*, and the documents from the Council of Nicea, we see quite different Christian approaches to Church organization; perhaps these diverse approaches reflect diverse social contexts and diverse experiences of the use of power. In the *Gospel of Thomas*, by contrast, Church organization and community seem relatively unimportant. In the works by Origen, Nazianzen, Chrysostom, and Leo we observe different approaches to interpreting Scripture; in the background we may discern the methods and premises of conflicting schools of philosophical thought. Ambrose, as we see in his two letters, invites himself into the conscience of the Emperor; in Paulinus and Simeon the Stylite we see ascetics who in different ways have sought to renounce the Emperor's world altogether. Augustine's vision of Christian community looks in some ways like a reaction against worldly social ideals, but in other ways like a "christianizing" of them. With Patrick and even more with Columbanus, Roman government and culture have grown remote, and Christianity has entered the world of the barbarians.

Finally, most of the documents say something about women, or at least about the issue of gender. I share the desire of most recent historians to discover the usually hidden role of women in society.

I have added my own introduction to each document, along with some study questions. My experience is that a neophyte in history faced with a strange historical document will usually ask, "What should I be looking for?" The best answer is that a new document, like a new friend, will disclose itself to one who is willing to listen. But I have found that the best answer is not always the most pedagogically effective answer. While I believe that beginning students are as capable as seasoned scholars of asking intelligent questions of a document, in fact in some ways more capable, beginning students also usually need at least a provisional context for interpretation and they need to develop confidence in their own common sense. The introductions and study questions are intended to serve these purposes. But it is the document, not the introduction, which is the primary source, and I hope very much that readers will not allow the introduction to control their intepretation of the document. I also hope that students will find more helpful approaches to take and better questions to ask than those which I have provided.

The documents range in date from very roughly the year 100 up to about the year 600. On the earlier end of the chronological range the New Testament is excluded, since by convention New Testament studies comprise an academic field distinct from Church history; those who want to explore the primary documents of the first century may want to consult Steve Mason and Tom Robinson, *An Early Christian Reader* (CSP, 1990). On the later end of the range, the year 600 is frequently taken as the symbolic end of the early period of Church history, before which Christianity is a largely Mediterranean religion, and after which it becomes a largely European religion.

Another teacher would select other documents for a collection such as this. I would not at all want to claim that these nineteen documents are the nineteen most important short documents from the early Church. Moreover, there are several documents which, although they exceed twenty pages, are necessary reading for anyone who is seeking even an elementary understanding of early Christianity. I always ask my own students to read Athanasius' *Life of Antony* and at least books II and III of Augustine's *Confessions*.

In my own teaching, I use these readings in conjunction with one of several available textbooks that survey early Church history in a narrative fashion. I do so for the pedagogical reason that students who know little history, and students who in high school or elsewhere learned to think of history as a chronological collection of personalities with names, events with dates, and ideas with genealogies, feel more secure in new historical territory if they have a story that orders the past into a manageable framework. But I know that if they continue in their study of history, they will sooner or later discover that every element of this manageable framework is undependable. They will discover a multiplicity of competing stories of early Christianity, each one papering over a profusion of cracks in the historical evidence, and each one with its own version of who was important and what motivated people and how things happened and why things happened the way they did. But by then they will have developed their skills in evaluating primary historical evidence, and they will be able to test each of these competing stories. To be free from dependence on someone else's understanding of the past, and to be able to build an understanding of how the world works by reflecting intelligently on dependable evidence, seems to me to be a pre-condition of intellectual, emotional, and spiritual maturity, and a primary goal of education.

I am grateful to my teaching assistants over the years for a number of things, and particularly, so far as this book is concerned, for helping me see which documents worked best in seminar discussions. They include Lawrin Armstrong, Byard Bennett, Craig Cameron, Paul Friesen, Jeannie Loughrey, Mark Steinacher, and Brad Walton. In former years the Toronto School of Theology course in early Christianity was very much a team effort, and even now, when it is divided into independent sections, several of us regularly share thoughts about it with one another. So I am grateful also that several of my colleagues have helped me see how documents might be selected, introduced, used, and interpreted: Phyllis Airhart, Robert Black, Robert Croken, John Grant, Brian Hogan, Thomas McIntire, and the late Michael Sheehan. My wife, the Reverend Morar Murray-Hayes, and my children, Jessica and Alexandra, have been not only very patient but also extremely supportive, and their love holds the rest of my life together. The book is dedicated to my mother, who not only biologically but also intellectually made it possible.

Writing a Short Essay

Where the documents in this book are used for a course in a university, theological school, or elsewhere, the instructor may ask students to write short essays on some of them. Here are guidelines for writing a short essay on an historical document.

1. In preparation for the essay, read the text of the document carefully, and ask yourself historiographical questions about it. An historiographical question is one which relates the document to its historical context. The following are examples of historiographical questions: Who (or what kind of person) wrote it? for what audience? for what reason? at what time and in what place? with what likely effect? What are the author's theological, cultural, and other premises? What particular issues seem to concern the author? Why did the author choose this particular genre of writing? Does the document show signs of being edited? If so, is it possible to distinguish the author's premises, purposes, and historical context from the editor's?

Needless to say, documents don't provide sure answers to all these questions, or to the other questions which you might ask of the document. For some questions the document will provide no evidence at all; for others it may provide ambiguous data that can be interpreted variously.

A key skill for the historian is what Herbert Butterfield called "sympathetic imagination". The unattainable ideal in reading an historical document is to know the author's mind from the inside, to know what the author thought and felt, and why.

2. An essay is the statement, development, and argument of a thesis.

3. The essay should include, usually in the introductory paragraph, a clear statement of a thesis. The thesis statement makes the main point of your essay. It differs from the statement of a theme (which states a topic to be discussed but not what will be said about it). It also differs from a summary (which summarizes the document but doesn't have a point to make about it). You can test whether an introductory statement is a thesis statement by seeing whether you can truthfully precede it with the clause, "This essay aims to demonstrate that...".

The thesis statement should be substantial, not truistic (incapable of being shown false) or trivial. To the question, "Can a valid argument be made against this thesis statement?" the answer should be "yes".

Example of a statement of a theme: "In this paper we will consider Perpetua's diary and explore the cost of her discipleship in a time of persecution."

Example of a summary: "Perpetua was a young woman who was arrested as a Christian in North Africa. The authorities tried very hard to make her recant. While she was in prison, she had several visions, which she recorded in her diary. In the first vision, she saw, etc., etc."

Example of a thesis statement: "[This paper aims to demonstrate that] Perpetua's diary was edited by someone who wanted to show that the authority of prophecy and inspired vision was greater than the authority of the Church's institutional order."

4. After the statement of the thesis in the first paragraph, the second and succeeding paragraphs support the thesis by clarifying it, developing it, qualifying it, and arguing it, with reference to the primary evidence, that is, the evidence of the text itself. This is by far the longest part of the paper, and is called the "exposition."

The exposition must show that the thesis statement, properly understood, is supported by *the primary evidence of the text you are examining*. The views that modern scholars take about the text have no value as evidence, even when they state their opinions very emphatically and publish them in influential textbooks or important journals or expensive encyclopedias. The views of modern scholars may, however, be valuable for sparking your own thinking about the document.

Your objective is to persuade the reader, not that your interpretation is true beyond question, but only that it is more probable than the alternatives. You should therefore identify and examine alternative possible interpretations, and show why you think your own interpretation is preferable. The exposition is thus a movement of persuasive arguments.

5. Each paragraph represents one argument or idea intended to clarify, develop, or support the thesis of the paper. This one argument or idea should be stated in a single topic sentence. This topic sentence should be clarified, developed, qualified, and argued in the rest of the paragraph by reference to one or more examples from the primary text you're considering. In other words, each paragraph supports its topic sentence in the same way that the essay as a whole supports its thesis statement.

Any paragraph which isn't clearly related to the thesis of the essay should either be omitted or else revised to make its relevance clear.

6. Transitions connect paragraphs smoothly so that the reader can follow the line of your argument and can see how each of your points relates to your thesis statement. A transition can be a sentence either at the end of one paragraph or at the beginning of the next. Or it can be a single word or a short phrase, such as "therefore" or "nevertheless".

7. A short essay should end with a paragraph which states a conclusion. The conclusion restates the thesis, sums up the points in the exposition, and connects the thesis to a broader perspective.

8. Avoid over-generalizing. The evidence of a single document is not conclusive proof of the mentality of the author, and it certainly cannot be used for drawing inferences about the entire history of Christianity or even about the early Church. For instance, it cannot be assumed that the liturgical texts found in Hippolytus' *Apostolic Tradition* represent the common practice of worship in the early centuries of the Church. In fact, it can't be demonstrated that the texts were ever used by any Christian community at all.

9. Stay in one tense, either past or present.

10. Don't moralize, and don't pass judgment on historical figures. You cannot know as much as God does about "the very secrets of the heart" or about the events and conditions that shaped the author's

outlook. Don't assume that our world is better than the past or that the past is better than our world. Aim to learn from the past, not to teach it something.

11. Be aware of your own premises, and of the perspective which you're bringing to your reading of the document. Be aware also of the limitations of your premises and your perspective.

A Word on the Texts

For most of the texts reproduced in this volume, many translations are available. I have tried to choose readable and reliable ones. Most texts are followed by endnotes. These are not my own. They reproduce the notes provided by the translator, or, in the case of Chapter 10, by the editor of the translation. Chapter citations of the Psalms will be inconsistent according to whether the translator is referring to a Roman Catholic text or a Protestant text.

1

The Pliny-Trajan Correspondence
Pliny's *Letters*, Book X, 96–97
(112?, Bithynia)

Pliny (Gaius Plinius Caecilius Secundus) was born in 61 or 62 into a wealthy and socially important family. His father died when he was young, and he was adopted by his uncle, whom we know as "the elder Pliny", a natural scientist and writer. He was well educated and won a reputation for his oratorical skills; he served as an advocate or lawyer in the Roman courts. He climbed the ladder of social achievement by being appointed to ever more important civil offices, reaching the pinnacle of prestige, the position of consul, in the year 100. He wrote numerous letters, carefully polished according to the highest rhetorical standards, for publication. In 109 or 110 or 111 the Emperor appointed him governor of the province of Bithynia and Pontus, in northwestern Asia Minor along the south coast of the Black Sea, where he served two years. He carried on a large administrative correspondence with the Emperor, which has been collected into Book X of his *Letters*. This collection includes not only Pliny's letters but also the Emperor's official replies, or "rescripts". This is the only collection of administrative correspondence between a Roman emperor and an imperial officer in Latin literature, and it is therefore an unusually important historical source. After writing these letters Pliny abruptly disappears from history, and there is reason to believe that he died in office in Bithynia.

Trajan (53–117) was born in Seville, in Roman Spain, and was adopted as heir by the Emperor Nerva. He followed Nerva to the imperial throne in 98. He was an efficient administrator who had the Roman infrastructure of roads, bridges, and other public works repaired and extended. He was also an accomplished military commander, popular with the army, and through conquests in Dacia (modern Romania) and Parthia (modern northeast Iran), enlarged the Roman Empire to its widest historical boundaries. In addition, he established a system of welfare for the poor children of Italy. According to a medieval legend, Pope Gregory the Great (540?–604), impressed with Trajan's love of justice, secured the release of his soul from hell.

Pliny, as a governor, enjoyed considerable authority and prestige in the imperial system. A governor was the overseer of a province. The whole Roman Empire outside Italy was divided into provinces (the word means "spheres of responsibility"), which were arrangements for administrative convenience without much regard to cultural, racial, or linguistic realities. In most provinces, the governor was appointed by the Emperor, as Pliny was. A governor would normally expect to serve for about three years. Within his jurisdiction the governor was the commander of military forces, the judge of serious criminal and civil cases, and the chief administrative officer. The province of Bithynia and Pontus had recently developed a reputation for financial irregularity, political disorder, and official corruption, and the Emperor expected Pliny to put matters right.

Many scholars have thought that Pliny wrote his letters primarily to impress the Emperor or to gratify his taste for letter-writing, but others have believed that a provincial governor was indeed expected to be in close contact with the Emperor. The rescripts of the Emperor had legal authority. Trajan's instructions regarding Christians, as reproduced below, guided imperial policy for some time to come. They were reinforced and elaborated by a rescript of Hadrian, Trajan's successor, in 124/125, which can now be read at the end of the *First Apology* of Justin Martyr, or in Eusebius' *Ecclesiastical History*, 4, 9.

Pliny's administrative letters of Book X were not polished literary exercises written for publication, as his other letters were. They were published after his death by an anonymous editor. The editor unfortunately excised the ceremonial greetings and conclusions, and the date and place of writing, which the letters originally must have contained. The letters were published in the early sixteenth century from a Latin manuscript of perhaps the sixth century, which has since been lost.

Questions on the reading

Is Pliny's letter a serious request for advice? If so, what is the problem that he is trying to solve? What information does he actually have about Christianity, and how credible is it? Is anything surprising in his understanding of Christian beliefs and practices? What impact were Christians having on society? What is Pliny's personal attitude towards the Christians, and why might he feel the way he does about them? What does he think of the informants? What appears to be the legal context for his correspondence, and how does he conceive his own role of political leadership in the midst of tensions between Christians and anti-Christians? What legal or political principles lie behind Trajan's rescript (reply)?

Pliny (the Younger) to Trajan

It is my rule, Sire, to refer to you in matters where I am uncertain. For who can better direct my hesitation or instruct my ignorance? I was never present at any trial of Christians; therefore I do not know what are the customary penalties or investigations, and what limits are observed. [2] I have hesitated a great deal on the question whether there should be any distinction of ages; whether the weak should have the same treatment as the more robust; whether those who recant should be pardoned, or whether a man who has ever been a Christian should gain nothing by ceasing to be such; whether the name itself, even if innocent of crime, should be punished, or only the crimes attaching to that name.

Source: Pliny-Trajan correspondence, in Henry Bettenson, ed., *Documents of the Christian Church*, 2nd ed., Oxford University Press, 1967, 3-4.

Meanwhile, this is the course that I have adopted in the case of those brought before me as Christians. [3] I ask them if they are Christians. If they admit it I repeat the question a second and a third time, threatening capital punishment; if they persist I sentence them to death. For I do not doubt that, whatever kind of crime it may be to which they have confessed, their pertinacity and inflexible obstinacy should certainly be punished. [4] There were others who displayed a like madness and whom I reserved to be sent to Rome, since they were Roman citizens.

Thereupon the usual result followed; the very fact of my dealing with the question led to a wider spread of the charge, and a great variety of cases were brought before me. [5] An anonymous pamphlet was issued, containing many names. All who denied that they were or had been Christians I considered should be discharged, because they called upon the gods at my dictation and did reverence, with incense and wine, to your image which I had ordered to be brought forward for this purpose, together with the statues of the deities; and especially because they cursed Christ, a thing which, it is said, genuine Christians cannot be induced to do. [6] Others named by the informer first said that they were Christians and then denied it; declaring that they had been but were so no longer, some having recanted three years or more before and one or two as long ago as twenty years. They all worshipped your image and the statues of the gods and cursed Christ. [7] But they declared that the sum of their guilt or error had amounted only to this, that on an appointed day they had been accustomed to meet before daybreak, and to recite a hymn antiphonally[1] to Christ, as to a god, and to bind themselves by an oath,[2] not for the commission of any crime but to abstain from theft, robbery, adultery and breach of faith, and not to deny a deposit when it was claimed. After the conclusion of this ceremony it was their custom to depart and meet again to take food; but it was ordinary and harmless food, and they had ceased this practice after my edict in which, in accordance with your orders, I had forbidden secret societies. [8] I thought it the more necessary, therefore, to find out what truth there was in this by applying torture to two maidservants, who were called deaconesses.[3] But I found nothing but a depraved and extravagant superstition, and I therefore postponed my examination and had recourse to you for consultation.

[9] The matter seemed to me to justify my consulting you, especially on account of the number of those imperilled; for many persons of all ages and classes and of both sexes are being put in peril by accusation, and this will go on. The contagion of this superstition has spread not only in the cities, but in the villages and rural districts as well; yet it seems capable of being checked and set right. [10] There is no shadow of doubt that the temples, which have been almost deserted, are beginning to be frequented once more, that the sacred rites which have been long neglected are being renewed, and that sacrificial victims are for sale everywhere, whereas, till recently, a buyer was rarely to be found. From this it is easy to imagine what a host of men could be set right, were they given a chance of recantation.

Trajan to Pliny

You have taken the right line, my dear Pliny, in examining the cases of those denounced to you as Christians, for no hard and fast rule can be laid down, of universal application. [2] They are not to be sought out; if they are informed against, and the charge is proved, they are to be punished, with this reservation — that if any one denies that he is a Christian, and actually proves it, that is by worshipping our gods, he shall be pardoned as a result of his recantation, however suspect he may have been with respect to the past. Pamphlets published anonymously should carry no weight in any charge whatsoever. They constitute a very bad precedent, and are also out of keeping with this age.

Notes

1   'carmen . . . dicere secum invicem' — 'carmen,' generally translated 'hymn,' may mean any set form of words; here perhaps a responsorial or antiphonal psalm, or some kind of litany.

2   'sacramentum' — the word chosen by the Christians — might suggest to Romans a conspiracy. The Catilinarian conspirators took a 'sacramentum' (Sall. *Cat.* xxii.).

5

3   'ministrae,' probably represents the Greek διάκονοι. If so, this is the last reference to 'deaconesses' till the fourth century, when they attained some importance in the East.

2

Didaché (Date and Place Unknown)

Ignatius, *To the Ephesians* (Between 98 and 117, Smyrna)

These two documents may possibly be roughly contemporary, and they both take an interest in how the Church should be governed. But their assumptions and perspectives are strikingly different. (Still a third view of Church government, roughly contemporary with Ignatius if not the *Didaché*, can be found in the First Letter of Clement of Rome, especially sections 40-44.)

"Didaché" is the Greek word for "teaching" or "instruction", and the full name of the document is "The Lord's Instruction to the Gentiles through the Twelve Apostles". This very important document was discovered only in modern times, in 1883. It may be a single composition by an individual author, or it may be a compilation of texts by an editor. The name of the author or editor is unknown. The date of the *Didaché* is very controversial, with estimates ranging from the second half of the first century to the early third century. Many who prefer an early date argue that the document reflects a primitive approach to Church government, not an elaborate or stabilized institutional development. Among those who disagree with this view, some question the assumption that institutions always develop from something that looks "primitive" to something that looks "elaborate" or "stabilized", and others think that the author or editor of the document for one reason or another was deliberately pretending to be living in a generation that was already long past. The geographical origins of the *Didaché* are also controversial. The best surviving manuscript copy, which is in the Greek language, comes from Jerusalem, but most of the text is also found copied into a fourth-century Syrian work, and some parts of the text are found as well in a fourth-century Egyptian work. Parts have also been found in Latin, Syriac, Arabic, Ethiopic, and Georgic; presumably these fragments represent translations from the Greek. Given the number of textual traditions and translations, we cannot know with assurance where the *Didaché* was written originally, but we are certainly entitled to conclude that it was widely circulated and well known. The *Didaché* is often classified as a "Church order", a manual of Church law giving instructions for governance, liturgy, and discipline. If it is as early as some think, it may be the model for all later Church orders.

Ignatius, bishop of Antioch, was martyred in Rome during the reign of the emperor Trajan, who ruled from 98 to 117. This we know from a friend of Ignatius' named Polycarp, writing a few years later. Before he was martyred, while he was being transported under guard from Antioch to Rome, Ignatius wrote six letters to Christian churches, and one letter to his friend Polycarp. The one to the Ephesians was written from Smyrna, a port city of western Asia Minor (now Izmir, Turkey). The authenticity of Ignatius' letters is now generally recognized; at one time some Protestant scholars doubted that anyone in the early second century could have made such strong claims for the authority of bishops. The letters are written in Greek, and the manuscript tradition appears to be based on a second-century recension, or manuscript version.

The selections raise the question, How was the Church organized? From reading these selections, you will probably agree that their witness is inconsistent.

Questions on the reading

How is the *Didaché* structured, and what natural divisions are there? To whom is it addressed? What is its purpose? Does it appear to be edited from various documents or written by a single hand? Looking at

Ignatius' *Letter*, how would you describe his personality? What are his chief interests? Now compare the two documents. To whom and for what purpose is each of the authors writing? How do the circumstances of the writing influence what each of them wants to say, and how each of them says it? What ambiguities are there in the text? What alternative forms of organization are apparent in the two documents? What is each author's implicit or explicit theological rationale for the form of organization described? Which comes first, the form of organization or the theological rationale? How can we explain the diversity between these two accounts of Church organization? When and where might you guess that the *Didaché* was written?

The Teaching of the Twelve Apostles, Commonly Called the Didaché

The Text

1. The Lord's Teaching to the Heathen by the Twelve Apostles:

There are two ways, one of life and one of death; and between the two ways there is a great difference.

Now, this is the way of life: "First, you must love God who made you, and second, your neighbor as yourself."[1] And whatever you want people to refrain from doing to you, you must not do to them.[2]

What these maxims teach is this: "Bless those who curse you," and "pray for your enemies." Moreover, fast "for those who persecute you." For "what credit is it to you if you love those who love you? Is that not the way the heathen act?" But "you must love those who hate you,"[3] and then you will make no enemies. "Abstain from carnal passions."[4] If someone strikes you "on the right cheek, turn to him the other too, and

---

Source: "Didaché", from *Early Christian Fathers* edited by Cyril C. Richardson, (Library of Christian Classics, vol. 1), Westminster, 1953, 171-179. Used by permission of Westminster John Knox Press.

you will be perfect."[5] If someone "forces you to go one mile with him, go along with him for two"; if someone robs you "of your overcoat, give him your suit as well."[6] If someone deprives you of "your property, do not ask for it back."[7] (You could not get it back anyway!) "Give to everybody who begs from you, and ask for no return."[8] For the Father wants his own gifts to be universally shared. Happy is the man who gives as the commandment bids him, for he is guiltless! But alas for the man who receives! If he receives because he is in need, he will be guiltless. But if he is not in need he will have to stand trial why he received and for what purpose. He will be thrown into prison and have his action investigated; and "he will not get out until he has paid back the last cent."[9] Indeed, there is a further saying that relates to this: "Let your donation sweat in your hands until you know to whom to give it."[10]

2. The second commandment of the Teaching: "Do not murder; do not commit adultery"; do not corrupt boys; do not fornicate; "do not steal"; do not practice magic; do not go in for sorcery; do not murder a child by abortion or kill a newborn infant. "Do not covet your neighbor's property; do not commit perjury; do not bear false witness";[11] do not slander; do not bear grudges. Do not be double-minded or double-tongued, for a double tongue is "a deadly snare."[12] Your words shall not be dishonest or hollow, but substantiated by action. Do not be greedy or extortionate or hypocritical or malicious or arrogant. Do not plot against your neighbor. Do not hate anybody; but reprove some, pray for others, and still others love more than your own life.

3. My child, flee from all wickedness and from everything of that sort. Do not be irritable, for anger leads to murder. Do not be jealous or contentious or impetuous, for all this breeds murder.

My child, do not be lustful, for lust leads to fornication. Do not use foul language or leer, for all this breeds adultery.

My child, do not be a diviner, for that leads to idolatry. Do not be an enchanter or an astrologer or a magician. Moreover, have no wish to observe or heed such practices, for all this breeds idolatry.

My child, do not be a liar, for lying leads to theft. Do not be avaricious or vain, for all this breeds thievery.

My child, do not be a grumbler, for grumbling leads to blasphemy. Do not be stubborn or evil-minded, for all this breeds blasphemy.

But be humble since "the humble will inherit the earth."[13] Be patient, merciful, harmless, quiet, and good; and always "have respect for the teaching"[14] you have been given. Do not put on airs or give yourself up to presumptuousness. Do not associate with the high and mighty; but be with the upright and humble. Accept whatever happens to you as good, in the realization that nothing occurs apart from God.

4. My child, day and night "you should remember him who preaches God's word to you,"[15] and honor him as you would the Lord. For where the Lord's nature is discussed, there the Lord is. Every day you should seek the company of saints to enjoy their refreshing conversation. You must not start a schism, but reconcile those at strife. "Your judgments must be fair."[16] You must no play favorites when reproving transgressions. You must not be of two minds about your decision.[17]

Do not be one who holds his hand out to take, but shuts it when it comes to giving. If your labor has brought you earnings, pay a ransom for your sins. Do not hesitate to give and do not give with a bad grace; for you will discover who He is that pays you back a reward with a good grace. Do not turn your back on the needy, but share everything with your brother and call nothing your own. For if you have what is eternal in common, how much more should you have what is transient!

Do not neglect your responsibility[18] to your son or your daughter, but from their youth you shall teach them to revere God. Do not be harsh in giving orders to your slaves and slave girls. They hope in the same God as you, and the result may be that they cease to revere the God over you both. For when he comes to call us, he will not respect our station, but will call those whom the Spirit has made ready. You slaves, for your part, must obey your masters with reverence and fear, as if they represented God.

You must hate all hypocrisy and everything which fails to please the Lord. You must not forsake "the Lord's commandments," but "observe" the ones you have been given, "neither adding nor subtracting anything."[19] At the church meeting you must confess your sins, and not approach prayer with a bad conscience. That is the way of life.

5. But the way of death is this: First of all, it is wicked and thoroughly blasphemous: murders, adulteries, lusts, fornications, thefts, idolatries, magic arts, sorceries, robberies, false witness, hypocrisies, duplicity,

deceit, arrogance, malice, stubbornness, greediness, filthy talk, jealousy, audacity, haughtiness, boastfulness.[20]

Those who persecute good people, who hate truth, who love lies, who are ignorant of the reward of uprightness, who do not "abide by goodness"[21] or justice, and are on the alert not for goodness but for evil: gentleness and patience are remote from them. "They love vanity,"[22] "look for profit,"[23] have no pity for the poor, do not exert themselves for the oppressed, ignore their Maker, "murder children,"[24] corrupt God's image, turn their backs on the needy, oppress the afflicted, defend the rich, unjustly condemn the poor, and are thoroughly wicked. My children, may you be saved from all this!

6. See "that no one leads you astray"[25] from this way of the teaching, since such a one's teaching is godless.

If you can bear the Lord's full yoke, you will be perfect. But if you cannot, then do what you can.

Now about food: undertake what you can. But keep strictly away from what is offered to idols, for that implies worshiping dead gods.

7. Now about baptism: this is how to baptize. Give public instruction on all these points, and then "baptize" in running water "in the name of the Father and of the Son and of the Holy Spirit."[26] If you do not have running water, baptize in some other. If you cannot in cold, then in warm. If you have neither, then pour water on the head three times "in the name of the Father, Son, and Holy Spirit."[27] Before the baptism, moreover, the one who baptizes and the one being baptized must fast, and any others who can. And you must tell the one being baptized to fast for one or two days beforehand.

8. Your fasts must not be identical with those of the hypocrites.[28] They fast on Mondays and Thursday; but you should fast on Wednesdays and Fridays.

You must not pray like the hypocrites,[29] but "pray as follows"[30] as the Lord bid us in his gospel:

"Our Father in heaven, hallowed be your name; your Kingdom come; your will be done on earth as it is in heaven; give us today our bread for the morrow; and forgive us our debts as we forgive our debtors. And do not lead us into temptation, but save us from the evil one, for yours is the power and the glory forever."

You should pray in this way three times a day.

9. Now about the Eucharist:[31] This is how to give thanks: First in connection with the cup:[32]

"We thank you, our Father, for the holy vine[33] of David, your child, which you have revealed through Jesus, your child. To you be glory forever."

Then in connection with the piece[34] [broken off the loaf]:

"We thank you, our Father, for the life and knowledge which you have revealed through Jesus, your child. To you be glory forever.

"As this piece [of bread] was scattered over the hills[35] and then was brought together and made one, so let your Church be brought together from the ends of the earth into your Kingdom. For yours is the glory and the power through Jesus Christ forever."

You must not let anyone eat or drink of your Eucharist except those baptized in the Lord's name. For in reference to this the Lord said, "Do not give what is sacred to dogs."[36]

10. After you have finished your meal, say grace[37] in this way:

"We thank you, holy Father, for your sacred name which you have lodged[38] in our hearts, and for the knowledge and faith and immortality which you have revealed through Jesus, your child. To you be the glory forever.

"Almighty Master, 'you have created everything'[39] for the sake of your name, and have given people food and drink to enjoy that they may thank you. But to us you have given spiritual food and drink and eternal life through Jesus, your child.

"Above all, we thank you that you are mighty. To you be glory forever.

"Remember, Lord, your Church, to save it from all evil and to make it perfect by your love. Make it holy, 'and gather' it 'together from the four winds'[40] into your Kingdom which you have made ready for it. For yours is the power and the glory forever."

"Let Grace[41] come and let this world pass away."

"Hosanna to the God of David!"[42]

"If anyone is holy, let him come. If not, let him repent."[43]

"Our Lord, come!"[44]

"Amen."[45]

In the case of the prophets, however, you should let them give thanks in their own way.[46]

11. Now, you should welcome anyone who comes your way and teaches you all we have been saying. But if the teacher proves himself a renegade and by teaching otherwise contradicts all this, pay no attention to him. But if his teaching furthers the Lord's righteousness and knowledge, welcome him as the Lord.

Now about the apostles and prophets: Act in line with the gospel precept.[47] Welcome every apostle on arriving, as if he were the Lord. But he must not stay beyond one day. In case of necessity, however, the next day too. If he stays three days, he is a false prophet. On departing, an apostle must not accept anything save sufficient food to carry him till his next lodging. If he asks for money, he is a false prophet.

While a prophet is making ecstatic utterances,[48] you must not test or examine him. For "every sin will be forgiven," but this sin "will not be forgiven."[49] However, not everybody making ecstatic utterances is a prophet, but only if he behaves like the Lord. It is by their conduct that the false prophet and the [true] prophet can be distinguished. For instance, if a prophet marks out a table in the Spirit,[50] he must not eat from it. If he does, he is a false prophet. Again, every prophet who teaches the truth but fails to practice what he preaches is a false prophet. But every attested and genuine prophet who acts with a view to symbolizing the mystery of the Church,[51] and does not teach you to do all he does, must not be judged by you. His judgment rests with God. For the ancient prophets too acted in this way. But if someone says in the Spirit, "Give me money, or something else," you must not heed him. However, if he tells you to give for others in need, no one must condemn him.

12. Everyone "who comes" to you "in the name of the Lord"[52] must be welcomed. Afterward, when you have tested him, you will find out about him, for you have insight into right and wrong. If it is a traveler who arrives, help him all you can. But he must not stay with you more than two days, or, if necessary, three. If he wants to settle with you and is an artisan, he must work for his living. If, however, he has no trade, use your judgment in taking steps for him to live with you as a Christian

without being idle. If he refuses to do this, he is trading on Christ. You must be on your guard against such people.

13. Every genuine prophet who wants to settle with you "has a right to his support." Similarly, a genuine teacher himself, just like a "workman, has a right to his support."[53] Hence take all the first fruits of vintage and harvest, and of cattle and sheep, and give these first fruits to the prophets. For they are your high priests. If, however, you have no prophet, give them to the poor. If you make bread, take the first fruits and give in accordance with the precept.[54] Similarly, when you open a jar of wine or oil, take the first fruits and give them to the prophets. Indeed, of money, clothes, and of all your possessions, take such first fruits as you think right, and give in accordance with the precept.

14. On every Lord's Day — his special day[55] — come together and break bread and give thanks, first confessing your sins so that your sacrifice may be pure. Anyone at variance with his neighbor must not join you, until they are reconciled, lest your sacrifice be defiled. For it was of this sacrifice that the Lord said, "Always and everywhere offer me a pure sacrifice; for I am a great King, says the Lord, and my name is marveled at by the nations."[56]

15. You must, then, elect for yourselves bishops and deacons who are a credit to the Lord, men who are gentle, generous, faithful, and well tried. For their ministry to you is identical with that of the prophets and teachers. You must not, therefore, despise them, for along with the prophets and teachers they enjoy a place of honor among you.

Furthermore, do not reprove each other angrily, but quietly, as you find it in the gospel. Moreover, if anyone has wronged his neighbor, nobody must speak to him, and he must not hear a word from you, until he repents. Say your prayers, give your charity, and do everything just as you find it in the gospel of our Lord.

16. "Watch" over your life: do not let "your lamps" go out, and do not keep "your loins ungirded"; but "be ready," for "you do not know the hour when our Lord is coming."[57] Meet together frequently in your search for what is good for your souls, since "a lifetime of faith will be of no advantage"[58] to you unless you prove perfect at the very last. For in the final days multitudes of false prophets and seducers will appear. Sheep will turn into wolves, and love into hatred. For with the increase

of iniquity men will hate, persecute, and betray each other. And then the world deceiver will appear in the guise of God's Son. He will work "signs and wonders"[59] and the earth will fall into his hands and he will commit outrages such as have never occurred before. Then humankind will come to the fiery trial "and many will fall away"[60] and perish, "but those who persevere" in their faith "will be saved"[61] by the Curse himself.[62] Then "there will appear the signs"[63] of the Truth: first the sign of stretched-out [hands] in heaven,[64] then the sign of "a trumpet's blast,"[65] and thirdly the resurrection of the dead, though not of all the dead, but as it has been said: "The Lord will come and all his saints with him. Then the world will see the Lord coming on the clouds of the sky."[66]

Notes

1 Matt. 22:37-39; Lev. 19:18.
2 Cf. Matt. 7:12.
3 Matt. 5:44, 46, 47; Luke 6:27, 28, 32, 33.
4 I Peter 2:11.
5 Matt. 5:39, 48; Luke 6:29.
6 Matt. 5:40, 41.
7 Luke 6:30.
8 *Ibid.*
9 Matt. 5:26. This whole section 5 should be compared with Hermas, Mand. 2:4-7, on which it is apparently dependent.
10 Source unknown.
11 Ex. 20:13-17; cf. Matt. 19:18; 5:33.
12 Prov. 21:6.
13 Ps. 37:11; Matt. 5:5.
14 Isa. 66:2.
15 Heb. 13:7.
16 Deut. 1:16, 17; Prov. 31:9.
17 Meaning uncertain.
18 Literally, "Do not withold your hand from . . ."
19 Deut. 4:2; 12:32.

20   Cf. Matt. 15:19; Mark 7:21, 22; Rom. 1:29-31; Gal. 5:19-21.

21   Rom. 12:9.

22   Ps. 4:2.

23   Isa. 1:23.

24   Wis. 12:6.

25   Matt. 24:4.

26   Matt. 28:19.

27   *Ibid.*

28   I.e., the Jews. Cf. Matt. 6:16.

29   Matt. 6:5.

30   Cf. Matt. 6:9-13.

31   I.e., "the Thanksgiving." The term, however, had become a technical one in Christianity for the special giving of thanks at the Lord's Supper. One might render the verbal form ("give thanks"), which immediately follows, as "say grace," for it was out of the Jewish forms for grace before and after meals (accompanied in the one instance by the breaking of bread and in the other by sharing a common cup of wine) that the Christian thanksgivings of the Lord's Supper developed.

32   It is a curious feature of the Didaché that the cup has been displaced from the end of the meal to the very beginning. Equally curious is the absence of any direct reference to the body and blood of Christ.

33   This may be a metaphorical reference to the divine life and knowledge revealed through Jesus (cf. ch. 9:3). It may also refer to the Messianic promise (cf. Isa. 11:1), or to the Messianic community (cf. Ps. 80:8), i.e., the Church.

34   An odd phrase, but one that refers to the Jewish custom (taken over in the Christian Lord's Supper) of grace before meals. The head of the house would distribute to each of the guests a piece of bread broken off a loaf, after uttering the appropriate thanksgiving to God.

35   The reference is likely to the sowing of wheat on the hillsides of Judea.

36   Matt. 7:6.

37   Or "give thanks." See note 31.

38   For the phrase cf. Neh. 1:9.

39   Wis. 1:14; Sir. 18:1; Rev. 4:11.

40   Matt. 24:31.

41   A title for Christ.

42   Cf. Matt. 21:9, 15.

43   Or perhaps "be converted."

44   Cf. I Cor. 16:22.

45   These terse exclamations may be versicles and responses. More likely they derive from the Jewish custom of reading verses concerning Israel's future redemption and glory, after the final benediction.

46   I.e., they are not bound by the texts given.

47   Matt. 10:40, 41.

48   Literally, "speaking in a spirit," i.e., speaking while possessed by a divine or demonic spirit. This whole passage (ch. 11:7-12) is a sort of parallel to Matt. 12:31ff. There is an interpretation of the sin against the Holy Ghost, followed by a comment on good and evil conduct (cf. Matt. 12:33-37), and concluded by the prophets' signs which are suggested by the sign of the Son of Man (Matt. 12:38 ff.).

49   Matt. 12:31.

50   The sense is not clear, but suggests a dramatic portrayal of the Messianic banquet. It was characteristic of the Biblical prophets to drive home their teaching by dramatic and symbolic actions (cf. Jer., ch. 19; Acts 21:11; etc.).

51   Literally, "acts with a view to a worldly mystery of the Church." The meaning is not certain, but some dramatic action, symbolizing the mystical marriage of the Church to Christ, is probably intended. The reference may, indeed, be to the prophet's being accompanied by a spiritual sister (cf. I Cor. 7:36 ff.).

52   Matt. 21:9; Ps. 118:26; cf. John 5:43.

53   Matt. 10:10. The provision for the prophet or teacher to settle and to be supported by the congregation implies the birth of the monarchical episcopate. Note the connection of this with the high priesthood (cf. Hippolytus, Apost. Trad. 3:4) and tithing. No provision is made for the support of the local clergy in ch. 15.

54   Deut. 18:3-5.

55   Literally, "On every Lord's Day of the Lord."

56   Mal. 1:11. 14.

57   Matt. 24:42, 44; Luke 12:35.

58   Barn. 4:9.

59   Matt. 24:24.

60   Matt. 24:10.

61   Matt. 10:22; 24:13.

62   An obscure reference, but possibly meaning the Christ who suffered the death of one accursed (Gal. 3:13; Barn. 7:9). Cf. two other titles for the Christ: Grace (ch. 10:6) and Truth (v. 6).

[63] Matt. 24:32.

[64] Another obscure reference, possibly to the belief that the Christ would appear on a glorified cross. Cf. Barn. 12:2-4.

[65] Matt. 24:31.

[66] Zech. 14:5; I Thess. 3:13; Matt. 24:30.

$\wp$

The Letter of Ignatius, Bishop of Antioch, To the Ephesians

Heartiest greetings of pure joy in Jesus Christ from Ignatius, the "God-inspired,"[1] to the church at Ephesus in Asia.[2] Out of the fullness[3] of God the Father you have been blessed with large numbers and are predestined from eternity to enjoy forever continual and unfading glory. The source of your unity and election is genuine suffering which you undergo by the will of the Father and of Jesus Christ, our God. Hence you deserve to be considered happy.

1. I gave a godly welcome to your church which has so endeared itself to us by reason of your upright nature, marked as it is by faith in Jesus Christ, our Saviour, and by love of him. You are imitators of God; and it was God's blood that stirred you up once more to do the sort of thing you do naturally and have now done to perfection. For you were all zeal to visit me when you heard that I was being shipped as a prisoner from Syria for the sake of our common Name[4] and hope. I hope, indeed, by your prayers to have the good fortune to fight with wild beasts in Rome, so that by doing this I can be a real disciple. In God's name, therefore, I received your large congregation in the person of Onesimus,[5] your bishop in this world,[6] a man whose love is beyond

Source: Ignatius, "To the Ephesiians", in Cyril C. Richardson, ed., *Early Christian Fathers* (Library of Christian Classics, vol. 1), Westminster, 1953, 87-93. Used by permission of Westminster John Knox Press

words. My prayer is that you should love him in the spirit of Jesus Christ and all be like him. Blessed is He who let you have such a bishop. You deserved it.

2. Now about my fellow slave[7] Burrhus, your godly deacon, who has been richly blessed. I very much want him to stay with me. He will thus bring honor on you and the bishop. Crocus too, who is a credit both to God and to you, and whom I received as a model of your love, altogether raised my spirits (May the Father of Jesus Christ grant him a similar comfort!), as did Onesimus, Burrhus, Euplus, and Fronto. In them I saw and loved you all. May I always be glad about you, that is, if I deserve to be! It is right, then, for you to render all glory to Jesus Christ, seeing he has glorified you. Thus, united in your submission, and subject to the bishop and the presbytery, you will be real saints.

3. I do not give you orders as if I were somebody important. For even if I am a prisoner for the Name, I have not yet reached Christian perfection. I am only beginning to be a disciple, so I address you as my fellow students. I needed your coaching in faith, encouragement, endurance, and patience. But since love forbids me to keep silent about you, I hasten to urge you to harmonize your actions with God's mind. For Jesus Christ — that life from which we can't be torn — is the Father's mind, as the bishops too, appointed the world over, reflect the mind of Jesus Christ.

4. Hence you should act in accord with the bishop's mind, as you surely do. Your presbytery, indeed, which deserves its name and is a credit to God, is as closely tied to the bishop as the strings to a harp. Wherefore your accord and harmonious love is a hymn to Jesus Christ. Yes, one and all, you should form yourselves into a choir,[8] so that, in perfect harmony and taking your pitch from God, you may sing in unison and with one voice to the Father through Jesus Christ. Thus he will heed you, and by your good deeds he will recognize you are members of his Son. Therefore you need to abide in irreproachable unity if you really want to be God's members forever.

5. If in so short a time I could get so close to your bishop — I do not mean in a natural way, but in a spiritual — how much more do I congratulate you on having such intimacy with him as the Church enjoys with Jesus Christ, and Jesus Christ with the Father. That is how unity and

harmony come to prevail everywhere. Make no mistake about it. If anyone is not inside the sanctuary,[9] he lacks God's bread.[10] And if the prayer of one or two has great avail, how much more that of the bishop and the total Church. He who fails to join in your worship shows his arrogance by the very fact of becoming a schismatic. It is written, moreover, "God resists the proud."[11] Let us, then, heartily avoid resisting the bishop so that we may be subject to God.

6. The more anyone sees the bishop modestly silent, the more he should revere him. For everyone the Master of the house sends on his business, we ought to receive as the One who sent him. It is clear, then, that we should regard the bishop as the Lord himself. Indeed, Onesimus spoke very highly of your godly conduct, that you were all living by the truth and harboring no sectarianism. Nay, you heed nobody beyond what he has to say truthfully about Jesus Christ.[12]

7. Some, indeed, have a wicked and deceitful habit of flaunting the Name about, while acting in a way unworthy of God. You must avoid them like wild beasts. For they are mad dogs which bite on the sly. You must be on your guard against them, for it is hard to heal their bite. There is only one physician — of flesh yet spiritual, born yet unbegotten, God incarnate, genuine life in the midst of death, sprung from Mary as well as God, first subject to suffering then beyond it — Jesus Christ our Lord.[13]

8. Let no one mislead you, as, indeed, you are not misled, being wholly God's. For when you harbor no dissension that can harass you, then you are indeed living in God's way. A cheap sacrifice[14] I am, but I dedicate myself to you Ephesians — a church forever famous. Carnal people cannot act spiritually,[15] or spiritual people carnally, just as faith cannot act like unbelief, or unbelief like faith. But even what you do in the flesh you do spiritually. For you do everything under Christ's control.[16]

9. I have heard that some strangers came your way with a wicked teaching. But you did not let them sow it among you. You stopped up your ears to prevent admitting what they disseminated. Like stones of God's Temple, ready for a building of God the Father, you are being hoisted up by Jesus Christ, as with a crane (that's the cross!), while the rope you use is the Holy Spirit. Your faith is what lifts you up, while love is the way you ascend to God.

You are all taking part in a religious procession,[17] carrying along with you your God, shrine, Christ, and your holy objects, and decked out from tip to toe in the commandments of Jesus Christ. I too am enjoying it all, because I can talk with you in a letter, and congratulate you on changing your old way of life and setting your love on God alone.

10. "Keep on praying"[18] for others too, for there is a chance of their being converted and getting to God. Let them, then, learn from you at least by your actions. Return their bad temper with gentleness; their boasts with humility; their abuse with prayer. In the face of their error, be "steadfast in the faith."[19] Return their violence with mildness and do not be intent on getting your own back. By our patience let us show we are their brothers, intent on imitating the Lord, seeing which of us can be the more wronged, robbed, and despised. Thus no devil's weed will be found among you; but thoroughly pure and self-controlled, you will remain body and soul united to Jesus Christ.

11. The last days are here. So let us abase ourselves and stand in awe of God's patience, lest it turn out to be our condemnation. Either let us fear the wrath to come or let us value the grace we have: one or the other. Only let our lot be genuine life in Jesus Christ. Do not let anything catch your eye besides him, for whom I carry around these chains — my spiritual pearls! Through them I want to rise from the dead by your prayers. May I ever share in these, so that I may be numbered among the Ephesian Christians who, by the might of Jesus Christ, have always been of one mind with the very apostles. 12. I realize who I am and to whom I am writing. I am a convict; you have been freed. I am in danger; you are safe. You are the route for God's victims.[20] You have been initiated into the [Christian] mysteries with Paul, a real saint and martyr, who deserves to be congratulated. When I come to meet God may I follow in his footsteps, who in all his letters[21] mentions your union with Christ Jesus.

13. Try to gather together more frequently to celebrate God's Eucharist and to praise him. For when you meet with frequency, Satan's powers are overthrown and his destructiveness is undone by the unanimity of your faith. There is nothing better than peace, by which all strife in heaven and earth is done away.

14. You will not overlook any of this if you have a thorough belief in Jesus Christ and love him. That is the beginning and end of life: faith the beginning and love the end.[22] And when the two are united you have God, and everything else that has to do with real goodness is dependent on them. No one who professes faith falls into sin, nor does one who has learned to love, hate. "The tree is known by its fruit."[23] Similarly, those who profess to be Christ's will be recognized by their actions. For what matters is not a momentary act of professing, but being persistently motivated by faith.

15. It is better to keep quiet and be real, than to chatter and be unreal. It is a good thing to teach if, that is, the teachers practice what they preach. There was one such Teacher, who "spoke and it was done"[24]; and what he did in silence[25] is worthy of the Father. They who have really grasped what Jesus said can appreciate his silence. Thus they will be perfect: their words will mean action, and their very silence will reveal their character.

The Lord overlooks nothing. Even secrets are open to him. Let us, then, do everything as if he were dwelling in us. Thus we shall be his temples[26] and he will be within us as our God — as he actually is. This will be clear to us just to the extent that we love him rightly.

16. Make no mistake, my brothers: adulterers will not inherit God's Kingdom.[27] If, then, those who act carnally suffer death, how much more shall those who by wicked teaching corrupt God's faith for which Jesus Christ was crucified. Such a vile creature will go to the unquenchable fire along with anyone who listens to him.

17. The reason the Lord let the ointment be poured on his head was that he might pass on the aroma of incorruption to the Church. Do not be anointed with the foul smell of the teaching of the prince of this world, lest he capture you and rob you of the life ahead of you. Why do we not all come to our senses by accepting God's knowledge, which is Jesus Christ? Why do we stupidly perish, ignoring the gift which the Lord has really sent?

18. I am giving my life (not that it's worth much!)[28] for the cross, which unbelievers find a stumbling block, but which means to us salvation and eternal life. "Where is the wise man? Where is the debater?"[29] Where are the boasts of those supposedly intelligent? For our God, Jesus the

Christ, was conceived by Mary, in God's plan being sprung both from the seed of David[30] and from the Holy Spirit. He was born and baptized that by his Passion he might hallow water.

19. Now, Mary's virginity and her giving birth escaped the notice of the prince of this world, as did the Lord's death — those three secrets crying to be told, but wrought in God's silence.[31] How, then, were they revealed to the ages? A star [32] shone in heaven brighter than all the stars. Its light was indescribable and its novelty caused amazement. The rest of the stars, along with the sun and the moon, formed a ring around it; yet it outshone them all, and there was bewilderment whence this unique novelty had arisen. As a result all magic lost its power and all witchcraft ceased. Ignorance was done away with, and the ancient kingdom [of evil] was utterly destroyed, for God was revealing himself as a man, to bring newness of eternal life.[33] What God had prepared was now beginning. Hence everything was in confusion as the destruction of death was being taken in hand.

20. If Jesus Christ allows me, in answer to your prayers, and it is his will, I will explain to you more about [God's] plan in a second letter I intend to write. I have only touched on this plan in reference to the New Man Jesus Christ, and how it involves believing in him and loving him, and entails his Passion and resurrection. I will do this especially if the Lord shows me that you are all, every one of you, meeting together under the influence of the grace that we owe to the Name,[34] in one faith and in union with Christ, who was "descended from David according to the flesh"[35] and is Son of man and Son of God. At these meetings you should heed the bishop and presbytery attentively, and break one loaf, which is the medicine of immortality, and the antidote which wards off death but yields continuous life in union with Jesus Christ.

21. I am giving my life for you and for those whom you, to God's honor, sent to Smyrna. I am writing to you from there, giving the Lord thanks and embracing Polycarp and you too in my love. Bear me in mind, as Jesus Christ does you. Pray for the church in Syria, whence I am being sent off to Rome as a prisoner. I am the least of the faithful there — yet I have been privileged to serve God's honor. Farewell in God the Father and in Jesus Christ, our common hope.

Notes

1   "Theophorus," literally "God-bearer." It is probably not a proper name but an epithet indicating his prophetic gifts. He is "full of God" (cf. Ignatius' letter to the Magnesians, ch. 14). Perhaps the church at Antioch dubbed him thus.

2   Ephesus, the scene of Paul's mission and traditionally of John's later activity, was the capital of the Roman province of Asia. It was, too, the central port of the trade route which joined the Aegean with the East. Hence the reference in ch. 12:2.

3   The term has a Gnostic ring, *pleroma* referring in later Gnostic systems to the sphere of the divine.

4   I.e., the name of "Christian."

5   In welcoming Onesimus, Ignatius felt that he received the whole Ephesian church which the bishop represented.

6   In contrast to their heavenly bishop, Christ.

7   A Pauline reminiscence. All Christians are slaves of Christ.

8   The many musical metaphors in Ignatius led to the later legend that he had introduced antiphonal singing into the Church (Socrates, *Hist. eccl.*, VI, ch. 8).

9   The metaphor is taken from that area of the Temple in which faithful Jews gathered for the usual sacrifices. It is contrasted with the outer Court of the Gentiles. The point here is that the true Holy Place is the faithful congregation regularly assembled under its bishop.

10   Cf. John 6:33.

11   Prov. 3:34.

12   Adopting the reading of Lightfoot.

13   The first of several compact credal statements in Ignatius. While they are stamped with his originality, they doubtless draw upon primitive formulas used in catechetical instruction and baptism.

14   The term *peripsema* (scum, filth), which occurs several times in Ignatius, was used of common criminals who were sacrificed in times of adversity to avert the wrath of the gods. Ignatius uses it as an expression of humility and devotion, to refer to his anticipated martyrdom.

15   Cf. Rom. 8:5, 8.

16   Literally "in Christ," a phrase which has a wide variety of meaning in Ignatius and is derived from Saint Paul. In the latter, as probably here in Ignatius, the underlying idea parallels that of demon possession (cf. Mark 1:23, "*in* an unclean spirit"). The Christian is "possessed by Christ," is "under his control" and "influence."

17 An abrupt change of metaphor, suggested by the building of a temple. This time the reference is to a heathen procession — perhaps in honor of the Ephesian Artemis. The devotees would be in festive attire and would carry small shrines and amulets of the goddess.

18 I Thess. 5:17.

19 Col. 1:23.

20 Ephesus lay on the route by which criminals from the provinces would be brought to Rome to supply victims for the amphitheater.

21 An exaggeration of the fact that in several of Paul's letters he refers to Ephesus and Ephesians.

22 Cf. I Tim. 1:5.

23 Matt. 12:33.

24 Ps. 33:9.

25 I.e., unobtrusively, and with special reference to his silence at his trial.

26 Cf. I Cor. 3:16.

27 Cf. I Cor. 6:9, 10.

28 See note 14.

29 I Cor. 1:20.

30 Cf. Rom. 1:3.

31 God's modesty and reserve in the incarnation were something for which Satan was unprepared.

32 An expansion of the story in Matt. 2:2, and influenced by Gen. 37:9.

33 Cf. Rom. 6:4.

34 I.e., the name of "Christian."

35 Rom. 1:3.

3 Gospel of Thomas (150? Syria?)

The Gospel of Thomas is one of the New Testament apocrypha. The word "apocrypha" means "hidden". In part an apocryphal work is hidden in that it usually intends to communicate secret knowledge, but more precisely it is hidden in that it is not in the public use of the Church. In other words, an apocryphal work is not Scripture, not recognized as the Church's public written standard of truth or "canon" (a Greek word meaning "measuring stick"). Nevertheless, not every non-canonical work is apocryphal. A work is not apocryphal unless it claims to offer authoritative knowledge about Jesus or the Apostles, or resembles one of the genres of canonical Scripture, such as gospel, epistle, sayings, or acts.

The Gospel of Thomas is also usually, though not always, considered a product of the school of thought called "Christian Gnosticism", which was reasonably widespread in the second century. The term "Gnosticism" describes any movement, school of thought, or theological tendency with certain characteristics. There was never a single organization or philosophy called "Gnosticism", and no single characteristic qualifies a school of thought as Gnostic. Perhaps the most common characteristic of Gnosticism, however, is the view that through knowledge of the truth (the Greek word for "knowledge" is "gnosis") a person might be redeemed from the limitations of human physical nature, especially death. By contrast, the orthodox idea of redemption through the death of Christ on the Cross is quite foreign to Gnosticism. It is often suggested that in the second century Christian Gnosticism was more likely to appeal to the intellectual elite, Christian Orthodoxy to the proletariat. Other common characteristics of Gnosticism include a dualistic view of the universe (spirit is good, matter is evil), arcane speculation about the creation of the universe, and claims of a secret tradition of knowledge. The historical origins of Gnosticism are not known.

Until a few years ago, Gnostic writings were known almost entirely through the quotations and unsympathetic summaries of its orthodox Christian enemies. For instance, the Gospel of Thomas was quoted, on a single occasion, by Hippolytus, a theological controversialist in Rome at the beginning of the third century. And Greek papyri that were later identified as pieces of the Gospel of Thomas were discovered in the late nineteenth century at the ancient site of Oxyrhynchus (now called Behnasa), in middle Egypt, where several Christian monasteries and convents were once located. It was not until December 1945 that the first complete copy of the Gospel of Thomas was found. The story is that two farmers in upper Egypt, who had gone searching for a kind of soil that was useful for fertilizer, were digging at the base of a cliff across the Nile River from Nag Hammadi. They found an ancient jar, about a meter high. When they broke it open, out fell a horde of fourth-century codices (books), most of them previously unknown. The codices were written in Coptic, a form of the Egyptian language which developed in the second century C.E., and which, unlike its predecessors, was written with the Greek alphabet, supplemented by a few extra signs. Along with the Gospel of Thomas, there were 52 other texts. It is believed that most of these Coptic texts were translations of Greek documents, but some scholars make an exception for the Gospel of Thomas. Because of a local blood feud, international politics, and academic intrigues, it was several years before the texts began to be made available, and it was only in 1977 that the entire collection was published. The collection is now often called "the Nag Hammadi library".

It is impossible to know when the various books of the Nag Hammadi library might have been written. With the Gospel of Thomas, an important clue is that some of the Oxyrhynchus papyri are believed to date from perhaps as early as 150. For this and several other reasons, most scholars date the Gospel of Thomas not later than the year 150. Some date it much earlier. Generally, those who believe that the Gospel of Thomas is derived from the Gospels of Matthew and Luke date it later; those who believe that it represents an independent historical tradition, or that it shares a common source with the canonical gospels, date it as early as 60 or 70. Many believe, on grounds of language, content, and circumstance, that it was written in Syria or Mesopotamia.

The Gospel of Thomas is by no means characteristic of the Nag Hammadi collection. Many of the other tractates are highly speculative, nearly to the point of unintelligibility. The Gospel of Thomas is the one, however, which so far has attracted the greatest interest, especially among New Testament scholars, and it is probably the easiest to follow.

Questions on the reading

What is the genre of this work? How might the sayings be categorized? In what various ways do the sayings relate to those in the canonical gospels of Matthew and Luke? What might explain the similarities? What might explain the differences? What might have been the historical relationship between the gospels of Matthew and Luke and the Gospel of Thomas? What historical value does it have, if any, as a source for the teaching of Jesus? To what audience does the Gospel of Thomas appear to be addressed? What is its picture of Jesus? What is its understanding of creation; the relation of matter and spirit; revelation; salvation; holiness; gender? From what you know of Gnosticism, is this is a Gnostic work? Where and when might it have been written or compiled?

The Gospel of Thomas

These are the secret sayings which the living Jesus spoke and which Didymos Judas Thomas wrote down.

(1) And he said, "Whoever finds the interpretation of these sayings will not experience death."

(2) Jesus said, "Let him who seeks continue seeking until he finds. When he finds, he will become troubled. When he becomes troubled, he will be astonished, and he will rule over the all."

(3) Jesus said, "If those who lead you say to you, 'See, the kingdom is in the sky,' then the birds of the sky will precede you. If they say to you, 'It is in the sea,' then the fish will precede you. Rather, the kingdom is inside of you, and it is outside of you. When you come to know yourselves, then you will become known, and you will realize that it is you who are the sons of the living father. But if you will not know yourselves, you dwell in poverty and it is you who are that poverty."

(4) Jesus said, "The man old in days will not hesitate to ask a small child seven days old about the place of life, and he will live. For many who are first will become last, and they will become one and the same."

(5) Jesus said, "Recognize what is in your (sg.) sight, and that which is hidden from you (sg.) will become plain to you (sg.). For there is nothing hidden which will not become manifest."

(6) His disciples questioned him and said to him, "Do you want us to fast? How shall we pray? Shall we give alms? What diet shall we observe?"

Jesus said, "Do not tell lies, and do not do what you hate, for all things are plain in the sight of heaven. For nothing hidden will not become manifest, and nothing covered will remain without being uncovered."

(7) Jesus said, "Blessed is the lion which becomes man when consumed by man; and cursed is the man whom the lion consumes, and the lion becomes man."

Source: "The Gospel of Thomas," trans. H. Koester and T.O. Lambdin, in James Robinson, gen. ed., *The Nag Hammadi Library*, Harper San Francisco, 1988, 124-138.

(8) And he said, "The man is like a wise fisherman who cast his net into the sea and drew it up from the sea full of small fish. Among them the wise fisherman found a fine large fish. He threw all the small fish back into the sea and chose the large fish without difficulty. Whoever has ears to hear, let him hear."

(9) Jesus said, "Now the sower went out, took a handful (of seeds), and scattered them. Some fell on the road; the birds came and gathered them up. Others fell on rock, did not take root in the soil, and did not produce ears. And others fell on thorns; they choked the seed(s) and worms ate them. And others fell on the good soil and it produced good fruit: it bore sixty per measure and a hundred and twenty per measure."

(10) Jesus said, "I have cast fire upon the world, and see, I am guarding it until it blazes."

(11) Jesus said, "This heaven will pass away, and the one above it will pass away. The dead are not alive, and the living will not die. In the days when you consumed what is dead, you made it what is alive. When you come to dwell in the light, what will you do? On the day when you were one you became two. But when you become two, what will you do?"

(12) The disciples said to Jesus, "We know that you will depart from us. Who is to be our leader?"

Jesus said to them, "Wherever you are, you are to go to James the righteous, for whose sake heaven and earth came into being."

(13) Jesus said to his disciples, "Compare me to someone and tell me whom I am like."

Simon Peter said to him, "You are like a righteous angel."

Matthew said to him, "You are like a wise philosopher."

Thomas said to him, "Master, my mouth is wholly incapable of saying whom you are like."

Jesus said, "I am not your (sg.) master. Because you (sg.) have drunk, you (sg.) have become intoxicated from the bubbling spring which I have measured out."

And he took him and withdrew and told him three things. When Thomas returned to his companions, they asked him, "What did Jesus say to you?"

Thomas said to them, "If I tell you one of the things which he told me, you will pick up stones and throw them at me; a fire will come out of the stones and burn you up."

(14) Jesus said to them, "If you fast, you will give rise to sin for yourselves; and if you pray, you will be condemned; and if you give alms, you will do harm to your spirits. When you go into any land and walk about in the districts, if they receive you, eat what they will set before you, and heal the sick among them. For what goes into your mouth will not defile you, but that which issues from your mouth — it is that which will defile you."

(15) Jesus said, "When you see one who was not born of woman, prostrate yourselves on your faces and worship him. That one is your father."

(16) Jesus said, "Men think, perhaps, that it is peace which I have come to cast upon the world. They do not know that it is dissension which I have come to cast upon the earth: fire, sword, and war. For there will be five in a house: three will be against two, and two against three, the father against the son, and the son against the father. And they will stand solitary."

(17) Jesus said, "I shall give you what no eye has seen and what no ear has heard and what no hand has touched and what has never occurred to the human mind."

(18) The disciples said to Jesus, "Tell us how our end will be."

Jesus said, "Have you discovered, then, the beginning, that you look for the end? For where the beginning is, there will the end be. Blessed is he who will take his place in the beginning; he will know the end and will not experience death."

(19) Jesus said, "Blessed is he who came into being before he came into being. If you become my disciples and listen to my words, these stones will minister to you. For there are five trees for you in Paradise which remain undisturbed summer and winter and whose leaves do not fall. Whoever becomes acquainted with them will not experience death."

(20) The disciples said to Jesus, "Tell us what the kingdom of heaven is like."

He said to them, "It is like a mustard seed. It is the smallest of all seeds. But when it falls on tilled soil, it produces a great plant and becomes a shelter for birds of the sky."

(21) Mary said to Jesus, "Whom are your disciples like?"

He said, "They are like children who have settled in a field which is not theirs. When the owners of the field come, they will say, 'Let us have back our field.' They (will) undress in their presence in order to let them have back their field and to give it back to them. Therefore I say, if the owner of a house knows that the thief is coming, he will begin his vigil before he comes and will not let him dig through into his house of his domain to carry away his goods. You (pl.), then, be on your guard against the world. Arm yourselves with great strength lest the robbers find a way to come to you, for the difficulty which you expect will (surely) materialize. Let there be among you a man of understanding. When the grain ripened, he came quickly with his sickle in his hand and reaped it. Whoever has ears to hear, let him hear."

(22) Jesus saw infants being suckled. He said to his disciples, "These infants being suckled are like those who enter the kingdom."

They said to him, "Shall we then, as children, enter the kingdom?"

Jesus said to them, "When you make the two one, and when you make the inside like the outside and the outside like the inside, and the above like the below, and when you make the male and the female one and the same, so that the male not be male nor the female female; and when you fashion eyes in place of an eye, and a hand in place of a hand, and a foot in place of a foot, and a likeness in place of a likeness; then will you enter [the kingdom]."

(23) Jesus said, "I shall choose you, one out of a thousand, and two out of ten thousand, and they shall stand as a single one."

(24) His disciples said to him, "Show us the place where you are, since it is necessary for us to seek it."

He said to them, "Whoever has ears, let him hear. There is light within a man of light, and he lights up the whole world. If he does not shine, he is darkness."

(25) Jesus said, "Love your (sg.) brother like your soul, guard him like the pupil of your eye."

(26) Jesus said, "You (sg.) see the mote in your brother's eye, but you do not see the beam in your own eye. When you cast the beam out of your own eye, then you will see clearly to cast the mote from your brother's eye."

(27) <Jesus said,> "If you do not fast as regards the world, you will not find the kingdom. If you do not observe the Sabbath as a Sabbath, you will not see the father."

(28) Jesus said, "I took my place in the midst of the world, and I appeared to them in flesh. I found all of them intoxicated; I found none of them thirsty. And my soul became afflicted for the sons of men, because they are blind in their hearts and do not have sight; for empty they came into the world, and empty too they seek to leave the world. But for the moment they are intoxicated. When they shake off their wine, then they will repent."

(29) Jesus said, "If the flesh came into being because of spirit, it is a wonder. But if spirit came into being because of the body, it is a wonder of wonders. Indeed, I am amazed at how this great wealth has made its home in this poverty."

(30) Jesus said, "Where there are three gods, they are gods. Where there are two or one, I am with him."

(31) Jesus said, "No prophet is accepted in his own village; no physician heals those who know him."

(32) Jesus said, "A city being built on a high mountain and fortified cannot fall, nor can it be hidden."

(33) Jesus said, "Preach from your (pl.) housetops that which you (sg.) will hear in your (sg.) ear. For no one lights a lamp and puts it under a bushel, nor does he put it in a hidden place, but rather he sets it on a lampstand so that everyone who enters and leaves will see its light."

(34) Jesus said, "If a blind man leads a blind man, they will both fall into a pit."

(35) Jesus said, "It is not possible for anyone to enter the house of a strong man and take it by force unless he binds his hands; then he will (be able to) ransack his house."

(36) Jesus said, "Do not be concerned from morning until evening and from evening until morning about what you will wear."

(37) His disciples said, "When will you become revealed to us and when shall we see you?"

Jesus said, "When you disrobe without being ashamed and take up your garments and place them under your feet like little children and tread on them, then [will you see] the son of the living one, and you will not be afraid."

(38) Jesus said, "Many times have you desired to hear these words which I am saying to you, and you have no one else to hear them from. There will be days when you will look for me and will not find me."

(39) Jesus said, "The pharisees and the scribes have taken the keys of knowledge (gnosis) and hidden them. They themselves have not entered, nor have they allowed to enter those who wish to. You, however, be as wise as serpents and as innocent as doves."

(40) Jesus said, "A grapevine has been planted outside of the father, but being unsound, it will be pulled up by its roots and destroyed."

(41) Jesus said, "Whoever has something in his hand will receive more, and whoever has nothing will be deprived of even the little he has."

(42) Jesus said, "Become passers-by."

(43) His disciples said to him, "Who are you, that you should say these things to us?"

<Jesus said to them,> "You do not realize who I am from what I say to you, but you have become like the Jews, for they (either) love the tree and hate its fruit (or) love the fruit and hate the tree."

(44) Jesus said, "Whoever blasphemes against the father will be forgiven, and whoever blasphemes against the son will be forgiven, but whoever blasphemes against the holy spirit will not be forgiven either on earth or in heaven."

(45) Jesus said, "Grapes are not harvested from thorns, nor are figs gathered from thistles, for they do not produce fruit. A good man brings forth good from his storehouse; an evil man brings forth evil things from his evil storehouse, which is in his heart, and says evil things. For out of the abundance of the heart he brings forth evil things."

(46) Jesus said, "Among those born of women, from Adam until John the Baptist, there is no one so superior to John the Baptist that his eyes should not be lowered (before him). Yet I have said, whichever one of you comes to be a child will be acquainted with the kingdom and will become superior to John."

(47) Jesus said, "It is impossible for a man to mount two horses or to stretch two bows. And it is impossible for a servant to serve two masters; otherwise, he will honor the one and treat the other contemptuously. No man drinks old wine and immediately desires to drink new wine. And new wine is not put into old wineskins, lest they burst; nor is old wine put into a new wineskin, lest it spoil it. An old patch is not sewn into a new garment, because a tear would result."

(48) Jesus said, "If two make peace with each other in this one house, they will say to the mountain, 'Move away,' and it will move away."

(49) Jesus said, "Blessed are the solitary and elect, for you will find the kingdom. For you are from it, and to it you will return."

(50) Jesus said, "If they say to you, 'Where did you come from?', say to them, 'We came from the light, the place where the light came into being on its own accord and established [itself] and became manifest through their image.' If they say to you, 'Is it you?', say, 'We are its children, and we are the elect of the living father.' If they ask you, 'What is the sign of your father in you?,' say to them, 'It is movement and repose.'"

(51) His disciples said to him, "When will the repose of the dead come about, and when will the new world come?"

He said to them, "What you look forward to has already come, but you do not recognize it."

(52) His disciples said to him, "Twenty-four prophets spoke in Israel, and all of them spoke in you."

He said to them, "You have omitted the one living in your presence and have spoken (only) of the dead."

(53) His disciples said to him, "Is circumcision beneficial or not?"

He said to them, "If it were beneficial, their father would beget them already circumcised from their mother. Rather, the true circumcision in spirit has become completely profitable."

(54) Jesus said, "Blessed are the poor, for yours is the kingdom of heaven."

(55) Jesus said, "Whoever does not hate his father and his mother cannot become a disciple to me. And whoever does not hate his brothers and sisters and take up his cross in my way will not be worthy of me."

(56) Jesus said, "Whoever has come to understand the world has found (only) a corpse, and whoever has found a corpse is superior to the world."

(57) Jesus said, "The kingdom of the father is like a man who had [good] seed. His enemy came by night and sowed weeds among the good seed. The man did not allow them to pull up the weeds; he said to them, 'I am afraid that you will go intending to pull up the weeds and pull up the wheat along with them.' For on the day of the harvest the weeds will be plainly visible, and they will be pulled up and burned."

(58) Jesus said, "Blessed is the man who has suffered and found life."

(59) Jesus said, "Take heed of the living one while you are alive, lest you die and seek to see him and be unable to do so."

(60) <They saw> a Samaritan carrying a lamb on his way to Judea. He said to his disciples, "That man is round about the lamb."

They said to him, "So that he may kill it and eat it."

He said to them, "While it is alive, he will not eat it, but only when he has killed it and it has become a corpse."

They said to him, "He cannot do so otherwise."

He said to them, "You too, look for a place for yourselves within repose, lest you become a corpse and be eaten."

(61) Jesus said, "Two will rest on a bed: the one will die, and the other will live."

Salome said, "Who are you, man, that you . . . have come up on my couch and eaten from my table?"

Jesus said to her, "I am he who exists from the undivided. I was given some of the things of my father."

< . . . > "I am your disciple."

< . . . > "Therefore I say, if he is destroyed he will be filled with light, but if he is divided, he will be filled with darkness."

(62) Jesus said, "It is to those [who are worthy of my] mysteries that I tell my mysteries. Do no let your (sg.) left hand know what your (sg.) right hand is doing."

(63) Jesus said, "There was a rich man who had much money. He said, 'I shall put my money to use so that I may sow, reap, plant, and fill my storehouse with produce, with the result that I shall lack nothing.' Such were his intentions, but that same night he died. Let him who has ears hear."

(64) Jesus said, "A man had received visitors. And when he had prepared the dinner, he sent his servant to invite the guests. He went to the first one and said to him, 'My master invites you.' He said, 'I have claims against some merchants. They are coming to me this evening. I must go and give them my orders. I ask to be excused from the dinner.'" He went to another and said to him, 'My master has invited you.' He said to him, 'I have just bought a house and am required for the day. I shall not have any spare time.' He went to another and said to him, 'My master invites you.' He said to him, ' My friend is going to get married, and I am to prepare the banquet. I shall not be able to come. I ask to be excused from the dinner.' He went to another and said to him, 'My master invites you.' He said to him, 'I have just bought a farm, and I am on my way to collect the rent. I shall not be able to come. I ask to be excused.' The servant returned and said to his master, 'Those whom you invited to the dinner have asked to be excused.' The master said to his servant, 'Go outside to the streets and bring back those whom you happen to meet, so that they may dine.' Businessmen and merchants [will] not enter the places of my father."

(65) He said, "There was a good man who owned a vineyard. He leased it to tenant farmers so that they might work it and he might collect the produce from them. He sent his servant so that the tenants might give him the produce of the vineyard. They seized his servant and beat him, all but killing him. The servant went back and told his master. The master said, 'Perhaps he did not recognize them.' He sent another servant. The tenants beat this one as well. Then the owner sent his son and said, 'Perhaps they will show respect to my son.' Because the tenants knew that it was he who was the heir to the vineyard, they seized him and killed him. Let him who has ears hear."

(66) Jesus said, "Show me the stone which the builders have rejected. That one is the cornerstone."

(67) Jesus said, "If one who knows the all still feels a personal deficiency, he is completely deficient."

(68) Jesus said, "Blessed are you when you are hated and persecuted. Wherever you have been persecuted they will find no place."

(69) Jesus said, "Blessed are they who have been persecuted within themselves. It is they who have truly come to know the father. Blessed are the hungry, for the belly of him who desires will be filled."

(70) Jesus said, "That which you have will save you if you bring it forth from yourselves. That which you do not have within you [will] kill you if you do not have it within you."

(71) Jesus said, "I shall [destroy this] house, and no one will be able to build it [. . .]"

(72) [A man said] to him, "Tell my brothers to divide my father's possessions with me."

He said to him, "O man, who has made me a divider?"

He turned to his disciples and said to them, "I am not a divider, am I?"

(73) Jesus said, "The harvest is great but the laborers are few. Beseech the lord, therefore, to send out laborers to the harvest."

(74) He said, "O lord, there are many around the drinking trough, but there is nothing in the cistern."

(75) Jesus said, "Many are standing at the door, but it is the solitary who will enter the bridal chamber."

(76) Jesus said, "The kingdom of the father is like a merchant who had a consignment of merchandise and who discovered a pearl. That merchant was shrewd. He sold the merchandise and bought the pearl alone for himself. You too, seek his unfailing and enduring treasure where no moth comes near to devour and no worm destroys."

(77) Jesus said, "It is I who am the light which is above them all. It is I who am the all. From me did the all come forth, and unto me did the all extend. Split a piece of wood, and I am there. Lift up the stone, and you will find me there."

(78) Jesus said, "Why have you come out into the desert? To see a reed shaken by the wind? And to see a man clothed in fine garments [like

your] kings and your great men? Upon them are the fine garments, and they are unable to discern the truth."

(79) A woman from the crowd said to him, "Blessed are the womb which bore you and the breasts which nourished you."

He said to [her], "Blessed are those who have heard the word of the father and have truly kept it. For there will be days when you (pl.) will say, 'Blessed are the womb which has not conceived and the breasts which have not given milk.'"

(80) Jesus said, "He who has recognized the world has found the body, but he who has found the body is superior to the world."

(81) Jesus said, "Let him who has grown rich be king, and let him who possesses power renounce it."

(82) Jesus said, "He who is near me is near the fire, and he who is far from me is far from the kingdom."

(83) Jesus said, "The images are manifest to man, but the light in them remains concealed in the image of the light of the father. He will become manifest, but his image will remain concealed by his light."

(84) Jesus said, "When you see your likeness, you rejoice. But when you see your images which came into being before you, and which neither die nor become manifest, how much you will have to bear!"

(85) Jesus said, "Adam came into being from a great power and a great wealth, but he did not become worthy of you. For had he been worthy, [he would] not [have experienced] death."

(86) Jesus said, "[The foxes have their holes] and the birds have their nests, but the son of man has no place to lay his head and rest."

(87) Jesus said, "Wretched is the body that is dependent upon a body, and wretched is the soul that is dependent on these two."

(88) Jesus said, "The angels and the prophets will come to you and give to you those things you (already) have. And you too, give them those things which you have, and say to yourselves, 'When will they come and take what is theirs?'"

(89) Jesus said, "Why do you wash the outside of the cup? Do you not realize that he who made the inside is the same one who made the outside?"

(90) Jesus said, "Come unto me, for my yoke is easy and my lordship is mild, and you will find repose for yourselves."

(91) They said to him, "Tell us who you are so that we may believe in you."

He said to them, "You read the face of the sky and of the earth, but you have not recognized the one who is before you, and you do not know how to read this moment."

(92) Jesus said, "Seek and you will find. Yet, what you asked me about in former times and which I did not tell you then, now I do desire to tell, but you do not inquire after it."

(93) <Jesus said,> "Do not give what is holy to dogs, lest they throw them on the dung heap. Do not throw the pearls [to] swine, lest they . . . it [. . .]."

(94) Jesus [said], "He who seeks will find, and [he who knocks] will be let in."

(95) [Jesus said], "If you have money, do not lend it at interest, but give [it] to one from whom you will not get it back."

(96) Jesus said, "The kingdom of the father is like [a certain] woman. She took a little leaven, [concealed] it in some dough, and made it into large loaves. Let him who has ears hear."

(97) Jesus said, "The kingdom of the [father] is like a certain woman who was carrying a [jar] full of meal. While she was walking [on the] road, still some distance from home, the handle of the jar broke and the meal emptied out behind her [on] the road. She did not realize it; she had noticed no accident. When she reached her house, she set the jar down and found it empty."

(98) Jesus said, "The kingdom of the father is like a certain man who wanted to kill a powerful man. In his own house he drew his sword and stuck it into the wall in order to find out whether his hand could carry through. Then he slew the powerful man."

(99) The disciples said to him, "Your brothers and your mother are standing outside."

He said to them, "Those here who do the will of my father are my brothers and my mother. It is they who will enter the kingdom of my father."

(100) They showed Jesus a gold coin and said to him, "Caesar's men demand taxes from us."

He said to them, "Give Caesar what belongs to Caesar, give God what belongs to God, and give me what is mine."

(101) <Jesus said,> "Whoever does not hate his [father] and his mother as I do cannot become a [disciple] to me. And whoever does [not] love his [father and] his mother as I do cannot become a [disciple to] me. For my mother [. . .], but [my] true [mother] gave me life."

(102) Jesus said, "Woe to the pharisees, for they are like a dog sleeping in the manger of oxen, for neither does he eat nor does he [let] the oxen eat."

(103) Jesus said, "Fortunate is the man who knows where the brigands will enter, so that [he] may get up, muster his domain, and arm himself before they invade."

(104) They said to Jesus, "Come, let us pray today and let us fast."

Jesus said, "What is the sin that I have committed, or wherein have I been defeated? But when the bridegroom leaves the bridal chamber, then let them fast and pray."

(105) Jesus said, "He who knows the father and the mother will be called the son of a harlot."

(106) Jesus said, "When you make the two one, you will become the sons of man, and when you say, 'Mountain, move away,' it will move away."

(107) Jesus said, "The kingdom is like a shepherd who had a hundred sheep. One of them, the largest went astray. He left the ninety-nine and looked for that one until he found it. When he had gone to such trouble, he said to the sheep, 'I care for you more than the ninety-nine.'"

(108) Jesus said, "He who will drink from my mouth will become like me. I myself shall become he, and the things that are hidden will be revealed to him."

(109) Jesus said, "The kingdom is like a man who had a [hidden] treasure in his field without knowing it. And [after] he died, he left it to his [son]. The son [did] not know (about the treasure). He inherited the field and sold [it]. And the one who bought it went plowing and [found]

the treasure. He began to lend money at interest to whomever he wished."

(110) Jesus said, "Whoever finds the world and becomes rich, let him renounce the world."

(111) Jesus said, "The heavens and the earth will be rolled up in your presence. And the one who lives from the living one will not see death." Does not Jesus say, "Whoever finds himself is superior to the world"?

(112) Jesus said, "Woe to the flesh that depends on the soul; woe to the soul that depends on the flesh."

(113) His disciples said to him, "When will the kingdom come?"

<Jesus said,> "It will not come by waiting for it. It will not be a matter of saying 'here it is' or 'there it is'. Rather, the kingdom of the father is spread out upon the earth, and men do not see it."

(114) Simon Peter said to them, "Let Mary leave us, for women are not worthy of life."

Jesus said, "I myself shall lead her in order to make her male, so that she too may become a living spirit resembling you males. For every woman who will make herself male will enter the kingdom of heaven."

The Gospel

According to Thomas

4 Justin, *Second Apology* (150?, Rome)

Justin (100?-165) is usually called "Justin Martyr" because he was martyred in about 165. He is the most important of the second-century "apologists"; "apology" is used in the sense of "defence", and a Christian apologist is one who defends Christianity against its critics and persecutors. Three of Justin's works have survived. His *First and Second Apologies* are addressed to pagans, and portray Christianity as the fulfillment of the philosophical, educational, and humane ideals of pagan culture. In particular, they attempt to relate Christian truth quite closely to the school of thought derived from the ancient Greek philosopher Plato. Thus while arguing the superiority of Christianity, Justin is also building intellectual bridges to paganism. His *Dialogue with Trypho the Jew* is a Christian apology with the Church's educated Jewish opponents in mind. It is represented as a two-day debate between Justin and a Jewish rabbi named Trypho and some of his friends. In this work Justin claims the Old Testament for Christianity, and, following the strategy of the *Apologies*, argues the superiority of Christianity while also building intellectual bridges to Judaism.

Much of what we know about Justin personally comes from chapters 2–8 of the *Dialogue*, where he speaks of his own intellectual development and conversion. He was born of pagan parents in Samaria, and as a young man sought the meaning of life in various philosophical schools (Stoicism, Aristotelianism, Pythagoreanism, Platonism). In about 132 he converted to Christianity as the truest philosophy. He became an itinerant

Christian teacher, but he taught in the style of a pagan philosopher; he even dressed after the manner of a philosopher by wearing a pallium, a kind of cloak. At some point Justin seems to have moved to Rome, where he opened a Christian school. He wrote a large number of works, although only the two *Apologies* and the *Dialogue* have survived. His life drew to a close after a pagan philosophical opponent named Crescens, from the school of thought called Cynicism, denounced him to the authorities as a Christian. Justin was arrested, and he refused to abjure his Christianity. According to a narrative of his martyrdom which appears to be based on court records, he was scourged and beheaded, along with six companions.

Justin wrote in Greek. His three extant works have come to us through a manuscript copied in 1364. Although the manuscript distinguishes the *First* and *Second Apologies*, many modern critics believe that the *Second* is a conclusion or appendix of the *First*. Nevertheless, the *Second Apology* presented here can be read as a self-contained whole. The document is addressed to one Urbicus, who was consul under the Emperor Antoninus Pius, who reigned from 138 to 161.

Questions on the reading

What event, according to Justin, has prompted his letter? What can be known from the document about the social context in which it was written? Why does Justin think that the pagans are critical of Christianity? What does he mean, in chapter 12, by the phrase "who approves of the eating of human flesh"? Why does Justin think that Christians are being persecuted? How does Justin understand God; Christ; the promised end of the world; the Christian faith? How does he relate Christianity to paganism? What kinds of arguments and rhetorical techniques does he use? In what ways might his arguments be persuasive to his intended readers; in what ways not? How has Justin been influenced by his reading of philosophy? What is the character of the inter-faith dialogue being conducted by Crescens and Justin? Does this reading appear to be a self-contained document, or might it have at one point belonged to a larger one?

Justin, Second Apology

Chapter 1

The things that have lately taken place in your city under Urbicus, and the evil deeds that are likewise being perpetrated without reason by your governors, have forced me to compose this address for you Romans who are men of feelings like ours and are our brethren, even though you fail to realize it or refuse to admit it because of your pride in your so-called dignities. Everywhere, indeed, whoever is chastened by father, or neighbor, or child, or friend, or brother, or husband, or wife for any shortcoming, such as being stubborn, and pleasure-loving, and difficult to urge to good (except those who believe that the wicked and sensual shall suffer the punishment of eternal fire, but that the virtuous and Christ-like, *i.e.*, those who have become Christians, shall live with God free from all pain) — these and the wicked demons who hate us so, and have as their slaves and worshippers such men as the above-mentioned judges, compel them, like rulers under demoniacal influence, to put us to death. That you may clearly understand the reason for all that took place under Urbicus I will now tell you just what happened.

Chapter 2

There was a certain woman who lived with an unchaste husband, and she, too, had once been unchaste. After learning the doctrines of Christ, she became a self-controlled person and she tried to effect a similar change in her husband, explaining the Christian teachings and warning him of the eternal punishment by fire reserved for those who live without chastity or right reason. But by clinging to the same shameful conduct he lost his wife's affections, and she desired a divorce from him because she considered it sinful to live any longer with a husband who sought in every way those means of sensual pleasure contrary to the law of nature and in violation of every right. However, she forced herself to stay with him after her friends convinced her that it was advisable to remain with him in the hope that at some future time he might change

Source: Justin, *Second Apology*, trans. Thomas B. Falls (Fathers of the Church, vol. 6), N.Y.: Christian Heritage Inc., 1948, 119-135. Reprinted by permission of the Catholic University of America Press.

his ways. But when her husband went to Alexandria and the report reached her that his conduct was worse than ever, she, in order not to participate in his sinful and impious acts by continuing to live with him by sharing his table and his bed, gave him what you term a bill of divorce and left him. But that gallant and gentlemanly husband — instead of being delighted that those evil actions which she used to commit so recklessly with servants and employees in those days when she took pleasure in drunkenness and every wicked action, she had now discontinued, and wanted him to do the same — when she left him against his will, brought a charge against her, claiming that she was a Christian. And she presented a petition to you, O Emperor, asking that she might be permitted first to set her household affairs in order, and then, after that was done she would defend herself against the accusation. You gave your permission. When her former husband could not answer her, he thus turned his attack on a certain Ptolemaeus, who had instructed her in Christian doctrine, in the following way. He induced his personal friend, a centurion, to summon Ptolemaeus and ask him just one question: Was he a Christian? And Ptolemaeus, being of a truthful and not deceitful or mendacious nature, confessed that he was a Christian, and was therefore placed in chains by the centurion and mistreated in prison for a long time. At length, when he appeared before Urbicus for judgment, he was again asked this one question: Was he a Christian? And again, being aware of the benefits he had gained through the teaching of Christ, he confessed to be a member of the school of divine virtue. For he who denies anything, either does so because he condemns the thing itself, or he avoids confessing it because he deems himself unworthy of and alien to it; neither of which applies to the true Christian. When Urbicus ordered him to be led away to execution, a certain Lucius, also a Christian, realizing how unreasonable the sentence was, said to Urbicus: 'What is the reason for this sentence? Why have you punished this man who is not an adulterer, or fornicator, or murderer, or thief, or robber, nor in a word convicted of any crime at all, but only confesses that he bears the name of Christian. Your judgment, Urbicus, does not become the Emperor Pius, nor the Philosopher, son of Caesar, nor the sacred Senate.' The only answer he made to Lucius was this: 'You also seem to be one [of this class].' And when Lucius replied, 'I certainly am,' he ordered him also to be led away to execution. And Lucius expressed his thanks, since he knew that he would soon be freed from such evil rulers, and would go to the Father and King of Heaven. A third Christian also came forward, and was likewise condemned to punishment.

Chapter 3

I also expect to be the victim of a plot and to be affixed to the stake by those just mentioned, or perhaps even by Crescens, that lover of fanfare and ostentation. For that man does not deserve the name of lover of wisdom, since he accuses us publicly in matters of which he is ignorant, claiming that Christians are atheists and irreligious, and doing this just to please and to gain the support of the deceived mob. If, indeed, he attacks us without studying the teachings of Christ, he is positively wicked, and far worse than illiterate — persons are generally careful not to argue or lie about matters of which they are ignorant. On the other hand, if he has studied them [the teachings of Christ] and has not grasped their grandeur, or, if he has and acts as he does in order not to appear to be a Christian, he is much more vile and evil, because he is then inferior even to a slave in popular and unreasonable opinion and fear. I want you to know that I put certain questions to him on this matter and I learned most assuredly that he truly knows nothing. And to show that I speak the truth, I am prepared, if our debate has not already been reported to you, to repeat it in your presence. Such a permission would be an act worthy of a royal ruler. But if my questions and his replies were brought to your attention, it is evident to you that he knows nothing of our teachings, or, if he does know them, but, through fear of his hearers, dares not utter them, as Socrates would have, then he proves himself to be, as I said before, not a lover of wisdom, but a lover of false opinions, who disregards that praiseworthy saying of Socrates: 'But no man must be honored before the truth.' However, it is impossible for a Cynic like Crescens, who considers the last end to be indifferent, to recognize any good but indifference.

Chapter 4

Lest any one should say to us, 'All of you, go, kill yourselves and thus go immediately to God, and save us the trouble,' I will explain why we do not do that, and why, when interrogated, we boldly acknowledge our faith. We have been taught that God did not create the world without a purpose, but that He did so for the sake of humankind, for we have stated before that God is pleased with those who imitate His perfections, but is displeased with those who choose evil, either in word or in deed. If, then, we should all kill ourselves we would be the cause, as far as it is up to us, why no one would be born and be instructed in the divine doctrines, or even why the human race might cease to exist; if we do act thus, we ourselves will be opposing the will of God. But when we are interrogated we do not deny our faith, for we are not conscious of having done any wrong, but we do consider it ungodly always not to tell the truth, which we also realize is pleasing to God; and we also now want to free you from an unfair prejudice.

Chapter 5

But if anyone should think that, if we profess God to be our protector, we should not, as we admit, be overpowered and molested by unjust persons — this difficulty, too, I will remove. When God made the universe and put all earthly things under human dominion, and arranged the heavenly bodies for the increase of fruits and the change of seasons, and decreed a divine law for these, which He apparently also created for our sake, He appointed His angels, whom He placed over humankind, to look after people and all things under heaven. But the angels violated their charge, fell into sin with women and begot children who are called demons. Moreover, they subsequently subjected the human race to themselves, partly by magic writings, partly by the fear they instilled into them and the punishments they inflicted upon them, and partly by instructing them in the use of sacrifices, incense, and libations, which they really needed after becoming slaves of their lustful passions; and they engendered murders, wars, adulteries, all sorts of dissipation, and every species of sin. Thus it was that the poets and writers of legends, unaware that the bad angels and the demons begotten by them did those things to men and women, to cities and nations, ascribed them to [their] god himself [Jupiter] and to those whom they thought were sons of his seed and to the children of those whom they called his brothers, Neptune and Pluto, and to the children of their children. For they called them by the name each of the bad angels had bestowed upon himself and his children.

Chapter 6

No proper name has been bestowed upon God, the Father of all, since He is unbegotten. For, whoever has a proper name received it from a person older than himself. The words Father, and God, and Creator, and Lord, and Master are not real names, but rather terms of address derived from His beneficent deeds. But His Son, who alone is properly called Son, the Word, who was with Him [God, the Father] and was begotten before all things, when in the beginning He [God, the Father] created and arranged all things through Him [the Son], is called Christ, because He was anointed and because God the Father arranged all the things of creation through Him. This name also has an unknown meaning, just as the term 'God,' which is not a real name, but the expression of a human innate opinion of a thing that can scarcely be defined. But 'Jesus,' which is His name both as Man and Savior, has a meaning. For He also became man, as we stated, and was born in accordance with the will of God the Father for the benefit of believers, and for the defeat of the demons. Even now, your own eyes will teach you the truth of this last statement. For many demoniacs throughout the entire world, and even in your own city, were exorcised by many of our Christians in the name of Jesus Christ, who was crucified under Pontius Pilate; and our people cured them, and they still cure others by rendering helpless and dispelling the demons who had taken possession of these men, even when they could not be cured by all the other exorcists, and exploiters of incantations and drugs.

Chapter 7

Therefore God postpones the collapse and dissolution of the universe (through which the bad angels, the demons, and people would cease to exist), because of the Christian seed, which He knows to be the cause in nature [of the world's preservation]. If such were not the case, it would be impossible for you to do the things you do and be influenced by the evil demons; but the fire of judgment would descend and would completely dissolve everything, just as the flood waters once left no one but him, with his family, whom we call Noah and you call Deucalion, from whom in turn so many have been born, some of them bad, others good. In this manner, we claim that the world will finally be destroyed by fire, and not, as the Stoics believe, because all things change into one another according to their disgraceful doctrine of metamorphosis. Nor do we teach [as do the Stoics] that people act and suffer according to the dictates of fate, but that by their own free will people act either well or evilly; and that through the influence of evil demons good people, such as Socrates and the like, are persecuted and imprisoned, while Sardanapalus, Epicurus, and the like seem to be endowed with wealth and glory. But the Stoics, ignorant of this demoniacal influence, claimed that everything takes place by the necessity of fate. But, since God from the very beginning created the race of angels and human beings with free will, they will justly pay the penalty in everlasting fire for the sins they have committed. Indeed, every creature is capable, by nature, of vice and of virtue. Nor would any action of theirs be worthy of praise unless they had the power to incline to either [vice or virtue]. The truth of this is shown everywhere by those legislators and philosophers who, acting according to right reason, have ordered some things to be done and others to be avoided. The Stoic philosophers also, in their moral teaching, always respect the same principles, so it is easily seen how wrong they are in their teaching on principles and incorporeal beings. For, if they state that human acts occur by fate, they will admit either that God is nothing else than those things which continually turn and change and dissolve into the same elements, and will seem to understand only corruptible things, and to affirm that God himself both in part and in whole is in every sin; or else that neither vice nor virtue is anything — which is against every sound idea, reason, and mind.

Chapter 8

We know that the followers of the Stoic teaching, because they were praiseworthy at least in their ethics, as were also the poets in some respects, because of the seed of reason implanted in all mankind, were hated and killed. As examples, we could mention Heraclitus, as we already stated, and Musonius, of our own times, and others. For, as we pointed out, the demons always brought it about that everyone, who strives in any way to live according to right reason and to avoid evil, be an object of hatred. Nor is it surprising that the demons are proved to be the cause why they are much more hated who do not live according to only a part of the seminal word, but by the knowledge and consideration of the whole Word, which is Christ. But these demons shall suffer just punishment and torments, confined to everlasting fire; for the fact that they are overcome even now by people in the name of Jesus Christ is a sign that they and their followers will be punished in eternal fire. All the prophets foretold that it would happen thus, and so taught Jesus, our Teacher.

Chapter 9

Lest any one repeat the mistake of those so-called philosophers who claim that our statements that the sinners are punished in everlasting fire are just boastful words calculated to instill terror, and that we want people to live a virtuous life through fear, and not because such a life is pleasant, I will make this brief reply that, if it is not as we say, then there is no God; or, if there is a God, He is not concerned with people, and virtue and vice are nothing, and, as we already stated, legislators unjustly punish the transgressors of their excellent precepts. But, since these legislators are not unjust, and their Father instructs them through the Word to do as He Himself does, they who comply with these legislators are not unjust. If anyone should advance the remonstrance that human laws are different, and say that some people consider one thing good, another bad, while other people deem as good what the former considered bad, and as bad what they thought good, let him listen to this reply. We realize that the bad angels made laws suited to their own iniquity, which are pleasing to their counterparts among people; and the true Word, at His coming, proved that not all opinions and teachings are good, but that some are bad, and others good. Wherefore, I will repeat the same statements and utter similar ones to such people as these, and, if necessary, I shall develop them more at length. But for the present I must return to my subject.

Chapter 10

Beyond doubt, therefore, our teachings are more noble than all human teaching, because Christ, who appeared on earth for our sakes, became the whole Logos, namely, Logos and body and soul. Everything that the philosophers and legislators discovered and expressed well, they accomplished through their discovery and contemplation of some part of the Logos. But, since they did not have a full knowledge of the

Logos, which is Christ, they often contradicted themselves. And those who were born before Christ assumed human nature were dragged into law courts as irreligious and meddling persons, when they tried in human narrowness to think out and prove things by reason. Socrates, the most ardent of all in this regard, was accused of the very crimes that are imputed to us. They claimed that he introduced new deities and rejected the state-sponsored gods. But what he did was to ostracize Homer and the other poets, and to instruct people to expel the evil demons and those who perpetrated the deeds narrated by the poets; and to exhort people by meditation to learn more about God who was unknown to them, saying: 'It is not an easy matter to find the Father and Creator of all things, nor, when He is found, is it safe to announce Him to all people.' Yet, our Christ did all this through His own power. There was no one who believed so much in Socrates as to die for his teaching, but not only philosophers and scholars believed in Christ, of whom even Socrates had a vague knowledge (for He was and is the Logos who is in every person, and who predicted things to come first through the prophets and then in person when He assumed our human nature and feelings, and taught us these doctrines), but also workers and people wholly uneducated, who all scorned glory, and fear, and death. Indeed, this is brought about by the power of the ineffable Father, and not through the instrumentality of human reason.

Chapter 11

Neither should we Christians be put to death, nor would evil people and demons prevail over us, were it not for the fact that absolutely everyone who is born must also, by reason of a debt, be subject to death. Thus, when we liquidate this debt, we render thanks. Now, for the sake of Crescens and those who rant like him, we deem it proper and fitting to relate here what Xenophon wrote. Hercules, relates Xenophon, once came to a place where three roads met, and there he found Virtue and Vice, who appeared to him in the guise of women. And Vice, in a costly and seductive dress, with an expression made alluring by such adornments, and being instantly fascinating to look at, said to Hercules that, if he would follow her, she would see to it that his whole life would be one of pleasure and that he would be arrayed in the most brilliant finery, such as she herself was then wearing. And Virtue, who was loathsome in appearance and dress, said: 'If you will obey me, you will be adorned, not with passing and perishable ornaments or beauty, but with everlasting and precious adornments.' Indeed, we believe that the one who avoids what only appears to be good and strives for what is considered difficult and unreasonable, will attain happiness. For Vice, to disguise her own actions, appropriated the qualities of Virtue which really are excellent, by imitating what is incorruptible (for Vice neither possesses nor is able to effect incorruptibility) and enslaves low-minded people, attributing her own evil habits to Virtue. But, those who have understood the things that really are good are also unspoiled in virtue. Such persons, everyone who is intelligent should conclude, were the Christians, the athletes, and those who performed the deeds which the poets narrate of the so-called gods; and this conclusion should be drawn from the fact that we Christians scorn escaping from death.

Chapter 12

Indeed, when I myself revelled in the teachings of Plato, and heard the Christians misrepresented and watched them stand fearless in the face of death and of every other thing that was considered dreadful, I realized the impossibility of their living in sinful pleasure. For, what sensual or self-indulgent person, who approves of the eating of human flesh, would welcome death that he might be despoiled of his pleasures, and would not rather always try to continue in his present manner of life, and to elude the public officers; and much less would he be apt to denounce himself when the penalty was death? The evil demons have caused these things also to be effected by wicked people. For, after inflicting the death penalty on some because of the false charges lodged against us, they subjected or servants, some of them children and women, to torture, and forced from them by these terrible torments a confession of those fictitious crimes which they themselves publicly commit. But we are not in the least concerned about such crimes, since we do not commit them, having as witness of our thoughts and actions the Unbegotten and Ineffable God. For why did we not acknowledge that we consider these things good, and show how they are divine philosophy, affirming that the mysteries of Saturn have in homicide and in drinking blood the same effect as what you do before the idol you venerate, on which you sprinkle not only the blood of brute animals, but also of people, making a libation of the slain person's blood through the most distinguished and most noble person in your midst? And by imitating Jupiter and the other gods in sodomy and sinful relations with women, might they not, in defense of their actions, cite the writings of Epicurus and the poets? But, because we persuade people to avoid such customs and those who practice them, together with their imitators, as we now have striven hard to persuade you with these words, we are assailed in many ways. But we are not in the least worried, for we realize that God is the just supervisor of all. Would that even now someone would ascend a lofty platform and cry out in loud voice: 'Be ashamed and blush, you who accuse the innocent of the very crimes you yourselves openly commit; and things of which you and your gods are guilty, you charge to those persons who have not the slightest part in them. Change your ways, and come to your senses.'

Chapter 13

When I learned of the evil camouflage which the wicked demons had thrown around the divine doctrines of the Christians to deter others from following them, I had to laugh at the authors of these lies, at the camouflage itself, and at the popular reaction. I am proud to say that I strove with all my might to be known as a Christian, not because the teachings of Plato are different from those of Christ, but because they are not in every way similar; neither are those of other writers, the Stoics, the poets, and the historians. For each one of them, seeing, through his participation of the seminal Divine Word, what was related to it, spoke very well. But, they who contradict themselves in important matters evidently did not acquire the unseen [that is, heavenly] wisdom and the indisputable knowledge. The truths which people in all lands have rightly spoken belong to us Christians. For we worship and love, after God the Father, the Word who is from the Unbegotten and Ineffable God, since He even became Man for us, so that by sharing in our sufferings He also might heal us. Indeed, all writers, by means of the engrafted seed of the Word which was implanted in them, had a dim glimpse of the truth. For the seed of something and its imitation, given in proportion to one's capacity, is one thing, but the thing itself, which is shared and imitated according to His grace, is quite another.

Chapter 14

We therefore beseech you to publish this pronouncement, adding your comment to it, so that others may know our customs and be released from the bonds of false beliefs and of ignorance of good; for by their own fault they have become worthy of punishment. Promulgate these words, too, in order that these truths may be made public for everyone, because by nature people can know good and evil; and because by denouncing us, of whom they do not know whether they really do such disgraceful things as they pretend, and because they revel in their gods who committed such actions themselves and still permit humankind to commit them, and because by punishing us with death or chains or some such penalty, as if we committed such actions, they so condemn themselves that other judges are not needed.

Chapter 15

[Concerning my countryman Simon Magus, I looked with utter disdain upon his impious and deceitful teachings.] If you will only approve this writing, we will expose him in the eyes of all, so that, if at all possible, they may be converted. For this purpose only have we written these words. After a just deliberation you will find that our teachings are not disgraceful, but are more sublime than all human wisdom. If you do not think them so, at least they bear no resemblance to the teachings of the Sotadists, the Philaenidians, the Archestratians, the Epicureans, and other such doctrines of the poets, with which everyone can become familiar, both by hearing them as they are recited and reading them. And now, having done the best we could, we conclude with a prayer that people of every land be deemed fit to receive the truth. And may you also, as befits your piety and wisdom, judge the case with justice for your own sakes.

5

Martyrdom of Perpetua
(202 or 203, Carthage, North Africa)

Accounts of the last days of the Christian martyrs were an important genre of early Church literature, quite popular among ordinary Christians in the third century. Some of the martyrs whose deaths were recorded in this literature were important Church officials like bishops, but many were simple laypeople, or even catechumens (people learning the faith before being admitted into the Church by baptism). These accounts were composed or edited partly to honour the memories of those who had died for their faith, and partly also to inspire those who remained alive and might themselves have to confront the martyr's choice between denying Christ and suffering death.

Were you to read the accounts of the martyrs, you would begin noticing in many of them some recurring scenes, stock dialogue sections, and common narrative structures, with an emphasis on the miraculous. For these reasons, modern historians treat them skeptically, although they recognize that some of them may incorporate more credible evidence, such as court records or eye-witness reports. But the *Martyrdom of Perpetua* is not representative of the genre. For instance, there are no miracles in the usual sense, although Perpetua does have miraculous visions; and the writing seems fresh and direct, not simply derived from a literary model.

Most of the document (chapters 3-10) is represented as an excerpt from the diary of Perpetua, a 20-year-old catechumen who was the mother of an infant son. Another portion (chapters 11-13) is represented as the work of one of her fellow martyrs, named Saturus. The rest comes from the hand of a Christian editor. The purpose and the theology of the editor may be different from the purpose and the theology of the documents which the editor is transcribing. The place of martyrdom is Carthage, in North Africa, and the year is thought to be 202 or 203, when it is known that Christian and Jewish converts were suffering official persecution in various parts of the Empire.

Perpetua's diary is one of only four surviving documents from the first six Christian centuries that are presented as written by a woman. Many other early Christian documents are known to have been written by women, but they were not preserved.

There are versions of this text in Latin and Greek. The Latin is usually believed to be the original version. The translation below was made from the Latin.

Questions on the reading

What is the editor's stated purpose for making these documents available? What does he or she think the Church might learn from them? What is the editor's relation to Perpetua and Saturus? What might be inferred about the editor's theological position? What might be inferred about the social and ecclesiastical situation of the readers whom the editor is wanting to address? Is it possible to determine Perpetua's and Saturus' purpose and theological position, or are these obscured by the process of editorial selection and revision? What are Perpetua's social origins, and why might an early Christian audience be interested in them? How does Perpetua relate to her father and husband? What might be the meaning of the various visions she records? How does Perpetua, a female catechumen, relate to male Church officials, and what might be surprising in this respect? What evidence does the document give as to why martyrs were willing to suffer, and as to why persecutors persecuted?

The Martyrdom of Perpetua

1. If instances of ancient faith which both testified to the grace of God and edified persons were written expressly for God's honor and humans' encouragement, why shouldn't recent events be similarly recorded for those same purposes? For these events will likewise become part of the past and vital to posterity, in spite of the fact that contemporary esteem for antiquity tends to minimize their value. And those who maintain that there is a single manifestation of the one Holy Spirit throughout the ages ought to consider that since a fullness of grace has been decreed for the last days of the world these recent events should be considered of greater value because of their proximity to those days. For "In the last days," says the Lord, "I shall diffuse my spirit over all humanity and their sons and daughters shall prophesy; the young shall see visions, and the old shall dream dreams."[1]

Just as we valued those prophecies so we acknowledge and reverence the new visions which were promised. And we consider the other powers of the Holy Spirit to be instruments of the Church to which that same Spirit was sent to administer all gifts to all people, just as the Lord allotted. For this reason we deem it necessary to disseminate the written accounts for the glory of God, lest anyone with a weak or despairing faith might think that supernatural grace prevailed solely among the ancients who were honored either by their experience of martyrdom or visions. For God always fulfills what he promises, either as proof to non-believers or as an added grace to believers.

And so, brothers and dear ones, we share with you those things which we have heard and touched with our hands, so that those of you who were eye-witnesses of these deeds may be reminded of the glory of the Lord, and those of you now learning of it through this narration may associate yourselves with the holy martyrs and, through them, with the Lord Jesus Christ to whom there is glory and honor forever. Amen.

2. Arrested were some young catechumens; Revocatus and Felicitas (both servants), Saturninus, Secundulus, and Vibia Perpetua, a young

---

Source: "The Martyrdom of Perpetua," trans. Rosemary Rader, in Patricia Wilson-Kastner *et al.*, University Press of America, 1981, 19-31. Used by permission of University Press of America Inc.

married woman about twenty years old, of good family and upbringing. She had a father, mother, two brothers (one was a catechumen like herself), and an infant son at the breast. The following account of her martyrdom is her own, a record in her own words of her perceptions of the event.

3. While I was still with the police authorities (she said) my father out of love for me tried to dissuade me from my resolution. "Father," I said, "do you see here, for example, this vase, or pitcher, or whatever it is?" "I see it," he said. "Can it be named anything else than what it really is?" I asked, and he said, "No." "So I also cannot be called anything else than what I am, a Christian." Enraged by my words my father came at me as though to tear out my eyes. He only annoyed me, but he left, overpowered by his diabolical arguments.

For a few days my father stayed away. I thanked the Lord and felt relieved because of my father's absence. At this time we were baptized and the Spirit instructed me not to request anything from the baptismal waters except endurance of physical suffering.[2]

A few days later we were imprisoned. I was terrified because never before had I experienced such darkness. What a terrible day! Because of crowded conditions and rough treatment by the soldiers the heat was unbearable. My condition was aggravated by my anxiety for my baby. Then Tertius and Pomponius, those kind deacons who were taking care of our needs, paid for us to be moved for a few hours to a better part of the prison where we might refresh ourselves. Leaving the dungeon we all went about our own business. I nursed my child, who was already weak from hunger. In my anxiety for the infant I spoke to my mother about him, tried to console my brother, and asked that they care for my son. I suffered intensely because I sensed their agony on my account. These were the trials I had to endure for many days. Then I was granted the privilege of having my son remain with me in prison. Being relieved of my anxiety and concern for the infant, I immediately regained my strength. Suddenly the prison became my palace, and I loved being there rather than any other place.

4. Then my brother said to me, "Dear sister, you already have such a great reputation that you could ask for a vision indicating whether you will be condemned or freed." Since I knew that I could speak with the

Lord, whose great favors I had already experienced, I confidently promised to do so. I said I would tell my brother about it the next day. Then I made my request and this is what I saw.

There was a bronze ladder of extraordinary height reaching up to heaven, but it was so narrow that only one person could ascend at a time. Every conceivable kind of iron weapon was attached to the sides of the ladder: swords, lances, hooks, and daggers. If anyone climbed up carelessly or without looking upwards, he/she would be mangled as the flesh adhered to the weapons. Crouching directly beneath the ladder was a monstrous dragon who threatened those climbing up and tried to frighten them from ascent.

Saturus went up first. Because of his concern for us he had given himself up voluntarily after we had been arrested. He had been our source of strength but was not with us at the time of the arrest. When he reached the top of the ladder he turned to me and said, "Perpetua, I'm waiting for you, but be careful not to be bitten by the dragon." I told him that in the name of Jesus Christ the dragon could not harm me. At this the dragon slowly lowered its head as though afraid of me. Using its head as the first step, I began my ascent."

At the summit I saw an immense garden, in the center of which sat a tall, grey-haired man dressed like a shepherd, milking sheep. Standing around him were several thousand white-robed people. As he raised his head he noticed me and said, "Welcome, my child." Then he beckoned me to approach and gave me a small morsel of the cheese he was making. I accepted it with cupped hands and ate it. When all those surrounding us said "Amen," I awoke, still tasting the sweet cheese. I immediately told my brother about the vision, and we both realized that we were to experience the sufferings of martyrdom. From then on we gave up having any hope in this world.

5. A few days later there was a rumor that our case was to be heard. My father, completely exhausted from his anxiety, came from the city to see me, with the intention of weakening my faith. "Daughter", he said, "have pity on my grey head. Have pity on your father if I have the honor to be called father by you, if with these hands I have brought you to the prime of your life, and if I have always favored you above your brothers, do not abandon me to the reproach of men. Consider your brothers;

consider your mother and your aunt; consider your son who cannot live without you. Give up your stubbornness before you destroy all of us. None of us will be able to speak freely if anything happens to you."

These were the things my father said out of love, kissing my hands and throwing himself at my feet. With tears he called me not daughter, but woman. I was very upset because of my father's condition. He was the only member of my family who would find no reason for joy in my suffering. I tried to comfort him saying, "Whatever God wants at this tribunal will happen, for remember that our power comes not from ourselves but from God." But utterly dejected, my father left me.

6. One day as we were eating we were suddenly rushed off for a hearing. We arrived at the forum and the news spread quickly throughout the area near the forum, and a huge crowd gathered. We went up to the prisoners' platform. All the others confessed when they were questioned. When my turn came my father appeared with my son. Dragging me from the step, he begged: "Have pity on your son!"

Hilarion, the governor, who assumed power after the death of the proconsul Minucius Timinianus,[3] said, "Have pity on your father's grey head; have pity on your infant son; offer sacrifice for the emperors' welfare". But I answered, "I will not." Hilarion asked, "Are you a Christian?" And I answered, "I am a Christian." And when my father persisted in his attempts to dissuade me, Hilarion ordered him thrown out, and he was beaten with a rod. My father's injury hurt me as much as if I myself had been beaten, and I grieved because of his pathetic old age. Then the sentence was passed; all of us were condemned to the beasts. We were overjoyed as we went back to the prison cell. Since I was still nursing my child who was ordinarily in the cell with me, I quickly sent the deacon Pomponius to my father's house to ask for the baby, but my father refused to give him up. Then God saw to it that my child no longer needed my nursing, nor were my breasts inflamed. After that I was no longer tortured by anxiety about my child or by pain in my breasts.

7. A few days later while all of us were praying, in the middle of a prayer I suddenly called out the name "Dinocrates." I was astonished since I hadn't thought about him till then. When I recalled what had happened to him I was very disturbed and decided right then that I had not only the right, but the obligation, to pray for him. So I began to pray repeatedly and to make moaning sounds to the Lord in his behalf.

During that same night I has this vision: I saw Dinocrates walking away from one of many very dark places. He seemed very hot and thirsty, his face grimy and colorless. The wound on his face was just as it had been when he died. This Dinocrates was my blood-brother who at the age of seven died very tragically from a cancerous disease which so disfigured his face that his death was repulsive to everyone. It was for him that I now prayed. But neither of us could reach the other because of the great distance between. In the place where Dinocrates stood was a pool filled with water, and the rim of the pool was so high that it extended far above the boy's height. Dinocrates stood on his toes as if to drink the water but in spite of the fact that the pool was full, he could not drink because the rim was so high!

I realized that my brother was in trouble, but I was confident that I could help him with his problem. I prayed for him every day until we were transferred to the arena prison where we were to fight wild animals on the birthday of Geta Caesar.[4] And I prayed day and night for him, moaning and weeping so that my petition would be granted.

8. On that day that we were kept in chains, I had the following vision: I saw the same place as before, but Dinocrates was clean, well-dressed, looking refreshed. In place of the wound there was a scar, and the fountain which I had seen previously now had its rim lowered to the boy's waist. On the rim, over which water was flowing constantly, there was a golden bowl filled with water. Dinocrates walked up to it and began to drink; the bowl never emptied. And when he was no longer thirsty, he gladly went to play as children do. Then I awoke, knowing that he had been relieved of his suffering.

9. A few days passed. Pudens, the official in charge of the prison (the official who had gradually come to admire us for our persistence), admitted many prisoners to our cell so that we might mutually encourage each other. As the day of the games drew near, my father, overwhelmed with grief, came again to see me. He began to pluck out his beard and throw it on the ground. Falling on his face before me, he cursed his old age, repeating such things as would move all creation. And I grieved because of his old age.

10. The day before the battle in the arena, in a vision I saw Pomponius the deacon coming to the prison door and knocking very loudly. I went

to open the gate for him. He was dressed in a loosely fitting white robe, wearing richly decorated sandals. He said to me, "Perpetua, come. We're waiting for you!" He took my hand and we began to walk over extremely rocky and winding paths. When we finally arrived short of breath, at the arena, he led me to the center saying, "Don't be frightened! I'll be here to help you." He left me and I stared out over a huge crowd which watched me with apprehension. Because I knew that I had to fight with the beasts, I wondered why they hadn't yet been turned loose in the arena. Coming towards me was some type of Egyptian, horrible to look at, accompanied by fighters who were to help defeat me. Some handsome young men came forward to help and encourage me. I was stripped of my clothing, and suddenly I was a man. My assistants began to rub me with oil as was the custom before a contest, while the Egyptian was on the opposite side rolling in the sand. Then a certain man appeared, so tall that he towered above the amphitheatre. He wore a loose purple robe with two parallel stripes across the chest; his sandals were richly decorated with gold and silver. He carried a rod like that of an athletic trainer, and a green branch on which were golden apples. He motioned for silence and said, "If this Egyptian wins, he will kill her with the sword; but if she wins, she will receive this branch." Then he withdrew.

We both stepped forward and began to fight with our fists. My opponent kept trying to grab my feet but I repeatedly kicked his face with my heels. I felt myself being lifted up into the air and began to strike at him as one who was no longer earth-bound. But when I saw that we were wasting time, I put my two hands together, linked my fingers, and put his head between them. As he fell on his face I stepped on his head. Then the people began to shout and my assistants started singing victory songs. I walked up to the trainer and accepted the branch.[5] He kissed me and said, "Peace be with you, my daughter." And I triumphantly headed towards the Sanavivarian Gate.[6] Then I woke up realizing that I would be contending not with wild animals but with the devil himself. I knew, however, that I would win. I have recorded the events which occurred up to the day before the final contest. Let anyone who wishes to record the events of the contest itself, do so."

11. The saintly Saturus also related a vision which he had and it is recorded here in his own hand. Our suffering had ended (he said), and we were being carried towards the east by four angels whose hands

never touched us. And we floated upward, not in a supine position, but as though we were climbing a gentle slope. As we left the earth's atmosphere we saw a brilliant light, and I said to Perpetua who was at my side, "This is what the Lord promised us. We have received his promise."

And while we were being carried along by those four angels we saw a large open space like a splendid garden landscaped with rose trees and every variety of flower. The trees were as tall as cypresses whose leaves rustled gently and incessantly. And there in that garden-sanctuary were four other angels, more dazzling than the rest. And when they saw us they showed us honor, saying to the other angels in admiration, "Here they are! They have arrived."

And those four angels who were carrying us began trembling in awe and set us down. And we walked through a violet-strewn field where we met Jocundus, Saturninus, and Artaxius who were burned alive in that same persecution, and Quintus, also a martyr, who had died in prison. We were asking them where they had been, when the other angels said to us, "First, come this way. Go in and greet the Lord."

12. We went up to a place where the walls seemed constructed of light. At the entrance of the place stood four angels who put white robes on those who entered. We went in and heard a unified voice chanting endlessly, "Holy, holy, holy." We saw a white haired man sitting there who, in spite of his snowy white hair, had the features of a young man. His feet were not visible. On his right and left were four elderly gentlemen and behind them stood many more. As we entered we stood in amazement before the throne. Four angels supported us as we went up to kiss the aged man, and he gently stroked our faces with his hands. The other elderly men said to us, "Stand up." We rose and gave the kiss of peace. Then they told us to enjoy ourselves. I said to Perpetua, "You have your wish." She answered, "I thank God, for although I was happy on earth, I am much happier here right now."

13. Then we went out, and before the gates we saw Optatus the bishop on the right and Aspasius the priest and teacher on the left, both looking sad as they stood there separated from each other. They knelt before us saying, "Make peace between us, for you've gone away and left us this way." But we said to them, "Aren't you our spiritual father,

and our teacher? Why are you kneeling before us?" We were deeply touched and we embraced them. And Perpetua began to speak to them in Greek and we invited them into the garden beneath a rose tree. While we were talking with them, the angels said to them, "Let them refresh themselves, and if you have any dissensions among you, forgive one another." This disturbed both of them and the angels said to Optatus, "Correct your people who flock to you as though returning from the games, fighting about the different teams." It seemed to us that they wanted to close the gates, and there we began to recognize many of our friends, among whom were martyrs. We were all sustained by an indescribable fragrance which completely satisfied us. Then in my joy, I awoke.

14. The remarkable visions narrated above were those of the blessed martyrs Saturus and Perpetua, just as they put them in writing. As for Secundulus, while he was still in prison God gave him the grace of an earlier exit from this world, so that he could escape combat with the wild beasts. But his body, though not his soul, certainly felt the sword.

15. As for Felicitas, she too was touched by God's grace in the following manner. She was pregnant when arrested, and was now in her eighth month. As the day of the contest approached she became very distressed that her martyrdom might be delayed, since the law forbade the execution of a pregnant woman. Then she would later have to shed her holy and innocent blood among common criminals. Her friends in martyrdom were equally sad at the thought of abandoning such a good friend to travel alone on the same road to hope.

And so, two days before the contest, united in grief they prayed to the Lord. Immediately after the prayers her labor pains began. Because of the additional pain natural for an eighth-month delivery, she suffered greatly during the birth, and one of the prison guards taunted her; "If you're complaining now, what will you do when you'll be thrown to the wild beasts? You didn't think of them when you refused to sacrifice." She answered, "Now it is I who suffer, but then another shall be in me to bear the pain for me, since I am now suffering for him." And she gave birth to a girl whom one of her sisters reared as her own daughter.

16. Since the Holy Spirit has permitted, and by permitting has willed, that the events of the contest be recorded, we have no choice but to

carry out the injunction (rather, the sacred trust) of Perpetua, in spite of the fact that it will be an inferior addition to the magnificent events already described. We are adding an instance of Perpetua's perseverance and lively spirit. At one time the prisoners were being treated with unusual severity by the commanding officer because certain deceitful men had intimated to him that the prisoners might escape by some magic spells. Perpetua openly challenged him; "Why don't you at least allow us to freshen up, the most noble of the condemned, since we belong to Caesar and are about to fight on his birthday? Or isn't it to your credit that we should appear in good condition on that day?" The officer grimaced and blushed, then ordered that they be treated more humanely and that her brothers and others be allowed to visit and dine with them. By this time the prison warden was himself a believer.

17. On the day before the public games, as they were eating the last meal commonly called the free meal, they tried as much as possible to make it instead an *agape*.[7] In the same spirit they were exhorting the people, warning them to remember the judgment of God, asking them to be witnesses to the prisoners' joy in suffering, and ridiculing the curiosity of the crowd. Saturus told them, "Won't tomorrow's view be enough for you? Why are you so eager to see something you hate? Friends today, enemies tomorrow! Take a good look so you'll recognize us on that day." Then they all left the prison amazed, and many of them began to believe.

18. The day of their victory dawned, and with joyful countenances they marched from the prison to the arena as though on their way to heaven. If there was any trembling it was from joy, not fear. Perpetua followed with quick step as a true spouse of Christ, the darling of God, her brightly flashing eyes quelling the gaze of the crowd. Felicitas too, joyful because she had safely survived childbirth and was now able to participate in the contest with the wild animals, passed from one shedding of blood to another; from midwife to gladiator, about to be purified after child-birth by a second baptism. As they were led through the gate they were ordered to put on different clothes; the men, those of the priests of Saturn, the women, those of the priestesses of Ceres. But that noble woman stubbornly resisted even to the end. She said, "We've come this far voluntarily in order to protect our rights, and we've pledged our lives not to recapitulate on any such matter as this. We made this agreement

with you." Injustice bowed to justice and the guard conceded that they could enter the arena in their ordinary dress. Perpetua was singing victory psalms as if already crushing the head of the Egyptian. Revocatus, Saturninus and Saturus were warning the spectators, and as they came within sight of Hilarion they informed him by nods and gestures: "You condemn us; God condemns you." This so infuriated the crowds that they demanded the scourging of these men in front of the line of gladiators. But the ones so punished rejoiced in that they had obtained yet another share in the Lord's suffering.

19. Whoever said, "Ask and you shall receive," granted to these petitioners the particular death that each one chose. For whenever the martyrs were discussing among themselves their choice of death, Saturus used to say that he wished to be thrown in with all the animals so that he might wear a more glorious crown. Accordingly, at the outset of the show he was matched against a leopard but then called back; then he was mauled by a bear on the exhibition platform. Now Saturus detested nothing as much as a bear and he had already decided to die by one bite from the leopard. Consequently, when he was tied to a wild boar the professional gladiator who had tied the two together was pierced instead and died shortly after the games ended, while Saturus was merely dragged about. And when he was tied up on the bridge in front of the bear, the bear refused to come out of his den; and so a second time Saturus was called back unharmed.

20. For the young women the devil had readied a mad cow, an animal not usually used at these games, but selected so that the women's sex would be matched with that of the animal. After being stripped and enmeshed in nets, the women were led into the arena. How horrified the people were as they saw that one was a young girl and the other, her breasts dripping with milk, had just recently given birth to a child. Consequently both were recalled and dressed in loosely fitting gowns.

Perpetua was tossed first and fell on her back. She sat up, and being more concerned with her sense of modesty than with her pain, covered her thighs with her gown which had been torn down one side. Then finding her hair-clip which had fallen out, she pinned back her loose hair thinking it not proper for a martyr to suffer with dishevelled hair; it might seem that she was mourning in her hour of triumph. Then she stood up. Noticing that Felicitas was badly bruised, she went to her, reached out her hands and helped her to her feet. As they stood there the cruelty of the crowds seemed to be appeased and they were sent to the Sanavivarian Gate. There Perpetua was taken care of by a certain catechumen, Rusticus, who stayed near her. She seemed to be waking from a deep sleep (so completely had she been entranced and imbued with the Spirit). She began to look around her and to everyone's astonishment asked, "When are we going to be led out to that cow, or whatever it is." She would not believe that it had already happened until she saw the various markings of the tossing on her body and clothing. Then calling for her brother she said to him and to the catechumen, "Remain strong in your faith and love one another. Do not let our excruciating sufferings become a stumbling block for you."

21. Meanwhile, at another gate Saturus was similarly encouraging the soldier, Pudens. "Up to the present," he said, "I've not been harmed by any of the animals, just as I've foretold and predicted. So that you will now believe completely, watch as I go back to die from a single leopard bite." And so at the end of that contest, Saturus was bitten once by the leopard that had been set loose, and bled so profusely from that one wound that as he was coming back the crowd shouted in witness to his second baptism: "Salvation by being cleansed; Salvation by being cleansed."[8] And that man was truly saved who was cleansed in this way.

Then Saturus said to Pudens the soldier, "Goodbye, and remember my faith. Let these happenings be a source of strength for you, rather than a cause for anxiety." Then asking Pudens for a ring from his finger, he dipped it into the wound and returned it to Pudens as a legacy, a pledge and remembrance of his death. And as he collapsed he was thrown with the rest to that place reserved for the usual throat-slitting. And when the crowd demanded that the prisoners be brought out into the open so that they might feast their eyes on death by the sword, they voluntarily arose and moved where the crowd wanted them. Before doing so they kissed each other so that their martyrdom would be completely perfected by the rite of the kiss of peace.

The others, without making any movement or sound, were killed by the sword. Saturus in particular, since he had been the first to climb the ladder and was to be Perpetua's encouragement, was the first to die. But Perpetua, in order to feel some of the pain, groaning as she was struck between the ribs, took the gladiator's trembling hand and guided it to her throat. Perhaps it was that so great a woman, feared as she was by the unclean spirit, could not have been slain had she not herself willed it.

O brave and fortunate martyrs, truly called and chosen to give honor to our Lord Jesus Christ! And anyone who is elaborating upon, or who reverences or worships that honor, should read these more recent examples, along with the ancient, as sources of encouragement for the Christian community. In this way, there will be new examples of courage witnessing to the fact that even in our day the same Holy Spirit is still efficaciously present, along with the all powerful God the Father and Jesus Christ our Lord, to whom there will always be glory and endless power. Amen.

Notes

[1] Acts 2:17–18. Cf. Joel 2:28.

[2] Apparently after baptism the newly baptized could pray for a special grace or gift. Cf. Tertullian "On Baptism", 20.

[3] There is no real information about Minucius Timianus, but Hilarion is mentioned as an African proconsul by Tertullian, *Ad Scapulam* 3:1. Hilarion was evidently temporarily serving as governor until a new one would be appointed.

[4] This incidental reference to the celebration of games on Geta's birthday helps establish the date of the martyrdom somewhere between 200 and 205.

[5] The branch was the reward presented to the victor in any kind of official combat or contest.

[6] The Porta Sanavivaria (Gate of Life) was the gate by which the victors would exit. Those who were defeated were carried out through the Porta Libitinensis.

[7] The agape or "love feast" was the common meal shared by the early Christian communities. It was the visible expression of the love Christians felt for each other as co-sharers of the love of Christ.

[8] One of the customary greetings of good omen before and after the public baths was "Salvum lotum," here used ironically by the crowd in the amphitheater.

6 Hippolytus? *Apostolic Tradition?* (215?, Rome?)

The work we now know as the *Apostolic Tradition* was first published in 1848 from a manuscript in one of the six dialects of Coptic. This mysterious work was clearly a "Church order", like the *Didaché*, but longer. It included instructions for the celebration of ordination, baptism, and the Eucharist, and descriptions of various Church offices.

Later in the nineteenth century scholars discovered manuscripts of the same work (but with detailed differences) in another dialect of Coptic and in Arabic, Ethiopic, and Latin. The work was also identified as being closely related to three other early Christian documents (known as the *Apostolic Constitutions* Book 8, the *Epitome*, and the *Canons of Hippolytus*). And there were "fragments" of the work, that is, quotations in other writings. It came to be agreed, for various reasons, that the original language of the work must have been Greek; but no manuscripts of the Greek text exist.

There is no evidence in the text itself for the title "Apostolic Tradition," and none for the date or place of its composition. But one fragment, and two of the works to which the document is closely related (the *Epitome* and the *Canons of Hippolytus*), do credit the influence of a person named Hippolytus. Now, as it happens, an important though not quite orthodox theologian named Hippolytus lived at Rome in the early third century, and several of his works are known. A statue of this Hippolytus was excavated in Rome in 1551, and carved in its base were the titles of several works, some of them known as Hippolytus' and some of them not known. One title which was not known was "Apostolic Tradition". Scholarly studies in 1906, 1910, and 1916 tried to make the obvious connection. They argued that the mysterious work that had first been published in 1848 from a Coptic manuscript was in fact a translation of the "Apostolic Tradition" of Hippolytus.

Many liturgical scholars, especially, received the theory eagerly. If the ascription to Hippolytus were correct, this work was by far the earliest evidence for the liturgical life of Rome, and given how frequently it was translated and how many other early Christian writers drew from it, it must have been extremely influential in the early Church. When the modern movement for liturgical revision gathered momentum in the early 1960s, notably in the Roman Catholic, Anglican, and Lutheran communions, liturgical revisers embraced the *Apostolic Tradition* as one of the crucial models for their task. For this reason, few works from the early Church have been more widely read in the past thirty years than this one; several editions, both popular and scholarly, have been published, and numerous books and articles have been written about it.

More recently, the ascription of this work to Hippolytus has been increasingly challenged. It rests mainly on the identification of the name "Hippolytus", connected with a few manuscripts of the work, with the Hippolytus whose statue was excavated. This identification is by no means sure. The statue itself, as a matter of fact, is curious; it seems originally to have been the statue of a woman, re-fashioned into a male figure in the sixteenth century, perhaps on the grounds that a woman could not have written the books whose titles were listed. No textual evidence connects the document to Rome or to the early third century. In any event, there is some reason to believe that the Hippolytus of the statue may have been in schism from the Catholic Church; in this case, if he did write this work, he may have done so simply in order to justify the possibly eccentric practices of his little breakaway constituency.

The English translation below is based on the Latin version of what is believed to be a Greek original. Additions and alterations taken from manuscripts other than the Latin text are printed in italics.

Questions on the reading

What authority does the author claim for the regulations given here? Why might the document have been written? How does the author understand the Church? liturgical prayer? What seems to distinguish the offices of bishop, presbyter, and deacon? What controversy about confessors appears to be in the historical background? What moral and disciplinary standards does the document establish? How does the author's church community appear to relate to the secular world? How can the two examples of a Eucharist prayer be compared and contrasted? What is the understanding of Christian initiation? How might one explain the differences in substance and tone between the Didaché and this document? Are there clues that this document did or did not have authority for an historical Christian community?

[The Apostolic Tradition]

1. We have set down those things which were worthy of note about the gifts which God has bestowed on humanity from the beginning according to his own will, presenting to himself that image which had gone astray. And now, led on by love for all the saints, we have proceeded to the summit of the tradition which *befits* the churches, in order that those who have been well *taught* by our exposition may guard that tradition which has remained up to now, and by recognising it may remain firm — because of that backsliding or error which was recently invented through ignorance — and that those who are ignorant (since the holy Spirit bestows perfect grace on those who believe rightly) may know how those who preside over the Church should hand down and guard all things.

Source: Hippolytus, *[Apostolic Tradition:] A Text For Students*, ed. G.J. Cuming, Bramcote, Notts.: Grove Books, 1976, 8-31, omitting notes.

Of Bishops

2. Let him be ordained bishop who has been chosen by all the people; and when he has been named and accepted by all, let the people assemble, together with the presbytery and those bishops who are present, on the Lord's day. When all give consent, they shall lay hands on him, and the presbytery shall stand by and be still. And all shall keep silence, praying in their hearts for the descent of the Spirit; after which one of the bishops present, being asked by all, shall lay his hand on him who is being ordained bishop, and pray, saying thus:

The Prayer for Ordination of a Bishop

3. *God and Father of our Lord Jesus Christ, Father of mercies and God of all comfort, you dwell on high and look on that which is lowly; you know all things before they come to pass; you gave ordinances in the Church through the word of your grace; you foreordained from the beginning a race of righteous men from Abraham; you appointed princes and priests, and did not leave your sanctuary without a ministry. From the beginning of the age it was your good pleasure to be glorified in those whom you have chosen: now pour forth that power which is from you, of the princely Spirit which you granted through your beloved Son Jesus Christ to your holy apostles who established the Church in every place as your sanctuary, to the unceasing glory and praise of your name.*

You who know the hearts of all, bestow upon this your servant, whom you have chosen for the episcopate, to feed your holy flock and to exercise the high-priesthood before you blamelessly, serving night and day; to propitiate your countenance unceasingly, and to offer to you the gifts of your holy Church; and by the spirit of high-priesthood to have the power to forgive sins according to your command, to confer orders according to your bidding, to loose every bond according to the power which you gave to the apostles, to please you in gentleness and a pure heart, offering to you a sweet-smelling savour; through your child Jesus Christ our Lord, with whom be glory and power and honour to you, with the holy Spirit, both now and to the ages of ages. Amen.

4. And when he has been made bishop, all shall offer the kiss of peace, greeting him because he has been made worthy. Then the deacons

shall present the offering to him; and he, laying his hands on it with all the presbytery, shall give thanks, saying:

The Lord be with you;

and all shall say:

And with your spirit.
Up with your hearts.
We have them with the Lord.
Let us give thanks to the Lord.
It is fitting and right.

And then he shall continue thus:

We render thanks to you, O God, through your beloved child Jesus Christ, whom in the last times you sent to us as saviour and redeemer and angel of your will; who is your inseparable Word, through whom you made all things, and in whom you were well pleased. You sent him from heaven into the Virgin's womb; and, conceived in the womb, he was made flesh and was manifested as your Son, being born of the holy Spirit and the Virgin. Fulfilling your will and gaining for you a holy people, he stretched out his hands when he should suffer, that he might release from suffering those who have believed in you.

And when he was betrayed to voluntary suffering that he might destroy death, and break the bonds of the devil, and tread down hell, and shine upon the righteous, and fix a term, and manifest the resurrection, he took bread and gave thanks to you, saying, 'Take, eat; this is my body, which shall be broken for you'. Likewise also the cup, saying, 'This is my blood, which is shed for you; when you do this, you make my remembrance'.

Remembering therefore his death and resurrection, we offer to you the bread and the cup, giving you thanks because you have held us worthy to stand before you and minister to you. And we ask that you would send your holy Spirit upon the offering of your holy Church; that, gathering (it) into one, you would grant to all who partake of the holy things (to partake) for the fullness of the holy Spirit for the strengthening of faith in truth, that we may praise and glorify you through your child Jesus Christ, through whom be glory and honour to you, with the holy Spirit, in your holy Church, both now and to the ages of ages. Amen.

Of the Offering of Oil

5. If anyone offers oil, (the bishop) shall render thanks in the same way as for the offering of bread and wine, not saying it word for word, but to similar effect, saying:

> O God, sanctifier of this oil, as you give health to those who are anointed and receive that with which you anointed kings, priests, and prophets, so may it give strength to all those who taste it, and health to all that are anointed with it.

(Of the Offering of Cheese and Olives)

6. Likewise, if anyone offers cheese and olives, he shall say thus:

> Sanctify this milk which has been coagulated, coagulating us also to your love. Make this fruit of the olive not to depart from your sweetness, which is an example of your richness which you have poured from the tree for life to those who hope in you.

But in every blessing shall be said:

> To you be glory, to the Father and the Son with the holy Spirit, in the holy Church, both now and always and to all the ages of ages.

Of Presbyters

7. And when a presbyter is ordained, the bishop shall lay his hand on his head, the presbyters also touching him; and he shall say according to what was said above, as we said before about the bishop, praying and saying:

> God and Father of our Lord Jesus Christ, look upon this your servant, and impart the Spirit of grace and counsel of the presbyterate, that he may help and govern your people with a pure heart; just as you looked upon your chosen people, and commanded Moses to choose presbyters whom you filled with your Spirit which you granted to your servant. And now, Lord, grant the Spirit of your grace to be preserved unfailingly in us, and make us worthy to minister to you in faith and in simplicity

of heart, praising you through your child Christ Jesus; through whom be glory and power to you with the holy Spirit, in the holy Church, both now and to the ages of ages. Amen.

Of Deacons

8. And when a deacon is ordained, let him be chosen according to what was said above, the bishop alone laying on hands, in the same way as we also directed above. In the ordination of a deacon, the bishop alone shall lay on hands, because he is not being ordained to the priesthood, but to the service of the bishop, to do what is ordered by him. For he does not share in the counsel of the presbyterate, but administers and informs the bishop of what is fitting; he does not receive the common spirit of seniority in which the presbyters share, but that which is entrusted to him under the bishop's authority. For this reason the bishop alone shall ordain a deacon; but on a presbyter the presbyters alone shall lay hands, because of the common and like spirit of their order. For a presbyter has authority only to receive; he has not authority to give. For this reason he does not ordain the clergy, but at the ordination of a presbyter he seals, while the bishop ordains.

Over a deacon, then, (the bishop) shall say thus:

God, who created all things and ordered them by your Word, Father of our Lord Jesus Christ, whom you sent to serve your will and make known to us your desire, give the holy Spirit of grace and caring and diligence to this your servant whom you have chosen to serve your Church and to present

in your holy of holies that which is offered to you by your appointed high-priest to the glory of your name; that, serving blamelessly and purely, he may attain the rank of a higher order, and praise and glorify you through your Son Jesus Christ our Lord; through whom be glory and power and praise to you, with the holy Spirit, now and always and to the ages of ages. Amen.

Of Confessors

9. *But a confessor, if he was in chains for the name of the Lord, shall not have hands laid on him for the diaconate or the presbyterate, for he*

has the honour of the presbyterate by his confession. But if he is appointed bishop, hands shall be laid on him.

But if there is a confessor who was not brought before the authorities, nor punished with chains, nor shut up in prison, nor condemned to any other penalty, but has only been derided on occasion for the name of our Lord, and punished with a domestic punishment: if he confessed, let hands be laid on him for any order of which he is worthy.

And the bishop shall give thanks according to what we said above. It is not at all necessary for him to utter the same words as we said above, as though reciting them from memory, when giving thanks to God; but let each pray according to his ability. If indeed anyone has the ability to pray at length and with a solemn prayer, it is good. But if anyone, when he prays, utters a brief prayer, do not prevent him. Only, he must pray what is sound and orthodox.

Of Widows

10. *When a widow is appointed, she is not ordained, but is chosen by name. If her husband has been dead a long time, let her not be taken on trust; even if she is old, let her be tested for a time, for often the passions grow old with him who makes a place for them in himself. A widow shall be appointed by word only, and shall join the rest. But hands shall not be laid on her, because she does not offer the offering, nor has she a liturgical duty. Ordination is for the clergy, on account of their liturgical duties; but a widow is appointed for prayer, which belongs to all.*

Of a Reader

11. *A reader is appointed by the bishop giving him the book, for he does not have hands laid on him.*

Of a Virgin

12. *Hands shall not be laid on a virgin: her choice alone makes her a virgin.*

Of a Subdeacon

13. *Hands shall not be laid on a subdeacon, but he shall be named in order that he may follow the deacons.*

Of Gifts of Healing

14. *If anyone says, 'I have received a gift of healing by a revelation', hands shall not be laid on him, for the facts themselves will show whether he has spoken the truth.*

Of Newcomers to the Faith

15. *Those who come forward for the first time to hear the word shall first be brought to the teachers before all the people arrive, and shall be questioned about their reason for coming to the faith. And those who have brought them shall bear witness about them, whether they are capable of hearing the word. They shall be questioned about their state of life: has he a wife? Is he the slave of a believer? Does his master allow him? Let him hear the word. If his master does not bear witness about him that he is a good man, he shall be rejected. If his master is a heathen, teach him to please his master, that there be no scandal. If any man has a wife, or a woman a husband, they shall be taught to be contented, the man with his wife and the woman with her husband. But if any man is not living with a wife, he shall be instructed not to fornicate, but to take a wife lawfully or remain as he is. If anyone is possessed by a demon, he shall not hear the word of teaching until he is pure.*

Of Crafts and Professions

16. *Inquiry shall be made about the crafts and professions of those who are brought for instruction. If a man is a brothel-keeper, let him cease or be rejected. If anyone is a sculptor or a painter, let them be instructed not to make idols; let them cease or be rejected. If anyone is an actor or gives theatrical performances, let him cease or be rejected. He who teaches children had best cease; but if he has no craft, let him have permission.*

Similarly, a charioteer who competes in the games, or goes to them, let him cease or be rejected. One who is a gladiator or teaches gladiators to fight, or one who fights with beasts in the games, or a public official employed on gladiatorial business, let him cease or be rejected.

If anyone is a priest, or keeper of idols, let him cease or be rejected.

A soldier under authority shall not kill a man. If he is ordered to, he shall not carry out the order; nor shall he take the oath. If he is unwilling, let him be rejected. He who has the power of the sword, or is a magistrate of a city who wears the purple, let him cease or be rejected. A catechumen or believer who want to become soldiers should be rejected, because they have despised God.

A prostitute, a profligate, a eunuch, or anyone else who does things of which it is a shame to speak, let them be rejected, for they are impure. Neither shall a magician be brought for examination. A charmer, an astrologer, a diviner, an interpreter of dreams, a mountebank, a cutter of fringes of clothes, or a maker of phylacteries, let them be rejected.

A man's concubine, if she is his slave and has reared her children and remained faithful to him alone, may be a hearer; otherwise, let her be rejected. Let any man who has a concubine cease, and take a wife lawfully; but if he is unwilling, let him be rejected.

If we have left anything out, the facts themselves will teach you; for we all have the Spirit of God.

Of the Time of Hearing the Word after (Examination of) Crafts and Professions

17. *Catechumens shall continue to hear the word for three years. But if a man is keen, and perseveres well in the matter, the time shall not be judged, but only his conduct.*

Of the Prayer of Those Who Hear the Word

18. *When the teacher has finished giving instruction, let the catechumens pray by themselves, separated from the faithful; and let the women, whether faithful or catechumens, stand by themselves in some place in the church when they pray. And when they have finished*

praying, they shall not give the Peace, for their kiss is not yet holy. But let only the faithful greet one another, men with men and women with women; but the men shall not greet the women. And let all the women cover their heads with a hood, but (not) just with a piece of linen, for that is no veil.

Of Laying Hands on the Catechumens

19. *After their prayer, when the teacher has laid hands on the catechumens, he shall pray and dismiss them. Whether the teacher is a cleric or a layman, let him act thus.*

If a catechumen is arrested for the name of the Lord, let him not be in two minds about his witness. For if he suffers violence and is killed (before he has received baptism) for the forgiveness of his sins, he will be justified, for he has received baptism in his blood.

Of Those Who Will Receive Baptism

20. *And when those who are to receive baptism are chosen, let their life be examined: have they lived good lives when they were catechumens? Have they honoured the widows? Have they visited the sick? Have they done every kind of good work? And when those who brought them bear witness to each: 'He has', let them hear the gospel.*

From the time that they were set apart, let hands be laid on them daily while they are exorcized. And when the day of their baptism approaches, the bishop shall exorcize each one of them, in order that he may know whether he is pure. And if anyone is not good or not pure, let him be put aside, because he has not heard the word with faith, for it is impossible that the Alien should hide himself for ever.

Those who are to be baptized should be instructed to bathe and wash themselves on the Thursday. And if a woman is in her period, let her be put aside, and receive baptism another day. Those who are to receive baptism shall fast on the Friday. On the Saturday those who are to receive baptism shall be gathered in one place at the bishop's decision. They shall all be told to pray and kneel. And he shall lay his hand on them and exorcize all alien spirits, that they may flee out of them and never return into them. And when he has finished exorcizing them, he shall breathe on their faces; and when he has signed their foreheads, ears, and noses, he shall raise them up.

And they shall spend the whole night in vigil; they shall be read to and instructed. Those who are to be baptized shall not bring with them any other thing, except what each brings for the eucharist. For it is suitable that he who has been made worthy should offer an offering then.

Of the Conferring of Holy Baptism

21. At the time when the cock crows, first let prayer be made over the water. Let the water be flowing in the font or poured over it. Let it be thus unless there is some necessity; if the necessity is permanent and urgent, use what water you can find. They shall take off their clothes. Baptize the little ones first. All those who can speak for themselves shall do so. As for those who cannot speak for themselves, their parents or someone from their family shall speak for them. Then baptize the men, and lastly the women, who shall have loosened all their hair, and laid down the gold and silver ornaments which they have on them. Let no-one take any alien object down into the water.

And at the time fixed for baptizing, the bishop shall give thanks over the oil, which he puts in a vessel: one calls it 'oil of thanksgiving'. And he shall also take other oil and exorcize it: one calls it 'oil of exorcism'. And a deacon takes the oil of exorcism and stands on the priest's left; and another deacon takes the oil of thanksgiving and stands on the priest's right. And when the priest takes each one of those who are to receive baptism, he shall bid him renounce, saying:

I renounce you, Satan, and all your service and all your works.

And when each one has renounced all this, he shall anoint him with the oil of exorcism, saying to him:

Let every spirit depart far from you.

And in this way he shall hand him over naked to the bishop or the priest who stands by the water to baptize. In the same way a deacon shall descend with him into the water and say, helping him to say:

I believe in one God, the Father almighty . . .

And he who receives shall say according to all this:

I believe in this way.

And the giver,

having his hand placed on his head, shall baptize him once.

And then he shall say:

Do you believe in Christ Jesus, the Son of God, who was born from the holy Spirit from the Virgin Mary, and was crucified under Pontius Pilate, and died, and rose again on the third day alive from the dead, and ascended into heaven, and sits at the right hand of the Father, and will come to judge the living and the dead?

And when he has said, 'I believe', he shall be baptized again.

And he shall say again:

Do you believe in the holy Spirit and the holy Church and the resurrection of the flesh?

Then he who is being baptized shall say, 'I believe', and thus he shall be baptized a third time.

And then, when he has come up, he shall be anointed from the oil *of thanksgiving* by the presbyter, who says:

I anoint you with holy oil in the name of Jesus Christ.

And so each of them shall wipe themselves and put on their clothes, and then they shall enter into the church.

And the bishop shall lay his hand on them and invoke, saying:

Lord God, you have made them worthy to receive remission of sins through the laver of regeneration of the holy Spirit: send upon them your grace, that they may serve you according to your will; for to you is glory, to Father and Son with the holy Spirit in the holy Church, both now and to the ages of ages. Amen.

Then, pouring the oil of thanksgiving from his hand and placing it on his head, he shall say:

I anoint you with holy oil in God the Father almighty and Christ Jesus and the holy Spirit.

And having signed him on the forehead, he shall give him a kiss and say:

> The Lord be with you.

And the one who has been signed shall say:

> And with your spirit.

So let him do with each one. And then they shall pray together with all the people: they do not pray with the faithful until they have carried out all these things. And when they have prayed, they shall give the kiss of peace.

And then the offering shall be presented by the deacons to the bishop; and he shall give thanks over the bread for the representation, which the Greeks call 'antitype', of the body of Christ; and over the cup mixed with wine for the antitype, which the Greeks call 'likeness', of the blood which was shed for all who have believed in him; and over milk and honey mixed together in fulfillment of the promise which was made to the fathers, in which he said, 'a land flowing with milk and honey', in which also Christ gave his flesh, through which those who believe are nourished like little children, making the bitterness of the heart sweet by the gentleness of his word; and over water, as an offering to signify the washing, that the inner person also, which is the soul, may receive the same things as the body. And the bishop shall give a reason for all these things to those who receive.

And when he breaks the bread, in distributing fragments to each, he shall say:

> The bread of heaven in Christ Jesus.

And he who receives shall answer:

> Amen.

And if there are not enough presbyters, the deacons also shall hold the cups, and stand by in good order and reverence: first, he who holds the water; second, the milk; third, the wine. And they who receive shall taste of each thrice, he who gives it saying:

> In God the Father almighty.

And he who receives shall say:

> Amen.
>
> And in the Lord Jesus Christ.
>
> (Amen).

And in the holy Spirit and the holy Church.

And he shall say:

Amen:

So shall it be done with each one.

When these things have been done, each one shall hasten to do good works *and to please God and to conduct himself rightly, being zealous for the Church, doing what he has learnt and advancing in piety.*

We have handed over to you in brief these things about holy baptism and the holy offering, for you have already been instructed about the resurrection of the flesh and the other things as it is written. But if there is anything else which ought to be said, the bishop shall say it privately to those who have received baptism. Unbelievers must not get to know it, unless they first receive baptism. This is the white stone of which John said, 'A new name is written on it, which no-one knows except him who receives the stone'.

(Of Administering the Communion)

22. *On Saturday and Sunday the bishop himself, if possible, shall distribute to all the people with his own hand; the deacons break, and the presbyters shall break the bread. When a deacon takes it to a presbyter, he shall hold out the paten, and the presbyter himself shall take it and distribute it to the people with his own hand. On other days they shall receive as the bishop directs.*

Of Fasting

23. *Widows and virgins shall fast often and pray for the Church. Presbyters shall fast if they wish, and laypeople likewise. A bishop cannot fast except when all the people do so. It happens that someone wishes to make an offering, and he cannot refuse him; but in all cases he breaks and tastes.*

Of Gifts to the Sick

24. *In an emergency a deacon shall give the sign to the sick with diligence, if no presbyter is present. And when he has given all that is*

needed for him to receive what is distributed, he shall give thanks, and they shall consume it there.

That Those Who Have Received Should Minister Diligently

If anyone has received anything to take to a widow, a sick person, or a church worker, he shall take it that day; and if he has not taken it, he shall take it the next day, adding to what there was from his own; because the bread of the poor remained with him.

Of the Bringing-In of Lambs at the Communal Supper

25. *When the bishop is present, and evening has come, a deacon brings in a lamp; and standing in the midst of all the faithful who are present, (the bishop) shall give thanks. First he shall say this greeting:*

> *The Lord be with you.*

And the people shall say:

> *With your spirit.*

> *Let us give thanks to the Lord.*

And they shall say:

> *It is fitting and right: greatness and exaltation with glory are his due.*

And he does not say, 'Up with your hearts', because that is said (only) at the offering. And he shall pray thus, saying:

> *We give you thanks, Lord, through your Son Jesus Christ our Lord, through whom you have shone upon us and revealed to us the inextinguishable light. So when we have completed the length of the day and have come to the beginning of the night, and have satisfied ourselves with the light of day which you created for our satisfying; and since now through your grace we do not lack the light of evening, we praise and glorify you through you Son Jesus Christ our Lord, through whom be glory and power and honour to you with the holy Spirit, both now and always and to the ages of ages. Amen.*

And all shall say:

> *Amen.*

They shall rise, then, after supper and pray; and the boys and the virgins shall say psalms.

And then the deacon, when he receives the mixed cup of the offering, shall say a psalm from those in which 'Alleluia' is written, and then, if the priest so directs, again from the same psalms. And after the bishop has offered the cup, he shall say the whole of a psalm which applies to the cup, with 'Alleluia', all joining in. When they recite psalms, all shall say, 'Alleluia', which means, 'We praise him who is God; glory and praise to him who created every age through his word alone'. And when the psalm is finished, he shall give thanks over the cup and distribute the fragments to all the faithful.

Of the Common Meal

26. *And when they have supper, the faithful who are present shall take from the bishop's hand a little bit of bread before they break their own bread; because it is blessed bread and not the eucharist, that is, the body of the Lord.*

Of the Time of the Meal

It is fitting that all, before they drink, should take a cup and give thanks over it, and so eat and drink in purity.

. . . you who are present, and so feast. But to the catechumens shall be given exorcized bread, and each shall offer a cup.

That Catechumens Ought Not to Eat with the Faithful

27. A catechumen shall not sit at the Lord's Supper. But through the whole meal he who *eats* should remember him who invited him; because that is why he besought him to enter under his roof.

That One Should Eat with Temperance and Moderation

28. When you eat and drink, do it discreetly and not to the point of drunkenness, and not so that anyone may laugh at you, or that he who invited you may be grieved by your disorderly behaviour, but so that he

may pray to be made worthy that the saints may come in to him; for he said, 'You are the salt of the earth'.

If an offering, which is called in Greek 'apophoreton', is made to all in common, accept some. If it is for all to eat, eat enough for there to be some over, which he who invited you may send to whom he wishes, as it were from the left-overs of the saints, and rejoice in confidence.

And let the guests, when they eat, receive in silence, not contending with words, but as the bishop allows; and if he has asked anything, an answer shall be given him. And when the bishop says a word, let all be modestly silent, until he asks another question.

If the bishop is absent, but the faithful are at the supper in the presence of a priest or a deacon, let them eat in the same orderly way. And all shall hasten to receive the blessed bread from the hand of the priest or the deacon. Likewise a catechumen shall receive the same, exorcized. If the laity are together, they must behave in an orderly way, for a layperson cannot make the blessed bread.

That One Should Eat with Thanksgiving

29. Let everyone eat in the name of the Lord. For this is pleasing to God, that we should compete among the heathen in being like-minded and sober.

Of Supper for Widows

30. If anyone wants widows to have a meal, let them be ripe in years, and let him send them away before the evening. And if he cannot (receive them) because of the charge which he has been allotted, let him give them food and wine, and send them away, and let them partake as they like at home.

Of the Fruits One Should Offer to the Bishop

31. Let all hasten to offer the new fruits to the bishop as firstfruits. And *as he* offers them, he shall bless them and name him who offered, saying:

We give you thanks, O God, and offer to you the firstfruits which you have granted us to receive; you nourished them by your word, and ordered the earth to bear all fruits for the joy and nourishment of people and for all animals. In all these things we praise you, O God, and in all the things with which you have helped us, adorning for us the whole creation with various fruits; through your child Jesus Christ our Lord, through whom be glory to you for the ages of ages. Amen.

Of the Blessing of Fruits

32. Fruits indeed are blessed, that is, grapes, figs, pomegranates, olives, pears, apples, mulberries, peaches, cherries, almonds, plums; but not pumpkins, melons, cucumbers, onions, garlic, or any other vegetable. But sometimes flowers also are offered.

So let roses and lilies be offered, but not others. And in all things which are eaten, they shall give thanks to the holy God, eating to his glory.

Than No-one Should Touch any Food at the Pascha before the Proper Time for Eating

33. At the Pascha no-one may eat before the offering is made. If anyone does so, it does not count for him as fasting. Anyone who is pregnant or ill, and cannot fast for two days, should fast (only) on the Saturday on account of their necessity, confining themselves to bread and water. Anyone who was at sea or found himself in some necessity, and did not know the day, when he has learned of it, shall observe the fast after Pentecost. For the type has passed away; that is why it ended in the second month; and when he has learned the truth, he should observe the fast.

That Deacons Should Attend on the Bishop

34. Each deacon, with the subdeacons, shall attend on the bishop. They shall inform him of those who are ill, so that, if he pleases, he may visit them. For sick people are greatly comforted when the high-priest remembers them.

Of the Time When One Ought to Pray

35. The faithful, as soon as they have woken and got up, before they turn to their work, shall pray to God, and so hasten to their work. If there is any verbal instruction, one should give preference to this, and go and hear the word of God, to the comfort of one's soul. Let one hasten to the church, where the Spirit flourishes.

That the Eucharist Should Be Received First, Whenever It Is Offered, before any Food Is Taken

36. Let all the faithful take steps to receive the eucharist before they eat anything else. For if they receive in faith, even if some deadly thing is given them, after that it shall not overpower them.

That the Eucharist Must Be Carefully Guarded

37. Let everyone take care that no unbeliever eats of the eucharist, nor any mouse or other animal, and that none of it falls and is lost. For it is the body of Christ, to be eaten by believers, and not to be despised.

Nothing Must Fall from the Cup

38. For having blessed (the cup) in the name of God, you received as it were the antitype of the blood of Christ. Therefore do not pour any out, as though you despised it, lest an alien spirit lick it up. You will be guilty of the blood, as one who despises the price with which one has been bought.

Of the Sign of the Cross

42A. *If you are tempted*, sign your forehead. For this sign of the passion is displayed against the Devil, if it is made in faith, not to please people, but through knowledge, presenting it like a breastplate. For when the Adversary sees the power of the Spirit (which comes) from the heart, outwardly displayed in the likeness of baptism, he will tremble and flee, when you do not strike him but breathe on him. Moses did this symbolically with the sheep which was sacrificed at the Passover. By sprinkling the blood on the threshold and by anointing the two doorposts, he signified that faith which is now in us, in the perfect sheep. Let us sign forehead and eyes with the hand, and escape from him who is trying to destroy us.

43A. And so, when these things are heard with thankfulness and true orthodox faith, they provide edification for the Church and eternal life for believers. I counsel those who are sensible to guard them. For to all who hear the apos(tolic tradition). . .

39. *The deacons and priests shall assemble daily at the place which the bishop appoints for them. Let the deacons not fail to assemble at all times, unless illness hinders them. When all have assembled, let them teach those who are in the church, and in this way, when they have prayed, let them go to the work which falls to each one of them.*

Of Cemeteries

40. *No one may be heavily charged for burying a person in the cemeteries; it is the property of all the poor. But the fee of the workman and the price of the tiles shall be paid to him who digs. The bishop shall provide for those who are in that place and look after it, so that there may be no heavy charge for those who come to those places.*

Of the Time When One Ought to Pray

41. *Let every faithful man and woman, when they have risen from sleep in the morning, before they touch any work at all, wash their hands and pray to God, and so go to their work. But if instruction in the word of God is given, each one should choose to go to that place, reckoning in the heart that it is God who is heard in the instructor.*

For the one who prays in the church will be able to pass by the wickedness of the day. Those who are pious should think it a great evil if they do not go to the place where instruction is given, and especially if they can read, or if a teacher comes. Let none of you be late in the church, the place where teaching is given. Then it shall be given to the speaker to say that is useful to each one; you will hear things which you do not think of, and profit from things which the holy Spirit will give you through the instructor. In this way your faith will be strengthened about the things you will have heard. You will also be told in that place what you ought to do at home. Therefore let each one be diligent in coming to the church, the place where the holy Spirit flourishes. If there is a day when there is no instruction, let each one, when at home, take up a holy book and read in it sufficiently what seems to bring profit.

And if you are at home, pray at the third hour and bless God. But if you are somewhere else at that moment, pray to God in your heart. For at that hour Christ was nailed to the tree. For this reason also in the Old (Testament) the Law prescribed that the shewbread should be offered continually as a type of the body and blood of Christ; and the slaughter of the lamb without reason is this type of the perfect lamb. For Christ is the shepherd, and also the bread which came down from heaven.

Pray likewise at the time of the sixth hour. For when Christ was nailed to the wood of the cross, the day was divided, and darkness fell. And so at that hour let them pray a powerful prayer, imitating the voice of him who prayed and made all creation dark for the unbelieving Jews.

And at the ninth hour let them pray also a great prayer and a great blessing, to know the way in which the soul of the righteous blesses God who does not lie, who remembered his saints and sent his word to give them light. For at that hour Christ was pierced in his side and poured out water and blood; giving light to the rest of the time of the day, he brought it to evening. Then, in beginning to sleep and making the beginning of another day, he fulfilled the type of the resurrection.

Pray before your body rests on the bed. Rise about midnight, wash you hands with water, and pray. If your wife is present also, pray both together; if she is not yet among the faithful, go apart into another room and pray, and go back to bed again. Do not be lazy about praying. He who is bound in the marriage-bond is not defiled.

Those who have washed have no need to wash again, for they are clean. By signing yourself with moist breath and catching your spittle in your hand, your body is sanctified down to your feet. For when (prayer) is offered with a believing heart as though from the font, the gift of the Spirit and the sprinkling of baptism sanctify the one who believes. Therefore it is necessary to pray at this hour.

For the elders who gave us the tradition taught us that at that hour all creation is still for a moment, to praise the Lord; stars, trees, waters stop for an instant, and all the host of angels (which) ministers to him praises

God with the souls of the righteous in this hour. That is why believers should take good care to pray at this hour.

Bearing witness to this, the Lord says thus, 'Lo, about midnight a shout was made of people saying, Lo, the bridegroom comes; rise to meet him'. And he goes on, saying, 'Watch therefore, for you know not at what hour he comes.'

And likewise rise about cockcrow, *and pray.* For at that hour, as the cock crew, the children of Israel denied Christ, whom we know by faith, our eyes looking towards that day in the hope of eternal light at the resurrection of the dead.

And if you act so, all you faithful, and remember these things, and teach them in your turn, and encourage the catechumens, you will not be able to be tempted or to perish, since you have Christ always in memory.

42B. Always reverently observe to sign your forehead. For this sign of the passion is known and approved against the devil, if you make it in faith, and not so that you may be seen by people, but through knowledge presenting it like a shield. For when the Adversary sees the power which comes from the heart, *and when he sees the inner rational person, signed within and without with the sign of the word of God, he flees at once, expelled by the holy Spirit, who is in (every) person who makes a place for him inside.* Moses did this symbolically with the sheep which was sacrificed at the Passover; by sprinkling the blood on the threshold and anointing the doorposts, he signified that faith which is now in us, in the perfect sheep. So let us sign forehead and eyes with the hand, and escape from him who is trying to destroy us.

43B. And so if these things are received with thankfulness and true faith, they provide edification in the Church and eternal life for believers. I counsel that these things should be guarded by all those who are sensible. For if all of you hear the apostolic tra(dition), *and follow it and keep it, no heretic or anyone at all can lead you into error. For in this way many heresies have grown, because the leaders were not willing to learn the purpose of the apostles, but did what they wanted, according to their own pleasure, and not what was fitting.*

If we have passed over anything, beloved, God will reveal it to those who are worthy, since he steers the Church to the haven of quietness.

7 Origen, "First Homily on the Song of Songs" (240?, Caesarea)

Origen (Origenes Adamantius) was born in or about 185 in Egypt, probably in Alexandria. Alexandria was the main port in Egypt, located on the west side of the delta where the Nile flowed into the Mediterranean, and it was one of the great cultural centres of the Roman Empire. It boasted the most important Jewish community outside Palestine, and it was the home of a brilliant tradition of Jewish Biblical, theological, and historical scholarship. Philo, a first-century Jewish scholar who influenced Christian thought in many ways, had been an Alexandrian; and it was in Alexandria that Jewish scholars had translated their Bible into the very influential Greek version known as the Septuagint. The philosophy called neoplatonism was born there, and neopythagoreanism may have been as well. Other philosophical traditions had academies in the city. The Mouseion (Museum) of Alexandria was one of the finest research institutes in the ancient world, with a "mother" library that housed half a million scrolls, and a "daughter" library which was even larger. Partly because Alexandrian Christianity had to answer the criticisms of the local non-Christian intelligentsia, and partly because it wanted to evangelize people whose way of thinking had been formed by other philosophical traditions, it grew accustomed to thinking and speaking in the categories of philosophy, especially the philosophy of Plato. And because it wanted to unlock the hidden meanings of Scripture, it borrowed academic tools of literary analysis from its cultured milieu.

According to Origen's best biographer, the very competent historian Eusebius of Caesarea, writing about 325, Origen was raised in a Christian home. In about 202, during the persecutions under the Emperor Septimius Severus, his father was martyred. About the same time the head of the diocesan school for catechumens fled the persecutions, and Origen in effect took his place, although he was still only a teenager. Later, the bishop appointed him to do what he was already doing. Origen proved a brilliant scholar and an inspiring and demanding teacher. He developed a curriculum for catechumens which began with philosophy, logic, and science, and then proceeded to ethics and theology. Meanwhile, he continued his own education, studying Hebrew with local Jewish scholars, attending lectures by the founder of neoplatonism, and reading Scripture very carefully. His lifestyle was highly ascetic, almost pathologically so. It was said that, inspired by Matthew 19:12, he castrated himself.

In 230, on a trip to Palestine, he allowed himself to be ordained without the permission of the bishop of Alexandria. His bishop was furious, and in 231 Origen found himself excommunicated. He then moved to Caesarea, the Roman capital of the province of Syria Palaestina, about 105 kilometers northwest of Jerusalem. Caesarea was an important sea-port and commercial centre, and it could boast an apostolic tradition dating back to Peter and Paul. Origen felt as if, like Israel, he had been released from the bondage of Pharaoh and had found freedom in the land of Canaan. He directed the school for catechumens there, and, being now a priest, began preaching homilies, or explanations of passages of Scripture. In a time when different churches and different synagogues were using different versions of Scripture, he used scientific means for establishing the true text. He wrote hundreds, possibly thousands of works. Because doubts later arose about his orthodoxy, and because many of his works were soaked in the philosophy of Plato, only a few of them have survived in their original Greek, and a few more in Latin translation. He is generally considered the most outstanding Christian scholar and thinker of the second and third centuries.

In 250 he was arrested during the persecutions under the Emperor Decius, and suffered long periods of torture. He died two or three years afterwards.

Most of Origen's works were on Biblical subjects, and his preferred method of interpretation was allegorical. This approach was a standard one in Alexandria, not only among pagan interpreters of the classics but also among Jewish interpreters of the Old Testament. The Christian justification for allegorical interpretation was Paul's use of it, as at Galatians 4:24 and I Cor. 9:9. Thus, Sarah and Hagar might be historical people at a merely literal level of interpretation, but at an allegorical level they represented the two covenants. Origen discussed the allegorical method in his work *On First Principles*, Book 4. A merely literal understanding of Scripture could lead to errors and absurdities, he believed, and anyway it missed the deeper truths. Every single word of Scripture had a purpose, and the task of interpretation was to see how each word figured spiritual and mystical realities. The letter killed, but the spirit gave life. It was enough for simple Christians to be satisfied with a basic faith in Christ crucified, but those who would be perfect would want to ascend to more sublime heights of contemplation through the knowledge of the spiritual truths of Scripture. After all, Jesus taught in figure to the many, and entrusted the deeper truths only to the few.

Origen wrote on all the books of the Old and New Testament. Some of his works were *scholia* or critical notes, some were homilies, and some were very detailed commentaries. One of the few homilies by Origen that has survived is the one below on the first part of the "Song of Songs". Almost everyone in the early Church (the fifth-century Antiochene Theodore of Mopsuestia was an exception) thought that allegorical interpretation was precisely suited to this book of the Bible. The synagogue had thought so, too; Rabbi Akiba (50-132), for example, understood the lovers in the book as God and Israel. Origen no doubt delivered the homily below during his years at Caesarea. The original Greek has not survived; the work is known through a Latin translation made a century and a half later by Jerome, the translator of the Bible into the Latin "Vulgate" version.

Questions on the reading

What interest does Origen take in the original historical context of the Song of Songs, or in the purpose of its author? What for Origen is the theme and purpose of the book? What does he regard as the significance of the Song of Songs, compared to the other songs recorded in the Bible? What in Origen's view is represented by the Bridegroom; the Bride; "kisses of his mouth"; "the odour of thy perfumes"; "embrace"; "little breast"; "bosom"; "breasts"; "perfume poured forth"; "black"; "queen of the south"; "fought against me"; "horse-rider"? What is the system of Origen's exegesis? What, from this document, appears to be his understanding of the Church (the Bride)? What might be the role of ordained ministry in the Church he envisions? Why might Origen's bishop have been glad to be rid of him?

Jerome's Prologue

Jerome to the Most Blessed Pope Damasus:

While Origen surpassed all writers in his other books, in his *Song of Songs* he surpassed himself. In ten full volumes, containing nearly twenty thousand lines, he expounded first the version of the Seventy, then those of Aquila, Symmachus, and Theodotion, and finally a fifth, which he tells us that he found on the coast near Actium. And this exposition of his is so splendid and so clear, that it seems to me that the words, *The King brought me into His chamber*, have found their fulfilment in him. I have passed over that work, for it would require far too much time and labour and expense worthily to render into Latin such a mighty theme. It is not strong meat that I offer here; instead of that, with greater faithfulness than elegance I have translated these two treatises which he composed for babes and sucklings into the speech of every day, to give you just a sample of his thinking, so that you may reflect how highly his great thoughts should be esteemed, when even his little ones can so commend themselves.

Source: Origen, "First Homily on the Song of Songs," in R.P. Lawson, trans., *Origen* (Ancient Christian Writers, vol. 26), Westminster, MD: Newman Press, 1957, 265-283.

The First Homily

On the beginning of the Song of Songs to the place
where the writer says: Until the King recline at his table.

1. As we have learned from Moses that some places are not merely
holy, but *holy of holies*, and that certain days are not sabbaths simply,
but are sabbaths of sabbaths: so now we are taught further by the pen of
Solomon that there are songs which are not merely songs, but songs of
songs. Blessed too is the one who enters holy places, but far more blest
the one who enters the holy of holies! Blessed is the one who observes
the sabbaths, but more blest the one who keeps sabbaths of sabbaths!
Blessed likewise is the one who understands songs and sings them — of
course nobody sings except on festal days — but much more blest is the
one who sings the Songs of Songs! And as the one who enters holy
places still needs much to be able to enter the holy of holies, and as the
one who keeps the sabbath which was ordained by God for the people
still requires many things before being able to keep the sabbath of
sabbaths: so also is it hard to find one competent to scale the heights of
the Songs of Songs, even one who has traversed all the songs in Scripture.

You must come out of Egypt and, when the land of Egypt lies
behind you, you must cross the Red Sea if you are to sing the first song,
saying: *Let us sing to the Lord, for He is gloriously magnified.* But though
you have uttered this first song, you are still a long way from the Song of
Songs. Pursue your spiritual journey through the wilderness, until you
come to *the well which the kings dug*, so that there you may sing the
second song. After that, come to the threshold of the holy land, that
standing on the bank of Jordan you may sing the song of Moses, saying:
*Hear, O heaven, and I will speak, and let the earth give ear to the words
of my mouth!* Again, you must fight under *Joshua* and possess the holy
land as your inheritance; and a bee must prophesy for you and judge
you — *Deborah*, you understand, means 'bee' — in order that you may
take that song also on your lips, which is found in the Book of Judges.
Mount up thence to the Book of Kings, and come to the song of David,
when he fled *out of the hand of all his enemies and out of the hand of
Saul, and said, 'The Lord is my stay and my strength and my refuge and
my saviour.'* You must go on next to Isaiah, so that with him you may
say: *I will sing to the Beloved the song of my vineyard.*

And when you have been through all the songs, then set your

course for greater heights, so that as a fair soul with her Spouse you may sing this Song of Songs too. I am not sure how many persons are concerned in it; but, as far as God has shown me in answer to your prayers, I seem to find four characters — the Husband and the Bride; along with the Bride, her maidens; and with the Bridegroom, a band of intimate companions. Some things are spoken by the Bride, others by the Bridegroom; sometimes too the maidens speak; so also do the Bridegroom's friends. It is fitting indeed that at a wedding the bride should be accompanied by a bevy of maidens and the bridegroom by a company of youths. You must not look without for the meaning of these; you must look no further than those who are saved by the preaching of the Gospel. By the Bridegroom understand Christ, and by the Bride the Church *without spot or wrinkle*, of whom it is written: *that He might present her to Himself a glorious Church, not having spot or wrinkle or any such thing, but that she might be holy and without blemish.* In the maidens who are with the Bride you must recognize those who, although they are faithful, do not come under the foregoing description, yet are regarded none the less as having in some sense obtained salvation — in short, they are the souls of believers. And in the men with the Bridegroom you must see the angels and those who have *come unto the perfect man.* We have thus four groups: the two individuals, the Bridegroom and the Bride; two choirs answering each other — the Bride singing with her maidens, and the Bridegroom with His companions. When you have grasped this, listen to the Song of Songs and make haste to understand it and to join with the Bride in saying what she says, so that you may hear also what she heard. And, if you are unable to join the Bride in her words, then, so that you may hear the things that are said to her, make haste at least to join the Bridegroom's companions. And if they also are beyond you, then be with the maidens who stay in the Bride's retinue and share her pleasures.

These are the characters in this book, which is at once a drama and a marriage-song. And it is from this book that the heathen appropriated the epithalamium, and here is the source of this type of poem; for it is obviously a marriage-song that we have in the Song of Songs. The Bride prays first and, even as she prays, forthwith is heard. She sees the Bridegroom present; she sees the maidens gathered in her train. Then the Bridegroom answers her; and, after He has spoken, while He is still suffering for her salvation, the companions reply that 'until the Bridegroom recline at his table' and rise from His Passion, they are going to make the Bride some ornaments.

2. We must consider now the actual words with which the Bride first voices her prayer: LET HIM KISS ME WITH THE KISSES OF HIS MOUTH. Their meaning is: 'How long is my Bridegroom going to send me kisses by Moses and kisses by the prophets? It is His own mouth that I desire now to touch; let Him come, let Him come down Himself!' So she beseeches the Bridegroom's Father saying: 'Let Him kiss me with the kisses of His mouth.' And because she is such that the prophetic word, *While thou are yet speaking, I will say, 'Lo, here am I!'* can be fulfilled upon her, the Bridegroom's Father listens to the Bride and sends His Son.

She, seeing Him for whose coming she prayed, leaves off her prayer and says to Him directly: THY BREASTS ARE BETTER THAN WINE, AND THE ODOUR OF THY PERFUMES BETTER THAN ALL SPICES. Christ the Bridegroom, therefore, whom the Father has sent, comes anointed to the Bride and it is said to Him: *Thou hast loved justice and hated iniquity: therefore God, Thy God, hath anointed Thee with the oil of gladness above Thy fellows.* If the Bridegroom has touched me, I too become of a good odour, I too am anointed with perfumes; and His perfumes are so imparted to me that I can say with the apostles: *We are the good odour of Christ in every place.*

But we, although we hear these things, still stink of the sins and vices concerning which the penitent speaks through the prophet, saying: *My sores are putrefied and corrupted because of my foolishness.* Sin has a putrid smell, virtue exhales sweet odours. Look up examples of them in the Book of Exodus; you will find there stacte, onyx, galbanum, and so on. Now these are to make incense; in addition, various perfumes, among them nard and stacte, are taken for the work of the perfumer. And God who made heaven and earth speaks to Moses, saying: *I have filled them with the spirit of wisdom and understanding, that they may make the things that belong to the perfumer's art;* and God teaches the perfumers. If these words are not to be spiritually understood, are they not mere tales? If they conceal no hidden mystery, are they not unworthy of God? He, therefore, who can discern the spiritual sense of Scripture or, if he cannot, yet desires so to do, must strive his utmost to live not after flesh and blood, so that he may become worthy of spiritual mysteries and — if I may speak more boldly — of spiritual desire and love, if such indeed there be. And as one sort of food is carnal and another is spiritual, and as there is one drink for the flesh and another for the spirit, so there is love of the flesh which comes from Satan, and there is also another love, belonging to the spirit, which has its origin in God; and nobody can be possessed by the two loves. If you are a lover of the flesh, you do not acquire the love of the spirit. If you have despised all bodily things — I do not mean flesh and blood, but money and property and the very earth and heaven, for these will pass away — if you have sent all these at nought and your soul is not attached to any of them, neither are you held back by any love of sinful practices, then you can acquire spiritual love.

We have put this here, because the opportunity arose to say something about spiritual love. And it is for us to follow Solomon's injunction, and still more His who spoke through Solomon concerning wisdom, saying: *Love her, and she will keep thee safe; enfold her, and she will exalt thee; render her honour, that she may embrace thee.* For there is a certain spiritual embrace, and O that the Bridegroom's more perfect embrace may enfold my Bride! Then I too shall be able to say what is written in this same book: *His left hand is under my head, and His right hand will embrace me.*

3. 'Let Him kiss me,' therefore, 'with the kisses of His mouth.' The Scriptures are wont to use the form of command, rather than that of wish. We have, for instance, *Our Father who art in heaven, hallowed be Thy name,* instead of 'O that it may be hallowed!'; and in the passage before us we read 'Let Him kiss me with the kisses of His mouth,' rather than 'O that He would kiss!'

Then she sees the Bridegroom. Fragrant with sweet oils He comes; and He could not otherwise approach the Bride, nor was it fitting for the Father to send His Son to the marriage in any other wise. He has anointed Him with divers perfumes, He has made Him the Christ, who comes breathing sweet odours and hears the Bride declare: 'Thy breasts are better than wine.' The Divine Word rightly has different names for the same thing, according to the context. When a victim is offered in the Law, and the Word wants to show exactly what is meant, it says: *The little breast that is set apart.* But when someone reclines with Jesus and enjoys full fellowship of thought with Him, then the expression is, not *little breast*, but *bosom*. And again, when the Bride speaks to the Bridegroom, because it is a marriage-song that is beginning, the word used is not *little breast*, as in the sacrifice, not *bosom*, as in the case of the disciple John, but *breasts* — 'Thy breasts are better than wine.'

Be you of one mind with the Bridegroom, like the Bride, and you will know that thoughts of this kind do inebriate and make the spirit glad. Wherefore, as *the inebriating chalice of the Lord, how surpassing good it is!* — so are the breasts of the Bridegroom better than any wine. 'For Thy breasts are better than wine' — this is how in the midst of her prayers she addresses herself to her Spouse — 'and the odour of Thy perfumes is above all spices.' Not with one perfume only does He come anointed, but with all. And if He will condescend to make my soul His Bride too and come to her, how fair must she then be to draw Him down from heaven to herself, to cause Him to come down to earth, that He may visit His beloved one! With what beauty must she be adorned, with what love must she burn that He may say to her the things which He said to the perfect Bride, about *thy neck, thine eyes, thy cheeks, thy hands, thy body*, thy shoulder, thy feet! God permitting, we will think about these questions, and consider why the Bride's members are thus differentiated and a special meed of praise accorded to each part; thus, when we have thought it out, we may try to have our own soul spoken to in the same way.

'Thy breasts,' then, 'are better than wine,' If you have seen the Bridegroom, you will know that what is spoken here is true: 'Thy breasts are better than wine, and the odour of Thy perfumes is above all spices.' Many people have had spices: the queen of the South brought spices to Solomon, and many others possessed them; but no matter what they had, their treasures could not be compared with the odours of Christ, of which the Bride says here: 'The odour of Thy perfumes is above all spices.' I think myself that Moses had spices too, and Aaron, and each one of the prophets; but if I have once seen Christ and have perceived the sweetness of His perfumes by their smell, forthwith I give my judgement in the words: 'The odour of Thy perfumes is above all spices.'

4. THY NAME IS AS PERFUME POURED FORTH. These words foretell a mystery: even so comes the name of Jesus to the world, and is 'as perfume poured forth' when it is proclaimed. In the Gospel, moreover, a woman took an alabaster vessel containing precious ointment of pure spikenard and

poured it on Jesus' head, and (another) on His feet. Note carefully which of the two women poured the perfume on the Saviour's head: the *sinner* poured it on His feet, and she who is not called a sinner poured it on His head. Notice, I say, and you will find that in this Gospel lesson the evangelists have written mysteries, and not just tales and stories. And so *the house was filled with the odour of the ointment.* We must take what the sinner brought with reference to the feet, and what the woman who was not a sinner brought with reference to the head. Small wonder that the house was filled with fragrance, since with this fragrance all the world is filled!

The same passage speaks of Simon the leper and his house. I think the leper is the prince of this world, and that the leper is called Simon: his house it is that at Christ's coming is filled with sweet odours, when a sinful woman repents and a holy one anoints the head of Jesus with sweet perfumes.

'Thy name is as perfume poured forth.' As perfume when it is applied scatters its fragrance far and wide, so is the name of Jesus poured forth. In every land His name is named, throughout all the world my Lord is preached; for His 'name is as perfume poured forth.' We hear the name of Moses now, though formerly it was not heard beyond the confines of Judea; for none of the Greeks makes mention of it, neither do we find anything written about him or about the others anywhere in pagan literature. But straight away, when Jesus shone upon the world, He led forth the Law and the Prophets along with Himself, and the words, 'Thy name is as perfume poured forth,' were indeed fulfilled.

5. THEREFORE HAVE THE VIRGINS LOVED THEE. Because *the charity of God is poured forth in our hearts by the Holy Spirit,* the mention of pouring forth, which is made here, is apt. As the Bride says the words, 'Thy name is as perfume poured forth,' she sees the maidens. When she made her petition to the Bridegroom's Father, and while she was talking directly to the Spouse Himself, the maidens were not present; but a band of virgins appears even as she is praying, and, praising them, she says, 'Therefore have the virgins loved Thee, AND HAVE DRAWN THEE.' And the maidens answer: WE WILL RUN AFTER THEE IN THE FRAGRANCE OF THY PERFUMES.

How fine a touch it is that the attendants of the Bride do not as yet have the Bride's own confidence! The Bride does not follow behind, she walks side by side with the Bridegroom; she takes His right hand, and in

His right hand her own hand is held. But the handmaidens follow after Him. *There are threescore queens, and fourscore concubines, and young maidens without number. One is my dove, my perfect one, she is the only one of her mother, she that conceived her hath no other one.* 'After thee,' therefore, 'we will run into the fragrance of thy perfumes.'

It was entirely appropriate that these words, 'we will run into the fragrance of thy perfumes,' were used of lovers; they accord with *I have finished the course, and they that run in the race all run indeed, but one receiveth the prize* — which prize is Christ. And these maidens who, as we know, are standing without because their love is only just beginning, are like *the friend of the Bridegroom, who standeth and heareth Him, and rejoiceth with joy because of the Bridegroom's voice.* The maidens undergo a like experience: when the Bridegroom enters, they remain without.

But when the Bride, the fair, the perfect one who is without spot or wrinkle, has entered the Bridegroom's chamber, the secret place of the King, she comes back to the maidens and, telling them the things that she alone has seen, she says: THE KING BROUGHT ME INTO HIS CHAMBER. She does not say: 'He brought us' — using the plural — 'into His chamber'; the others remain without, the Bride alone is brought into the chamber, that she may see there dark and hidden treasures and may take back word to the damsels: 'The King brought me into His chamber.'

Further, when the Bride has gone into the Bridegroom's chamber and is seeing there the riches of her Spouse, the maidens — the goodly company of those who are learning to be brides — sing together joyfully while they await her coming, saying: WE WILL BE GLAD AND REJOICE IN THEE. They are glad because of the Bride's perfection, for there is here no envy in respect of virtues; this love is pure, this is love free from fault.

'We will be glad and rejoice in thee. WE WILL LOVE THY BREASTS.' She who is greater is already enjoying the milk of those breasts, and she says in her joy: 'Thy breasts are above wine.' But these, because they are young maidens only, defer their joy and gladness; their love also they defer and say: 'We will be glad and rejoice in thee. We will love' — not 'we love,' but 'we will love' — 'Thy breasts MORE THAN WINE.' Then they say to the Bridegroom, 'EQUITY HAS LOVED THEE': they praise the Bride by calling her Equity, as denoting the sum of her characteristic virtues —

'Equity has loved Thee.'

6. The Bride then makes the maidens this reply: I AM BLACK AND
BEAUTIFUL, O YE DAUGHTERS OF JERUSALEM — we learn now that 'daughters of
Jerusalem' is what the maidens are — AS THE TENTS OF CEDAR, AS THE CURTAINS
OF SOLOMON. LOOK NOT AT ME, FOR THAT I AM BLACKENED; FOR THE SUN HAS LOOKED
DOWN ON ME.

Beautiful indeed is the Bride, and I can find out in what manner she
is so. But the question is, in what way is she black and how, if she lacks
whiteness, is she fair. She has repented of her sins, beauty is the gift
conversion has bestowed; that is the reason she is hymned as beautiful.
She is called black, however, because she has not yet been purged of
every stain of sin, she has not yet been washed unto salvation;
nevertheless she does not stay dark-hued, she is becoming white. When,
therefore, she arises towards greater things and begins to mount from
lowly things to lofty, they say concerning her: *Who is this that cometh
up, having been washed white?* And in order that the mystery may be
more clearly expressed, they do not say *leaning upon her Nephew's
arm*, as we read in most versions — that is to say, *episterizoméne*, but
epistethizoméne, that is, *leaning upon His breast*. And it is significant
that the expression used concerning the bride-soul and the Bridegroom-
Word is *lying upon His breast*, because there is the seat of our heart.
Forsaking carnal things, therefore, we must perceive those of the spirit
and understand that it is much better to love after this manner than to
refrain from love. She *cometh up*, then, *leaning on her Nephew's breast*,
and of her, who at the Canticle's beginning was set down as black, it is
sung at the end of the marriage-song: *Who is this that cometh up, having
been washed white?*

We understand, then, why the Bride is black and beautiful at one
and the same time. But, if you do not likewise practise penitence, take
heed lest *your* soul be described as black and ugly, and you be hideous
with a double foulness — black by reason of your past sins and ugly
because you are continuing in the same vices! If you have repented,
however, your soul will indeed be black because of your old sins, but
your penitence will give it something of what I may call an Ethiopian
beauty. And having once made mention of an Ethiopian, I want to
summon a Scriptural witness about this word too. *Aaron and Mary
murmur against Moses, because Moses has an Ethiopian wife.* Moses

weds an Ethiopian wife, because his Law has passed over to the Ethiopian woman of our Song. Let the Aaron of the Jewish priesthood murmur, and let the Mary of their synagogue murmur too. Moses cares nothing for their murmuring: He loves His Ethiopian woman, concerning whom it is said elsewhere through the prophet: *From the ends of the rivers of Ethiopia shall they bring offerings,* and again: *Ethiopia shall get her hands in first with God.* It is well said that she shall get in first; for, as in the Gospel the woman with the issue of blood received attention before the daughter of the ruler of the synagogue, so also has Ethiopia been healed while Israel is still sick. *By their offence salvation has been effected for the Gentiles, so as to make them jealous.*

'I am black and beautiful, O ye daughters of Jerusalem.' Address yourself to the daughters of Jerusalem, you member of the Church, and say: 'The Bridegroom loves me more and holds me dearer than you, who are the many daughters of Jerusalem; you stand without and watch the Bride enter the chamber.' [Let no one doubt that the black one is beautiful, for all she is called black. For we exist in order that we may acknowledge God, that we may tell forth songs of a song, that we may be those who have come from the borders of Ethiopia, from the ends of the earth, to hear the wisdom of the true Solomon.] And when the Saviour's voice is heard thundering out the words: *The queen of the South shall come to judgement and shall condemn the men of this generation, because she came from the ends of the earth to hear the wisdom of Solomon, and behold, a greater than Solomon is here,* you must understand what is said in a mystical sense: the queen of the South, who comes from the ends of the earth, is the Church; and the men of this generation whom she condemns, are the Jews, who are given over to flesh and blood. She comes from the ends of the earth to hear the wisdom, not of that Solomon about whom we read in the Old Testament, but of Him who is said in the Gospel to be greater than Solomon.

'I am black and beautiful, O daughters of Jerusalem, black as the tents of Cedar, beautiful as the curtains of Solomon.' The very names accord with the Bride's comeliness. The Hebrews say that *Cedar* is the word for darkness — 'I am black,' therefore, 'as the tents of Cedar,' as the Ethiopians, as Ethiopian tents; and 'beautiful as the curtains of Solomon,' which he prepared as adornments of the tabernacle at the time when he built the Temple with the utmost care and toil. Solomon was rich indeed, and no one surpassed him in any branch of wisdom. 'I am black and beautiful, O daughters of Jerusalem, as the tents of Cedar, as the curtains of Solomon. Look not at me, for that I am blackened.' She apologizes for her blackness; and being turned to better things through penitence, she tells the daughters of Jerusalem that she is black indeed, but beautiful for the reason which we gave above, and says: 'Look not at me, for that I am blackened.' 'Do not be surprised,' she says, 'that I am of a forbidding hue; the Sun has looked down on me. With full radiance His bright light has shone on me, and I am darkened by His heat. I have not indeed received His light into myself as it were fitting that I should, and as the Sun's own dignity required.'

By their offence salvation has been effected for the Gentiles. And again: *Through the unbelief of the Gentiles is the knowledge of Israel.* You find both these texts in the Apostle.

7. THE SONS OF MY MOTHER HAVE FOUGHT AGAINST ME. We must consider in what sense the Bride says: 'The sons of my mother have fought against me,' and at what time her brothers launched this attack. You have only to look at Paul, the persecutor of the Church, to see how a son of her mother fought against her. The persecutors of the Church have repented, and her opponents have turned to their sister's banners and have preached the faith which they formerly sought to destroy. Foreseeing this, the Bride now sings: THEY HAVE CONTENDED AGAINST ME, THEY HAVE MADE ME THE KEEPER IN THE VINEYARDS; MY VINEYARD I HAVE NOT KEPT. 'I, the Church, the spotless one,' she says, 'have been appointed keeper of many vineyards by my mother's sons, who once had fought against me. Harassed by the responsibility and care involved in guarding many vineyards, I have not kept my own.'

Apply these words to Paul or any other of the saints who care for the salvation of all people, and you will see how he guards others' vine-plantations while not guarding his own; how he himself bears loss in some respects so that he may gain others; and how, though he was free as to all, he made himself the servant of all that he might gain all, being made weak to the weak, a Jew to the Jews, as subject to the Law to those who are so subject, and so forth — how, in a word, he can say: 'My vineyard I have not kept.'

The Bride then beholds the Bridegroom; and He, as soon as she has seen Him, goes away. He does this frequently throughout the Song; and that is something nobody can understand who has not suffered it himself. God is my witness that I have often perceived the Bridegroom drawing near me and being most intensely present with me; then suddenly He has withdrawn and I could not find Him, though I sought to do so. I long, therefore, for Him to come again, and sometimes He does so. Then, when He has appeared and I lay hold of Him, He slips away once more; and, when He has so slipped away, my search for Him begins anew. So does He act with me repeatedly, until in truth I hold Him and go up, 'leaning on my Nephew's arm.'

8. TELL ME, THOU WHOM MY SOUL HAS LOVED, WHERE THOU FEEDEST, WHERE THOU LIEST IN THE MIDDAY. I am not asking about other times, I ask not where Thou feedest in the evening, or at daybreak, or when the sun goes down. I ask about the full day-time, when the light is brightest and Thou dwellest in the splendour of Thy majesty: 'Tell me, Thou whom my soul has loved, where Thou liest in the midday.'   .

Observe attentively where else you have read about midday. In the story of Joseph his brethren feast at noon; at noon the angels were entertained by Abraham, and there are other instances besides. You will find if you look into it, that Holy Scripture never uses any word haphazard and without a purpose. Who among us, do you think, is worthy to attain the midday, and to see where the Bridegroom feeds and where He lies at noon? 'Tell me, Thou whom my soul has loved, where Thou feedest, where Thou liest in the midday.' For, unless Thou tell me, I shall begin to be a vagrant, driven to and fro; while I am looking for Thee, I shall begin to run after other people's flocks and, because these other people make me feel ashamed, I shall begin to cover my face and my mouth. I am the beautiful Bride in sooth, and I show not my naked face to any save Thee only, whom I kissed tenderly but now. 'Tell me, Thou whom my soul has loved, where Thou feedest, where Thou liest in the midday, LEST I HAVE TO GO VEILED BESIDE THE FLOCKS OF THY COMPANIONS.' That I suffer not these things — that I may need not to go veiled nor hide my face; that, mixing with others, I run not the risk of beginning to love also them whom I know not — tell me, therefore, where I may seek and find Thee in the midday, 'lest I have to go veiled beside the flocks of Thy companions.'

9. After these words the Bridegroom warns her, saying: 'Either know thyself, that thou art the Bride of the King and beautiful, and made beautiful by me because I have presented to myself *a glorious Church, not having spot or wrinkle*; or understand that if thou hast not known thyself nor grasped thy dignity, thou must endure the things that follow.' What may these be?

IF THOU HAVE NOT KNOWN THYSELF, O FAIR ONE AMONG WOMEN, GO FORTH IN THE STEPS OF THE FLOCKS AND FEED — not the flocks of sheep, nor of lambs, but — THY GOATS. He will set the sheep on the right hand and the goats upon the left, assuredly. 'If thou have not known thyself, O fair one among women, go forth in the steps of the flocks and feed thy goats AMONG THE SHEPHERDS' TENTS.' 'In the steps of the flocks,' He says, 'wilt thou find thyself at the last, not among the sheep, but among the goats; and when thou dwellest with them thou canst not be with me — that is, with the Good Shepherd.

10. 'To MY COMPANY OF HORSEMEN AMONG PHARAO'S CHARIOTS HAVE I LIKENED THEE. If thou wouldst understand, O Bride, how thou must know thyself, think what it is to which I have compared thee. Then, when thou hast recognized thy likeness, thou wilt see that thou art such as must not be disgraced.'

What then is the meaning of these words: 'To my company of horsemen among Pharao's chariots have I likened thee'? I myself know that the Bridegroom is likened to a horseman in the words of the prophet: *Thy riding is salvation*; so thou art compared to 'my company of horsemen among Pharao's chariots.' As different is the company of horsemen that belongs to me, who am the Lord and drown the Pharao and his generals, his riders and his horsemen in the waves — as different, I tell you, is my cavalry from Pharao's horses as thou, the Bride, art better than all daughters, and thou, the soul belonging to the Church, art better than all souls that are not of the Church. 'To my company of horsemen among Pharao's chariots have I likened thee.'

He next describes the beauty of the Bride in terms of spiritual love: THY CHEEKS ARE AS THE TURTLE-DOVE'S. He praises her face, and is kindled to admiration by her rosy cheeks. A woman's beauty is considered to reside supremely in her cheeks. So let us likewise take the cheeks as revealing the beauty of the soul; by lips and tongue, however, let the intelligence be represented to us.

THY NECK IS AS A NECKLACE. Thy neck, that is to say, even when unadorned is of itself as much an ornament as is the little necklace called *hormiskos*, that virgins are wont to wear.

After these things the Spouse takes His repose. *He has reposed as a lion, and as a lion's whelp He has slept,* so that in due course He may hear: *Who shall arouse Him?* While He reposes, His companions the angels appear to the Bride and comfort her with these words: 'We cannot make thee golden ornaments — we are not so rich as is thy Spouse, who gives thee a necklace of gold; we will make thee likenesses of gold, for gold we have not got. Yet this also is matter for rejoicing, if we make likenesses of gold, if we make studs of silver. WE WILL MAKE THEE LIKENESSES OF GOLD WITH STUDS OF SILVER; but not for always, only until thy Spouse arises from His rest. For, when He has arisen, He Himself will make thee gold and silver, He will Himself adorn thy mind and thy understanding, and thou shalt be rich indeed, the Bride made perfect in the House of the Bridegroom, to whom be glory for ever and ever. Amen.'

8 Cyprian, *Treatise to Demetrianus* (252?, Carthage)

Cyprian (Thascius Caecilius Cyprianus, d. 258), bishop of Carthage, followed in a theological tradition laid out by an earlier Carthaginian Christian, Tertullian, who died fifteen or twenty years before Cyprian's conversion. Tertullian is considered a deeper theologian with a wider range of interests, Cyprian the clearer writer with the more practical bent and the more compassionate heart.

Cyprian was born into a cultured and wealthy pagan family, probably in Carthage, the premier city of North Africa, and the second most important city of the western Roman Empire after Rome. (Its ruins remain on its site on the Bay of Tunis, quite near modern Tunis in Tunisia.) He was classically educated, and made his living as a teacher of rhetoric. While the field of rhetoric could be, at its worst, simply the skill of speaking impressively in public and winning arguments, it could also be, at its best — as the philosopher Aristotle had explained it more than five centuries earlier — a sophisticated art that integrated philosophy, logic, dialectic, grammar, and literary analysis. Moreover, the rhetorician could be expected to serve as the remembrancer of the political and social traditions of the community. A good teacher of rhetoric, therefore, was an eminent person in classical culture. Cyprian gave up his social standing when he converted to Christianity at an unknown date under the influence of a Christian presbyter. He stopped reading pagan literature, and devoted himself to the study of Scripture instead. He apparently also gave away most of his wealth. Soon he was made a presbyter in the Church, and by early 249, reluctantly and after demonstrations by laypeople who supported him, he was made bishop. He had probably been a Christian only a few years, because several Carthaginian clergy opposed his consecration as bishop on the grounds that he was still new to the faith.

Cyprian had been bishop for only about a year when the Emperor Decius unleashed an intense persecution of the Church. Cyprian went into hiding. Some criticized him as a coward and a bad example, but he defended his decision as good strategy for the church, and he also quoted Revelation 18:4, "Come out of her, my people,. . . so that you do not share in her plagues," and Matthew 10:23, "When they persecute you in one town, flee to the next." From his refuge, he continued to administer his diocese. He returned to Carthage the following year.

In the wake of the persecution, the Church faced a very practical question: what should be done with the "lapsed", those who had in some measure denied their faith under duress? And what should be done with the "libellatici", those who had not exactly denied their faith, but who had obtained certificates ("libelli") stating that they had venerated the Roman gods? Two extreme positions split the Church in Carthage. Some, who may be called "the laxists," were willing to re-admit the lapsed and the "libellatici" immediately. Others, who may be called "the rigourists," maintained that their sin was unforgivable. Between the laxists and the rigourists Cyprian made his way to a mediating position. He persuaded his synod (the church council of his diocese) that all the lapsed might be reconciled to the Church, but only after a period of penance commensurate with the gravity of the offence, or else on their deathbed.

Two related matters troubled Cyprian. Among the laxists were some "confessors", Christians who had maintained their faith even through imprisonment and torture, but had not been martyred; and many of them were claiming authority from God to forgive the lapsed and to re-admit them into the Church. Did they really have this authority? Cyprian's answer was that they did not. Only the bishop and clergy could reconcile sinners on God's behalf. Moreover, some of the rigourists were setting up their own churches, in schism from the true Church. Were the people they baptized truly baptized? Cyprian answered that they were not; and should they later want to enter the Catholic Church, they would need a proper baptism. He thus contradicted the bishop of Rome of his day.

In 257 a new Emperor, Valerian, began a new persecution of Christians. Cyprian was forced into exile, and then finally, in 258, he was martyred, by beheading.

Most of Cyprian's works attend to churchy themes, but the treatise *To Demetrianus*, printed below, is an exception, at least at first sight. Instead it aims to answer a question which haunted another North African, St. Augustine, over a century and a half later: if Christianity is from God, then why did so many bad things start happening as soon as the Church began attracting people away from paganism? Written against a background of persecution, the work reflects some of the philosophical and other differences that divided Christian from pagan. Demetrianus was the proconsul of Africa. The work bears some resemblance to an *Apology* by Tertullian, whom Cyprian much admired. Cyprian, like Tertullian, wrote in Latin, and the manuscript tradition raises no unusual problems.

Questions on the reading

What prompts Cyprian to write? What, according to Cyprian, has Demetrianus been saying about the Christians? What tone does Cyprian take? What evidence of the social background of the controversy can be found within the text? To what extent is Cyprian really addressing Demetrianus personally, and to what extent a Christian or pagan public? What does Cyprian understand as authoritative evidence for his position? Would Demetrianus be impressed with citations of Scripture? What common understanding might they share, if any, as a basis of conversation? Is Cyprian's classical education in evidence in the document? What is Cyprian's understanding of the world, and how history works? What is his view of the day of judgment? What are the apologetic goals and strategies of the treatise? What might be considered distinctive of North African Christianity in this document?

$\wp$

Treatise to Demetrianus

1. I had frequently, Demetrianus, treated with contempt your railing and noisy clamour with sacrilegious mouth and impious words against the one and true God, thinking it more modest and better, silently to scorn the ignorance of a mistaken man, than by speaking to provoke the fury of a senseless one. Neither did I do this without the authority of the divine teaching, since it is written, "Speak not in the ears of a fool, lest when he hear thee he should despise the wisdom of thy words;"[1] and again, "Answer not a fool according to his folly, lest thou also be like unto him."[2] And we are, moreover, bidden to keep what is holy within our own knowledge, and not expose it to be trodden down by swine and dogs, since the Lord speaks, saying, "Give not that which is holy unto the dogs, neither cast ye your pearls before swine, lest they trample them under their feet, and turn again and rend you."[3] For when you used often to come to me with the desire of contradicting rather than with the wish to learn, and preferred impudently to insist on your own views, which you shouted with noisy words, to patiently listening to mine, it seemed to me foolish to contend with you; since it would be an easier and slighter thing to restrain the angry waves of a turbulent sea with shouts, than to check your madness by arguments. Assuredly it would be both a vain and ineffectual labour to offer light to a blind man, discourse to a deaf one, or wisdom to a brute; since neither can a brute apprehend, nor can a blind man admit the light, nor can a deaf man hear.

2. In consideration of this, I have frequently held my tongue, and overcome an impatient person with patience; since I could neither teach an unteachable person, nor check an impious one with religion, nor restrain a frantic person with gentleness. But yet, when you say that very

---

Source: Cyprian, *Treatise to Demetrianus*, in Alexander Roberts and James Donaldson, eds., *The Ante-Nicene Fathers*, volume 5, Buffalo, 1886, 457-465.

many are complaining that to us it is ascribed that wars arise more frequently, that plague, that famines rage, and that long droughts are suspending the showers and rains, it is not fitting that I should be silent any longer, lest my silence should begin to be attributed to mistrust rather than to modesty; and while I am treating the false charges with contempt, I may seem to be acknowledging the crime. I reply, therefore, as well to you, Demetrianus, as to others whom perhaps you have stirred up, and many of whom, by sowing hatred against us with malicious words, you have made your own partisans, from the budding forth of your own root and origin, who, however, I believe, will admit the reasonableness of my discourse; for he who is moved to evil by the deception of a lie, will much more easily be moved to good by the cogency of truth.

3. You have said that all these things are caused by us, and that to us ought to be attributed the misfortunes wherewith the world is now shaken and distressed, because your gods are not worshipped by us. And in this behalf, since you are ignorant of divine knowledge, and a stranger to the truth, you must in the first place know this, that the world has now grown old, and does not abide in that strength in which it formerly stood; nor has it that vigour and force which it formerly possessed. This, even were we silent, and if we alleged no proofs from the sacred Scriptures and from the divine declarations, the world itself is now announcing, and bearing witness to its decline by the testimony of its failing estate. In the winter there is not such an abundance of showers for nourishing the seeds; in the summer the sun has not so much heat for cherishing the harvest; nor in the spring season are the corn-fields so joyous; nor are the autumnal seasons so fruitful in their leafy products. The layers of marble are dug out in less quantity from the disembowelled and wearied mountains; the diminished quantities of gold and silver suggest the early exhaustion of the metals, and the impoverished veins are straitened and decreased day by day; the husbandman is failing in the fields, the sailor at sea, the soldier in the camp, innocence in the market, justice in the tribunal, concord in friendships, skilfulness in the arts, discipline in morals. Think you that the substantial character of a thing that is growing old remains so robust as that wherewith it might previously flourish in its youth while still new and vigorous? Whatever is tending downwards to decay, with its end nearly approaching, must of necessity be weakened. Thus, the sun at his setting darts his rays with a

less bright and fiery splendour; thus, in her declining course, the moon wanes with exhausted horns; and the tree, which before had been green and fertile, as its branches dry up, becomes by and by misshapen in a barren old age; and the fountain which once gushed forth liberally from its overflowing veins, as old age causes it to fail, scarcely trickles with a sparing moisture. This is the sentence passed on the world, this is God's law, that everything that has had a beginning should perish, and things that have grown should become old, and that strong things should become weak, and great things become small, and that, when they have become weakened and diminished, they should come to an end.

4. You impute it to the Christians that everything is decaying as the world grows old. What if the old should charge it on the Christians that they grow less strong in their old age; that they no longer, as formerly, have the same faculties, in the hearing of their ears, in the swiftness of their feet, in the keenness of their eyes, in the vigour of their strength, in the freshness of their organic powers, in the fulness of their limbs, and that although once a human life endured beyond the age of eight and nine hundred years, it can now scarcely attain to its hundredth year? We see grey hairs in boys — the hair fails before it begins to grow; and life does not cease in old age, but it begins with old age. Thus, even at its very commencement, birth hastens to its close;[4] thus, whatever is now born degenerates with the old age of the world itself; so that no one ought to wonder that everything begins to fail in the world, when the whole world itself is already in process of failing, and in its end.

5. Moreover, that wars continue frequently to prevail, that death and famine accumulate anxiety, that health is shattered by raging diseases, that the human race is wasted by the desolation of pestilence, know that this was foretold; that evils should be multiplied in the last times, and that misfortunes should be varied; and that as the day of judgment is now drawing nigh, the censure of an indignant God should be more and more aroused for the scourging of the human race. For these things happen not, as your false complaining and ignorant inexperience of the truth asserts and repeats, because your gods are not worshipped by us, but because God is not worshipped by you. For since He is Lord and Ruler of the world, and all things are carried on by His will and direction, nor can anything be done save what He Himself has done or allowed to be done, certainly when those things occur which show the anger of an

offended God, they happen not on account of us by whom God is worshipped, but they are called down by your sins and deservings, by whom God is neither in any way sought nor feared, because your vain superstitions are not forsaken, nor the true religion known in such wise that He who is the one God over all might alone be worshipped and petitioned.

6. In fine, listen to Himself speaking; Himself with a divine voice at once instructing and warning us: "Thou shalt worship the Lord thy God," says He, "and Him only shalt thou serve."[5] And again, "Thou shalt have none other gods but me."[6] And again, "Go not after other gods, to serve them; and worship them not, and provoke not me to anger with the works of your hands to destroy you."[7] Moreover, the prophet, filled with the Holy Spirit, attests and denounces the anger of God, saying, "Thus saith the Lord Almighty: Because of mine house that is waste, and ye run every man to his own house, therefore the heavens shall be stayed from dew, and the earth shall withhold her fruits: and I will bring a sword upon the earth, and upon the corn, and upon the wine, and upon the oil, and upon people, and upon cattle, and upon all labours of their hands."[8] Moreover, another prophet repeats, and says, "And I will cause it to rain upon one city, and upon another city I will cause it not to rain. One piece shall be rained upon, and the piece whereon I send no rain shall be withered. And two and three cities shall be gathered into one city to drink water, and shall not be satisfied; and ye are not converted unto me, saith the Lord."[9]

7. Behold, the Lord is angry and wrathful, and threatens, because you turn not unto Him. And you wonder or complain in this your obstinacy and contempt, if the rain comes down with unusual scarcity; and the earth falls into neglect with dusty corruption; if the barren glebe hardly brings forth a few jejune and pallid blades of grass; if the destroying hail weakens the vines; if the overwhelming whirlwind roots out the olive; if drought stanches the fountain; a pestilent breeze corrupts the air; the weakness of disease wastes away man; although all these things come as the consequence of the sins that provoke them, and God is more deeply indignant when such and so great evils avail nothing! For that these things occur either for the discipline of the obstinate or for the punishment of the evil, the same God declares in the Holy Scriptures, saying, "In vain have I smitten your children; they have not received

correction."[10] And the prophet devoted and dedicated to God answers to these words in the same strain, and says, "Thou has stricken them, but they have not grieved; Thou hast scourged them, but they have refused to receive correction."[11] Lo, stripes are inflicted from God, and there is no fear of God. Lo, blows and scourgings from above are not wanting, and there is no trembling, no fear. What if even no such rebuke as that interfered in human affairs? How much greater still would be people's audacity, if it were secure in the impunity of their crimes!

8. You complain that the fountains are now less plentiful to you, and the breezes less salubrious, and the frequent showers and the fertile earth afford you less ready assistance; that the elements no longer subserve your uses and your pleasures as of old. But do you serve God, by whom all things are ordained to your service; do you wait upon Him by whose good pleasure all things wait upon you? From your slave you yourself require service; and though a man, you compel your fellow-man to submit, and to be obedient to you; and although you share the same lot in respect of being born, the same condition in respect of dying; although you have like bodily substance and a common order of souls, and although you come into this world of ours and depart from it after a time with equal rights, and by the same law; yet, unless you are served by him according to your pleasure, unless you are obeyed by him in conformity to your will, you, as an imperious and excessive exactor of his service, flog and scourge him: you afflict and torture him with hunger, with thirst and nakedness, and even frequently with the sword and with imprisonment. And, wretch that you are, do you not acknowledge the Lord your God while you yourself are thus exercising lordship?

9. And therefore with reason in these plagues that occur, there are not wanting God's stripes and scourges; and since they are of no avail in this matter, and do not convert individuals to God by such terror of destructions, there remains after all the eternal dungeon, and the continual fire, and the everlasting punishment; nor shall the groaning of the suppliants be heard there, because here the terror of the angry God was not heard, crying by His prophet, and saying, "Hear the word of the Lord, ye children of Israel: for the judgment of the Lord is against the inhabitants of the earth; because there is neither mercy, nor truth, nor knowledge of God upon the earth. But cursing, and lying, and killing, and stealing, and committing adultery, is broken out over the land, they

mingle blood with blood. Therefore shall the land mourn, with every one that dwelleth therein, with the beasts of the field, with things that creep on the earth, and with the fowls of heaven; and the fishes of the sea shall languish, so that no one shall judge, no one shall rebuke."[12] God says He is wrathful and angry, because there is no acknowledgment of God in the earth, and God is neither known nor feared. The sins of lying, of lust, of fraud, of cruelty, of impiety, of anger, God rebukes and finds fault with, and no one is converted to innocency. Lo, those things are happening which were before foretold by the words of God; nor is any one admonished by the belief of things present to take thought for what is to come. Amongst those very misfortunes wherein the soul, closely bound and shut up, can scarcely breathe, there is still found opportunity for people to be evil, and in such great dangers to judge not so much of themselves as of others. You are indignant that God is angry, as if by an evil life you were deserving any good, as if all things of that kind which happen were not infinitely less and of smaller account than your sins.

10. You who judge others, be for once also a judge of yourself; look into the hiding-places of your own conscience; nay, since now there is not even any shame in your sin, and you are wicked, as if it were rather the very wickedness itself that pleased you, do you, who are seen clearly and nakedly by all other people, yourself also look upon yourself. For either you are swollen with pride, or greedy with avarice, or cruel with anger, or prodigal with gambling, or flushed with intemperance, or envious with jealousy, or unchaste with lust, or violent with cruelty; and do you wonder that God's anger increases in punishing the human race, when the sin that is punished is daily increasing? You complain that the enemy rises up, as if, though an enemy were wanting, there could be peace for you even among the very togas of peace. You complain that the enemy rises up, as if, even although external arms and dangers from barbarians were repressed, the weapons of domestic assault from the calumnies and wrongs of powerful citizens, would not be more ferocious and more harshly wielded within. You complain of barrenness and famine, as if drought made a greater famine than rapacity, as if the fierceness of want did not increase more terribly from grasping at the increase of the year's produce, and the accumulation of their price. You complain that the heaven is shut up from showers, although in the same

way the barns are shut up on earth. You complain that now less is produced, as if what had already been produced were given to the indigent. You reproach plague and disease, while by plague itself and disease the crimes of individuals are either detected or increased, while mercy is not manifested to the weak, and avarice and rapine are waiting open-mouthed for the dead. The same men are timid in the duties of affection, but rash in quest of impious gains; shunning the deaths of the dying, and craving the spoils of the dead, so that it may appear as if the wretched are probably forsaken in their sickness for this cause, that they may not, by being cured, escape: for he who enters so eagerly upon the estate of the dying, *probably* desired the sick man to perish.

11. So great a terror of destruction cannot give the teaching of innocency; and in the midst of a people dying with constant havoc, nobody considers that he himself is mortal. Everywhere there is scattering, there is seizure, there is taking possession; no dissimulation about spoiling, and no delay. As if it were all lawful, as if it were all becoming, as if he who does not rob were suffering loss and wasting his own property, thus every one hastens to the rapine. Among thieves there is at any rate some modesty in their crimes. They love pathless ravines and deserted solitudes; and they do wrong in such a way, that still the crime of the wrong-doers is veiled by darkness and night. Avarice, *however*, rages openly, and, safe by its very boldness, exposes the weapons of its headlong craving in the light of the market-place. Thence cheats, thence poisoners, thence assassins in the midst of the city, are as eager for wickedness as they are wicked with impunity. The crime is committed by the guilty, and the guiltless who can avenge it is not found. There is no fear from accuser or judge: the wicked obtain impunity, while modest men are silent; accomplices are afraid, and those who are to judge are for sale. And therefore by the mouth of the prophet the truth of the matter is put forth with the divine spirit and instinct: it is shown in a certain and obvious way that God can prevent adverse things, but that the evil deserts of sinners prevent His bringing aid. "Is the Lord's hand," says he, "not strong to save you; or has He made heavy His ear, that He cannot hear you? But your sins separate between you and God; and because of your sins He hath hid His face from you, that He may not have mercy."[13] Therefore let your sins and offences be reckoned up; let the wounds of your conscience be considered; and let those cease

complaining about God, or about us, who should perceive that they deserve what they suffer.

12. Look what that very matter is of which is chiefly our discourse — that you molest us, although innocent; that, in contempt of God, you attack and oppress God's servants. It is little, *in your account*, that your life is stained with a variety of gross vices, with the iniquity of deadly crimes, with the summary of all bloody rapines; that true religion is overturned by false superstitions; that God is neither sought at all, nor feared at all; but over and above this, you weary God's servants, and those who are dedicated to His majesty and His name, with unjust persecutions. It is not enough that you yourself do not worship God, but, over and above, you persecute those who do worship, with a sacrilegious hostility. You neither worship God, nor do you at all permit Him to be worshipped; and while others who venerate not only those foolish idols and images made by human hands, but even portents and monsters besides, are pleasing to you, it is only the worshipper of God who is displeasing to you. The ashes of victims and the piles of cattle everywhere smoke in your temples, and God's altars are either nowhere or are hidden. Crocodiles, and apes, and stones, and serpents are worshipped by you; and God alone in the earth is not worshipped, or if worshipped, not with impunity. You deprive the innocent, the just, the dear to God, of their home; you spoil them of their estate, you load them with chains, you shut them up in prison, you punish them with the sword, with the wild beasts, with the flames. Nor, indeed, are you content with a brief endurance of our sufferings, and with a simple and swift exhaustion of pains. You set on foot tedious tortures, by tearing our bodies; you multiply numerous punishments, by lacerating our vitals; nor can your brutality and fierceness be content with ordinary tortures; your ingenious cruelty devises new sufferings.

13. What is this insatiable madness for bloodshedding, what this interminable lust of cruelty? Rather make your election of one of two alternatives. To be a Christian is either a crime, or it is not. If it be a crime, why do you not put the man that confesses it to death? If it be not a crime, why do you persecute an innocent man? For I ought to be put to the torture if I denied it. If in fear of your punishment I should conceal, by a deceitful falsehood, what I had previously been, and the fact that I had not worshipped your gods, then I might deserve to be tormented,

then I ought to be compelled to confession of my crime by the power of suffering, as in other examinations the guilty, who deny that they are guilty of the crime of which they are accused, are tortured in order that the confession of the reality of the crime, which the tell-tale voice refuses to make, may be wrung out by the bodily suffering. But now, when of my own free will I confess, and cry out, and with words frequent and repeated to the same effect bear witness that I am a Christian, why do you apply tortures to one who avows it, and who destroys your gods, not in hidden and secret places, but openly, and publicly, and in the very market-place, in the hearing of your magistrates and governors; so that, although it was a slight thing which you blamed in me before, that which you ought rather to hate and punish has increased, that by declaring myself a Christian in a frequented place, and with the people standing around, I am confounding both you and your gods by an open and public announcement?

14. Why do you turn your attention to the weakness of our body? Why do you strive with the feebleness of this earthly flesh? Contend rather with the strength of the mind, break down the power of the soul, destroy our faith, conquer if you can by discussion, overcome by reason; or, if your gods have any deity and power, let them themselves rise to their own vindication, let them defend themselves by their own majesty. But what can they advantage their worshippers, if they cannot avenge themselves on those who worship them not? For if the one who avenges is of more account than the one who is avenged, then you are greater than your gods. And if you are greater than those whom you worship, you ought not to worship them, but rather to be worshipped and feared by them as their lord. Your championship defends them when injured, just as your protection guards them when shut up from perishing. You should be ashamed to worship those whom you yourself defend; you should be ashamed to hope for protection from those whom you yourself protect.

15. Oh, would you but hear and see them when they are adjured by us, and tortured with spiritual scourges, and are ejected from the possessed bodies with tortures of words, when howling and groaning at a human voice and the power of God, feeling the stripes and blows, they confess the judgment to come! Come and acknowledge that what we say is true; and since you say that you thus worship gods, believe even those whom you worship. Or if you will even believe yourself, he — i.e., the

demon — who has now possessed your breast, who has now darkened your mind with the night of ignorance, shall speak concerning yourself in your hearing. You will see that we are entreated by those whom you entreat, that we are feared by those whom you fear, whom you adore. You will see that under our hands they stand bound, and tremble as captives, whom you look up to and venerate as lords: assuredly even thus you might be confounded in those errors of yours, when you see and hear your gods, at once upon our interrogation betraying what they are, and even in your presence unable to conceal those deceits and trickeries of theirs.

16. What, then, is that sluggishness of mind; yea, what blind and stupid madness of fools, to be unwilling to come out of darkness into light, and to be unwilling, when bound in the toils of eternal death, to receive the hope of immortality, and not to fear God when He threatens and says, "He that sacrifices unto any gods, but unto the Lord only, shall by rooted out?"[14] And again: "They worshipped them whom their fingers made; and the mean man hath bowed down, and the great man hath humbled himself, and I will not forgive them."[15] Why do you humble and bend yourself to false gods? Why do you bow your body captive before foolish images and creations of earth? God made you upright; and while other animals are downlooking, and are depressed in posture bending towards the earth, yours is a lofty attitude; and your countenance is raised upwards to heaven, and to God. Look thither, lift your eyes thitherward, seek God in the highest, that you may be free from things below; lift your heart to a dependence on high and heavenly things. Why do you prostrate yourself into the ruin of death with the serpent whom you worship? Why do you fall into the destruction of the devil, by his means and in his company? Keep the lofty estate in which you were born. Continue such as you were made by God. To the posture of your countenance and of your body, conform your soul. That you may be able to know God, first know yourself. Forsake the idols which human error has invented. Be turned to God, whom if you implore He will aid you. Believe in Christ, whom the Father has sent to quicken and restore us. Cease to hurt the servants of God and of Christ with your persecutions, since when they are injured the divine vengeance defends them.

17. For this reason it is that none of us, when apprehended, makes resistance, nor takes vengeance against your unrighteous violence,

although our people are numerous and plentiful. Our certainty of a vengeance to follow makes us patient. The innocent give place to the guilty; the harmless acquiesce in punishments and tortures, sure and confident that whatsoever we suffer will not remain unavenged, and that in proportion to the greatness of the injustice of our persecution so will be the justice and the severity of the vengeance exacted for those persecutions. Nor does the wickedness of the impious ever rise up against the name we bear, without immediate vengeance from above attending it. To say nothing of the memories of ancient times, and not to recur with wordy commemoration to frequently repeated vengeance on behalf of God's worshippers, the instance of a recent matter is sufficient to prove that our defence, so speedily, and in its speed so powerfully, followed of late in the ruins of things, in the destruction of wealth, in the waste of soldiers, and the diminution of forts. Nor let any one think that this occurred by chance, or think that it was fortuitous, since long ago Scripture has laid down, and said. "Vengeance is mine; I will repay, saith the Lord."[16] And again the Holy Spirit forewarns, and says, "Say not thou, I will avenge myself of mine enemy, but wait on the Lord, that He may be thy help."[17] Whence it is plain and manifest, that not by our means, but for our sakes, all those things are happening which come down from the anger of God.

18. Nor let anybody think that Christians are not avenged by those things that are happening, for the reason that they also themselves seem to be affected by their visitation. People feel the punishment of worldly adversity, when all their joy and glory are in the world. They grieve and groan if it is ill with them in this life, with whom it cannot be well after this life, all the fruit of whose life is received here, all whose consolation is ended here, whose fading and brief life here reckons some sweetness and pleasure, but when it has departed hence, there remains for them only punishment added to sorrow. But they have no suffering from the assault of present evils who have confidence in future good things. In fact, we are never prostrated by adversity, nor are we broken down, nor do we grieve or murmur in any external misfortune or weakness of body: living by the Spirit rather than by the flesh, we overcome bodily weakness by mental strength. By those very things which torment and weary us, we know and trust that we are proved and strengthened.

19. Do you think that we suffer adversity equally with yourselves, when you see that the same adverse things are not borne equally by us

and by you? Among you there is always a clamorous and complaining impatience; with us there is a strong and religious patience, always quiet and always grateful to God. Nor does it claim for itself anything joyous or prosperous in this world, but, meek and gentle and stable against all the gusts of this tossing world, it waits for the time of the divine promise; for as long as this body endures, it must needs have a common lot with others, and its bodily condition must be common. Nor is it given to any of the human race to be separated one from another, except by withdrawal from this present life. In the meantime, we are all, good and evil, contained in one household. Whatever happens within the house, we suffer with equal fate, until, when the end of the temporal life shall be attained, we shall be distributed among the homes either of eternal death or immortality. Thus, therefore, we are not on the same level, and equal with you, because, placed in this present world and in this flesh, we incur equally with you the annoyances of the world and of the flesh; for since in the sense of pain is all punishment, it is manifest that one is not a sharer of your punishment who, you see, does not suffer pain equally with yourselves.

20. There flourishes with us the strength of hope and the firmness of faith. Among these very ruins of a decaying world our soul is lifted up, and our courage unshaken: our patience is never anything but joyous; and the mind is always secure of its God, even as the Holy Spirit speaks through the prophet, and exhorts us, strengthening with a heavenly word the firmness of our hope and faith. "The fig-tree," says He, "shall not bear fruit, and there shall be no blossom in the vines. The labour of the olive shall fail, and the fields shall yield no meat. The flock shall be cut off from the fold, and there shall be no herd in the stalls. But I will rejoice in the Lord, and I will joy in the God of my salvation."[18] He says that the man of God and the worshipper of God, depending on the truth of his hope, and founded on the stedfastness of his faith, is not moved by the attacks of this world and this life. Although the vine should fail, and the olive deceive, and the field parched with grass dying with drought should wither, what is this to Christians? what to God's servants whom paradise is inviting, whom all the grace and all the abundance of the kingdom of heaven is waiting for? They always exult in the Lord, and rejoice and are glad in their God; and the evils and adversities of the world they bravely suffer, because they are looking forward to gifts and

129

prosperities to come: for we who have put off our earthly birth, and are now created and regenerated by the Spirit, and no longer live to the world but to God, shall not receive God's gifts and promises until we arrive at the presence of God. And yet we always ask for the repulse of enemies, and for obtaining showers, and either for the removal or the moderating of adversity; and we pour forth our prayers, and, propitiating and appeasing God, we entreat constantly and urgently, day and night, for your peace and salvation.

21. Let no one, however, flatter himself, because there is for the present to us and to the profane, to God's worshippers and to God's opponents, by reason of the equality of the flesh and body, a common condition of worldly troubles, in such a way as to think from this, that all those things which happen are not drawn down by you; since by the announcement of God Himself, and by prophetic testimony, it has previously been foretold that upon the unjust should come the wrath of God, and that persecutions which humanly would hurt us should not be wanting; but, moreover, that vengeance, which should defend with heavenly defence those who were hurt, should attend them.

22. And how great, too, are those things which in the meantime are happening in that respect on our behalf! Something is given for an example, that the anger of an avenging God may be known. But the day of judgment is still future which the Holy Scripture denounces, saying, "Howl ye, for the day of the Lord is at hand, and destruction from God shall come; for, lo, the day of the Lord cometh, cruel with wrath and anger, to lay the earth desolate, and to destroy the sinners out of it."[19] And again: "Behold, the day of the Lord cometh, burning as an oven; and all the aliens and all that do wickedly shall be as stubble, and the day that cometh shall burn them up, saith the Lord."[20] The Lord prophesies that the aliens shall be burnt up and consumed; that is, aliens from the divine race, and the profane, those who are not spiritually new-born, nor made children of God. For that those only can escape who have been new-born and signed with the sign of Christ, God says in another place, when, sending forth His angels to the destruction of the world and the death of the human race, He threatens more terribly in the last time, saying, "Go ye, and smite, and let not your eye spare. Have no pity upon old or young, and slay the virgins and the little ones and the women, that they may be utterly destroyed. But touch not any one upon

whom is written the mark."[21] Moreover, what this mark is, and in what part of the body it is placed, God sets forth in another place, saying, "Go through the midst of Jerusalem, and set a mark upon the foreheads of those that sigh and that cry for all the abominations that be done in the midst thereof."[22] And that the sign pertains to the passion and blood of Christ, and that whoever is found in this sign is kept safe and unharmed, is also proved by God's testimony, saying, "And the blood shall be to you for a token upon the houses in which ye shall be; and I will see the blood, and will protect you, and the plague of diminution shall not be upon you when I smite the land of Egypt."[23] What previously preceded by a figure in the slain lamb is fulfilled in Christ, the truth which followed afterwards. As, then, when Egypt was smitten, the Jewish people could not escape except by the blood and the sign of the lamb; so also, when the world shall begin to be desolated and smitten, whoever is found in the blood and the sign of Christ alone shall escape.[24]

23. Look, therefore, while there is time, to the true and eternal salvation; and since now the end of the world is at hand, turn your minds to God, in the fear of God; nor let that powerless and vain dominion in the world over the just and meek delight you, since in the field, even among the cultivated and fruitful corn, the tares and the damel have dominion. Nor say ye that ill fortunes happen because your gods are not worshipped by us; but know that this is the judgment of God's anger, that He who is not acknowledged on account of His benefits may at least be acknowledged through His judgments. Seek the Lord even late; for long ago, God, forewarning by His prophet, exhorts and says, "Seek ye the Lord, and your soul shall live."[25] Know God even late; for Christ at His coming admonishes and teaches this, saying, "This is life eternal, that they might know Thee, the only true God, and Jesus Christ, whom Thou hast sent."[26] Believe Him who deceives not at all. Believe Him who foretold that all these things should come to pass. Believe Him who will give to all that believe the reward of eternal life. Believe Him who will call down on them that believe not, eternal punishments in the fires of Gehenna.

24. What will then be the glory of faith? What the punishment of faithlessness? When the day of judgment shall come, what joy of believers, what sorrow of unbelievers; that they should have been unwilling to believe here, and now that they should be unable to return that they

might believe! An ever-burning Gehenna will burn up the condemned, and a punishment devouring with living flames; nor will there be any source whence at any time they may have either respite or end to their torments. Souls with their bodies will be reserved in infinite tortures for suffering. Thus the man will be for ever seen by us who here gazed upon us for a season; and the short joy of those cruel eyes in the persecutions that they made for us will be compensated by a perpetual spectacle, according to the truth of Holy Scripture, which says, "Their worm shall not die, and their fire shall not be quenched; and they shall be for a vision to all flesh."[27] And again: "Then shall the righteous stand in great constancy before the face of those who have afflicted them, and have taken away their labours. When they see it, they shall be troubled with horrible fear, and shall be amazed at the suddenness of their unexpected salvation; and they, repenting and groaning for anguish of spirit, shall say within themselves, These are they whom we had some time in derision, and a proverb of reproach; we fools counted their life madness, and their end to be without honour. How are they numbered among the children of God, and their lot is among the saints! Therefore have we erred from the way of truth, and the light of righteousness hath not shined upon us, and the sun rose not on us. We wearied ourselves in the way of wickedness and destruction; we have gone through deserts where there lay no way; but we have not known the way of the Lord. What hath pride profited us, or what good hath the boasting of riches done us? All those things are passed away like a shadow."[28] The pain of punishment will then be without the fruit of penitence; weeping will be useless, and prayer ineffectual. Too late they will believe in eternal punishment who would not believe in eternal life.

25. Provide, therefore, while you may, for your safety and your life. We offer you the wholesome help of our mind and advice. And because we may not hate, and we please God more by rendering no return for wrong, we exhort you while you have the power, while there yet remains to you something of life, to make satisfaction to God, and to emerge from the abyss of darkling superstition into the bright light of true religion. We do not envy your comforts, nor do we conceal the divine benefits. We repay kindness for your hatred; and for the torments and penalties which are inflicted on us, we point out to you the ways of salvation. Believe and live, and do ye who persecute us in time rejoice

with us for eternity. When you have once departed thither, there is no longer any place for repentance, and no possibility of making satisfaction. Here life is either lost or saved; here eternal safety is provided for by the worship of God and the fruits of faith. Nor let any one be restrained either by sins or by age from coming to obtain salvation. To the one who still remains in this world no repentance is too late. The approach to God's mercy is open, and the access is easy to those who seek and apprehend the truth. Do you entreat for your sins, although it be in the very end of life, and at the setting of the sun of time; and implore God, who is the one and true God, in confession and faith of acknowledgment of Him, and pardon is granted to the one who confesses, and saving mercy is given from the divine goodness to the believer, and a passage is opened to immortality even in death itself. This grace Christ bestows; this gift of His mercy He confers upon us, by overcoming death in the trophy of the cross, by redeeming the believer with the price of His blood, by reconciling humanity to God the Father, by quickening our mortal nature with a heavenly regeneration. If it be possible, let us all follow Him; let us be registered in His sacrament and sign. He opens to us the way of life; He brings us back to paradise; He leads us on to the kingdom of heaven. Made by Him the children of God, with Him we shall ever live; with Him we shall always rejoice, restored by His own blood. We Christians shall be glorious together with Christ, blessed of God the Father, always rejoicing with perpetual pleasures in the sight of God, and ever giving thanks to God. For none can be other than always glad and grateful, who, having been once subject to death, has been made secure in the possession of immortality.

Notes

1   Prov. xxiii. 9.

2   Prov. xxvi. 4.

3   Matt. vii. 6.

4   Wisd. v. 13.

5   Deut. vi. 13.

6   Ex. xxix. 3.

7   Jer. xxv. 6.

8   Hag. i. 9.

9   Amos iv. 7.

10   Jer. ii. 30.

11   Jer. v. 3.

12   Hos. iv. 1-4.

13   Isa. lix. 1.

14   Ex. xxii. 20.

15   Isa. ii. 8.

16   Rom. xii. 19.

17   Prov. xx. 22.

18   Hab. iii. 17.

19   Isa. xiii. 6-9.

20   Mal. iv. 1.

21   Ezek. ix. 5.

22   Ezek. ix. 4.

23   Ex. xii. 13.

24   [Ezek. ix. 4; Rev. vii. 3, ix. 4.]

25   Amos v. 6.

26   John xvii. 3.

27   Isa. lxvi. 24.

28   Wisd. v. 1-9.

9 *Acts of the Council of Nicea* (325, Nicea)

The first Ecumenical Council of the Christian Church was convened by the Emperor Constantine in 325, and its agenda was to address some issues that were dividing the household of faith. Constantine's desire was a united religion in a united Empire. The delegates to the Council were bishops, mainly from the eastern part of the Roman Empire; a number had been victims of the Great Persecution not so many years before, permanently disabled by torture and the conditions of their imprisonment. The meetings were held at Nicea in Bithynia (now Iznik in Turkey), about a hundred kilometers southwest of the future capital, Constantinople, and quite close to the then capital, Nicomedia. The politicking was considerable, but it is not possible to know exactly how the Council proceeded; there are no records of the debates, and much of the historical evidence that does exist glosses over the disagreements. The outcomes were influenced not only by theological argument but also by the interventions of the Emperor, the interplay of the local interests represented, and personal relationships, among other things. The documents promulgated by the Council were the synodal letter, the creed, and the twenty canons (laws) presented below. It seems unlikely that there were other acts of the Council, though conceivably some may have been lost.

The concerns of the Council can be inferred from these documents. Some background may be helpful, however, concerning three specific controversies: Arianism, the treatment of the lapsed, and the paschal controversy.

Arius was a presbyter in a wealthy parish in Alexandria who, in disagreement with his bishop, asserted that "there was when the Son was not." He meant that the Son of God, who became incarnate in Jesus Christ, was not eternal, and therefore must have come into being, and therefore must have been made, and therefore was a creature, and therefore was not God. Controversy flared. Constantine's representatives could not settle the conflict. Perhaps, Constantine thought, a council of bishops could.

During the Decian persecution in 249 and 250, the Church at Rome had been divided between those who wanted to re-admit the lapsed on relatively lenient terms, and those who did not. The rigourist party went into schism, and consecrated a presbyter named Novatian as their own bishop of Rome. Similarly, in Egypt, during the Great Persecution from 303 to 313, a rigourist bishop named Melitius founded a schismatic church which refused to recognize the authority of the more lenient Catholics. The Novatianist and Melitian schisms went onto the agenda of Nicea.

The paschal controversy was a disagreement about when Easter ought to be celebrated. The churches in Asia Minor, for as long as anyone could remember, had always celebrated Easter on the first day of the Jewish Passover, whichever day of the week that might be. (That this was the anniversary of the crucifixion of Christ, not of his resurrection, did not bother them, since in their view the day of the crucifixion was the day of redemption, and therefore the Christian Passover.) The church in Rome, for as long as anyone could remember, had always thought it more fitting for the Eucharist of Easter to be celebrated on the Lord's Day, Sunday, and therefore commemorated the crucifixion of Christ on the Friday following the Jewish Passover, and Easter on the Sunday. Besides this controversy on the dating of Easter, there was another. The Jewish date of Passover was dependent on the date of the spring equinox, but in various parts of the Empire the date of the spring equinox was reckoned variously, and therefore the date of Easter was reckoned variously. Constantine thought, and the Council of Nicea agreed, that the Catholic Church should celebrate Easter on a common day.

The documents naturally cannot show how effective the Council of Nicea proved to be after it ended. It was certainly not very effective in the short run. The Arian controversy continued, and Arianism was supported by some of the Emperors who succeeded Constantine. The Nicene Creed did not pre-empt local creeds. The schismatic Novatian and Melitian churches survived for decades. Some groups, including the Celtic Church, which was not represented at Nicea, continued to calculate their own date of Easter.

The documents of the Council of Nicea were written in Greek. They are recorded in letters of two bishops, Eusebius of Caesarea and Athanasius, who were in attendance, as well as in early Church histories, in quotations within the acts of later councils, and elsewhere.

Questions on the reading

To whom is the synodal epistle addressed? How does the Council (which here calls itself "the Synod") understand its own authority? What, according to this epistle, was its agenda? How does it understand its achievement? What appears to be the Council's purpose in producing the Nicene Creed? What is its theology? (How does this creed differ from what is today often called "the Nicene Creed"?) What might be its sources? What errors, scandals, and disorders are the canons trying to address? What actions does the Council take to correct the problems? What are the chief administrative and political concerns of the Council, so far as the canons give evidence? What is the Council's understanding of sin after baptism, penance, and reconciliation?

Acts of the Council of Nicea
The Synodal Epistle

To the holy and great, by the grace of God, the Church of Alexandria, and to the beloved brethren who are in Egypt, and Libya, and Pentapolis,

Source: The Creed and Canons of the Council of Nicea, A.D. 325, in W.A. Hammond, ed., *The Definitions of Faith, and Canons of Discipline, of the Six Oecumenical Councils*, Oxford, 1843, 1-40, omitting notes.

the Bishops assembled at Nicæa, and composing the great and holy Synod; Health in the Lord.

Forasmuch as this great and holy Synod has been assembled at Nicæa, the grace of God, and our most religious sovereign Constantine bringing us together from different provinces and cities, it has appeared necessary that letters should be sent to you from the whole holy Synod, that you might know what things have been debated, and inquired into, and also what has been decreed and established.

First then, the matters relating to the impiety and transgression of Arius and his followers have been inquired into by all in the presence of our most religious sovereign Constantine; and it has been unanimously decreed, that his impious opinion should be anathematized, as well as the blasphemous words which he used, blaspheming the Son of God, saying that he had his origin from things which did not exist, and that he had no existence before he was begotten, and that there was a time when he did not exist, and that the Son of God is capable by his free will of vice and virtue, and is created and made. All these tenets the holy Synod has anathematized, not enduring so much as to listen to such impious sentiments, and such madness and blasphemous sayings. As regards however the charges against him, and what has been the result of them, if you have not already fully heard, you shall have a particular account, that we may not appear to press hardly upon a man who has only received a suitable recompense for his sins. His impiety however has prevailed so far as to ruin also Theonas of Marmorica, and Secundus of Ptolemais, for they have received the same sentence.

The grace of God having thus delivered Egypt from this evil doctrine, and impiety, and blasphemy, and from the persons who have dared to make disorder and division amongst a people heretofore at peace, the matters relating to the insolence of Meletius and of those who have been ordained by him, remained to be settled; and we now inform you, beloved brethren, of what has been decreed respecting him by the Synod. The holy Synod then, being disposed to deal gently with Meletius, (for according to strict justice he was deserving of no indulgence,) has decreed, that he shall remain in his own city, and shall have no authority either to select persons for any ecclesiastical office, or to ordain any one, nor shall appear in any place or city for such a purpose, but shall only enjoy his bare title of honour. That however those who have been appointed by him shall, after having been confirmed by a more holy ordination, be admitted to communion upon these terms; viz. that they shall have both the dignity and the right of officiating, but shall be altogether inferior to those ministers who are enrolled in any parish or Church, and who have been ordained by our most honourable colleague Alexander. That accordingly they shall have no authority to choose such persons as please them, or to suggest their names, or to do any thing at all, without the consent of the Bishops of the Catholic and Apostolic Church who are under Alexander; but that the authority to select and nominate persons who are worthy of the Ministry, and in short to do all things agreeable to the ecclesiastical laws and customs, shall belong to those Ministers who by the Grace of God and through your prayers have been discovered in no schism, but have continued without spot in the Catholic and Apostolic Church. If however it should happen that any of the Ministers who already belong to the Church should die, then those who have been lately received into it shall succeed to the dignity of the deceased, provided they appear worthy, and the people choose them, and the Bishop of the Catholic Church of Alexandria agrees to and confirms the nomination. Thus much has been conceded to the followers of Meletius; but as regards Meletius himself, this licence has not been extended to him, on account of his former disorderly conduct, and his rash and headstrong disposition; but it has been decreed that he shall have no power or authority at all, he being a man who is capable of committing again the same disorders.

These are the particulars which relate especially to Egypt, and to the most holy Church of Alexandria; but if any other matters have been established by canon or decree, in the presence of our most honourable Lord, and colleague, and brother Alexander, he will when he comes detail them more accurately to you, he having been both Lord, and partaker of those things which have been transacted.

We however declare to you the glad tidings of our agreement respecting our most holy feast of Easter; that by your prayers, this particular also has been rightly settled, so that all the brethren of the East, who formerly kept the feast with the Jews, and did not agree with the Romans, and with you, and with all those who have from the beginning kept it with us, shall from henceforth keep it with us.

Rejoicing therefore for these reformations, and for the common peace and agreement, and for the cutting off of every heresy, receive ye with greater honour, and more abundant love, our colleague, and your Bishop, Alexander, who gladdened us by his presence, and who has undergone so much labour at such an advanced age for the purpose of settling your affairs in peace. Pray also for all of us, that the things which have been decreed may prosper, and be rendered firm by the Almighty God, and our Lord Jesus Christ, having been done as we believe according to the good pleasure of God the Father, in the Holy Ghost, to whom be glory for ever and ever. Amen.

The Nicene Creed

We believe in one God, the Father Almighty, Maker of all things both visible and invisible. And in one Lord Jesus Christ, the Son of God, begotten of the Father, the only begotten, that is of the substance of the Father, God of God, Light of light, very God of very God, begotten not made, consubstantial with the Father, by whom all things were made, both those in heaven and those in earth: who for us men, and for our salvation, came down, and was incarnate, made man, suffered, and rose again the third day, ascended into the heavens, and will come to judge the living and the dead. And in the Holy Ghost. But those who say that there was once a time when he was not, and that he was not before he was begotten, and that he was made out of things which did not exist, or who say that he is of another substance or essence, or that the Son of God is created, capable of change, or alteration, the Catholic Church anathematizes.

The Canons of the Council of Nicea

If any one has been obliged to undergo a surgical operation from disease, or has been castrated by barbarians, let him continue in the Clergy. But if any one in good health has so mutilated himself, it is right that if he be enrolled amongst the Clergy he should cease from his ministrations; and that from henceforth no such person should be promoted. As however it is plain that this is said with reference to those who dare to mutilate themselves, therefore if any persons have been so mutilated by barbarians, or by their own masters, and in other respects are found worthy, the Canon allows them to be admitted to the Clerical office.

Since many things have been done by men either from necessity, or some other pressing cause, contrary to the Canons of the Church, as that persons who have come over to the faith from a heathen life, and have been taught for a short time, have been presently to the spiritual laver, and at the same time that they have been baptized, have been promoted to the Episcopate, or Presbytery; it appears right to determine, that nothing of the sort shall be done for the future: for some time is necessary for the state of a Catechumen, and a fuller probation after Baptism; for the Apostolic decree is clear, which says, "Not a novice, lest being lifted up with pride he fall into a snare, and the condemnation of the devil." But if in process of time any natural fault should be discovered about the person let him be deposed from the Clergy. Whosoever shall act contrary to these rules will endanger his own orders, as boldly opposing the great Synod.

III. The great Synod altogether forbids any Bishop, Presbyter, or Deacon, or any one of the Clergy, to have a woman dwelling with him excepting a mother, or sister, or aunt, or such persons only as are above all suspicion.

IV. It is most proper that a Bishop should be constituted by all the Bishops of the Province; but if this be difficult on account of some urgent necessity, or the length of the way, that at all events three should meet together at the same place, those who are absent also giving their suffrages, and their consent in writing, and then the ordination be performed. The confirming however of what is done in each Province, belongs to the Metropolitan of it.

V. Concerning those, whether of the Clergy or Laity, who have been excommunicated by the Bishops in the different Provinces, let the sentence of the Canon prevail, which pronounces, that those persons who have been cast out by one Bishop are not to be received again into communion by any others. Inquiry should however be made whether they have been excommunicated through the peevishness or contentiousness, or other such like bitterness, of the Bishop. And in order that this inquiry may be conveniently made, it is decreed to be proper, that Synods should be assembled twice every year in every Province, that all the Bishops of the Province being assembled together, such questions may be examined into, that so those who have confessedly offended against the Bishop may appear to be with reason excommunicated by all the Bishops, until it shall seem fit to their general assembly to pronounce a more lenient sentence upon them. And of these Synods, one is to be held before Lent, that all bitterness being removed, a pure gift may be offered to God. The other in the season of Autumn.

VI. Let the ancient customs be maintained, which are in Egypt and Libya, and Pentapolis, according to which the Bishop of Alexandria has authority over all those places. For this is also customary to the Bishop of Rome. In like manner in Antioch, and in the other Provinces, the privileges are to be preserved to the Churches. But this is clearly to be understood, that if any one be made a Bishop without the consent of the Metropolitan, the great Synod declares that he shall not be a Bishop. If however two or three Bishops shall from private contention oppose the common choice of all the others, it being a reasonable one, and made according to the Ecclesiastical Canons, let the choice of the majority hold good.

VII. Since a custom and ancient tradition has prevailed, that the Bishop of Ælia should be honoured, let him have the second place of honour, saving to the Metropolis the authority which is due it.

VIII. Concerning those who have formerly called themselves Cathari, but who come over to the Catholic and Apostolic Church, the holy Synod has decreed, that they having received imposition of hands, shall so remain in the Clergy. It is right, however, that they should in the first instance make profession in writing that they will agree to and follow the decrees of the Catholic Church; in particular that they will communicate with those persons who have been twice married, and with those who, having lapsed in persecution, have had a certain period of penitence assigned to them, and a time for reconciliation fixed; and, generally, that they will follow in all things the decrees of the Catholic Church. Wherever therefore, whether in villages or cities, all who have been ordained are found to be of this party only, let them continue in the Clergy in the same rank in which they are found. But if any of these come to a place where there is already a Bishop or Presbyter of the Catholic Church, it is clear that the Bishop of the Church is to have the Episcopal dignity, and he who had the name of a Bishop amongst those who are called Cathari, shall have the rank of a Presbyter, unless it shall seem fit to the Bishop to allow him to partake of the honour of the name. If the Bishop is not pleased to do so, he shall assign him the place of a Chorepiscopus or Presbyter, that he may indeed altogether appear to be in the Clergy, but that there may not be two Bishops in the city.

IX. If any Presbyters have been promoted without inquiry, or if upon examination they have confessed their sins, and notwithstanding their having confessed, any man has in opposition to the Canon laid hands upon them, the Canon does not admit persons so ordained. For the Church defends that which cannot be found fault with.

X. If any who have lapsed have been ordained in ignorance, or even if those who ordained them were aware of the fact, this does not prejudice the ecclesiastical Canon; for upon the circumstance being made known, they are deposed.

XI. Concerning those who have fallen away without necessity, or without the spoiling of their goods, or without being in danger, or any other such reason, as happened under the tyranny of Licinius, the Synod has decreed, that although they are undeserving of any kindness, they shall nevertheless be dealt with mercifully. As many therefore as shall truly repent, shall continue three years amongst the hearers as believers, and seven amongst the prostrators, and for two years they shall communicate with the people in prayer without the offering.

XII. Those who have been called by grace, and have at first displayed their ardour, and laid aside their girdles, but afterwards have run like dogs to their own vomit, (insomuch that some have spent money, and by means of gifts have acquired again their military station,) must continue amongst the prostrators for ten years, after having been for three years amongst the hearers. In all such cases, however, it is proper to examine into the purpose and appearance of their repentance; for as many as manifest their conversion in deed, and not in appearance only, by their fear, and tears, and patience, and good works, these having completed the prescribed time as hearers, may properly communicate in the prayers, and the Bishop may be allowed to determine yet more favourably respecting them. But those who hear their sentence with indifference, and think the form of entering into the Church sufficient for their conversion, must complete the whole time.

XIII. Concerning those who are likely to die, the old and Canonical law is still to be observed, that if any one is about to die, he must not be deprived of the perfect and most necessary provision for his journey. If however after having been given over, and having again received the Communion, he is again restored to health, let him continue amongst those who communicate in prayers only. But generally, and as regards every one who is likely to die, and who desires to partake of the Eucharist, the Bishop, after examination, shall impart to him of the offering.

XIV. Concerning those who are Catechumens, and who have lapsed, the holy and great Synod has decreed, that they shall be only three years amongst the Hearers, and after that shall pray with the Catechumens.

XV. On account of the great disturbance and disputes which have occurred, it seems right that the custom which has been admitted in some places contrary to the Canon, should by all means be done away, and that no Bishop, Presbyter, or Deacon, should remove from one city to another. But if any person after the decision of the holy and great Synod, shall attempt any such thing, or allow himself in such a practice, that which he has attempted shall be made utterly void, and he shall be restored to the Church in which he was ordained Bishop or Presbyter.

XVI. If any persons, rashly and inconsiderately, not having the fear of God before their eyes, nor regarding the Canons of the Church, whether they be Presbyters or Deacons, or any others who are enrolled in the list of the Clergy, shall remove from their own Church, they ought by no means to be received into any other, but they must be constrained to return to their own parish, or if they continue they must be without communion. And if any Bishop shall dare to usurp what belongs to another, and to ordain in his Church any such person without the consent of the proper Bishop from whom he has seceded, let the Ordination be void.

XVII. Since many persons of the Ecclesiastical order, being led away by covetousness, and a desire of filthy lucre, have forgotten the Holy Scripture, which says, "he gave not his money to usury," and in lending require the hundredth part, the holy and great Synod considers it right, that if any one after this decision shall be found receiving money for what he has advanced, or going about the business in any other way, as by requiring the whole and a half, or using any other device for filthy lucre's sake, he should be deposed from the Clergy, and struck out of the list.

XVIII. It has come to the knowledge of the holy Synod, that in certain places, and cities, the Deacons give the Eucharist to the Presbyters, whereas neither Canon nor custom allows that they who have no authority to offer, should give the Body of Christ to those who do offer. It has also been made known, that now some of the Deacons receive the Eucharist even before the Bishops. Let all such practices be done away, and let the Deacons keep within their proper bounds, knowing that they are the Ministers of the Bishop, and inferior to the Presbyters. Let them therefore receive the Eucharist according to their order, after the Presbyters, either the Bishop or Presbyter administering it to them. Further, the Deacons are not to be allowed to sit amongst the Presbyters, for this is done contrary to the Canon and due order. But if any one after this decision will not obey, let him be put out of the Diaconate.

XIX. Concerning the Paulianists[1] who have come over to the Catholic Church, the decision is, that they must by all means be baptized again. But if any of them have in time past been enrolled amongst the Clergy, if they appear to be blameless and without reproach, after they have been rebaptized, let them be ordained by the Bishop of the Catholic Church. If, however, upon examination they are found to be not qualified, they must be deposed. In like manner as regards the Deaconesses, and, in short, any who have been enrolled amongst the Clergy, the same form is to be observed. And we have mentioned particularly those Deaconesses who are enrolled as far as the dress, since they have not any imposition of hands, they are altogether to be reckoned amongst the laity.

XX. Since there are some persons who kneel on the Lord's day, and in the days of the Pentecost; in order that all things may be observed in like manner in every parish, the holy Synod has decreed that all should at those times offer up their prayers to God standing.

Notes

[1] The Paulianists derived their name from Paulus Samosatensis, who was elected Bishop of Anticoh, A.D. 260. The Canon requires the Paulianists to be rebaptized, because in baptizing they did not use the only lawful form, according to our Saviour's command, "In the name of the Father, the Son, and the Holy Ghost."

10 Gregory Nazianzen, *Letters 101, 102, 202*
Against the Apollinarians (383?, Cappadocia)

T he Roman province of Cappadocia, in east central Asia Minor, was a centre of Christian theological thought in the third and fourth centuries. How Christianity began there is unknown, but Cappadocians were among those who heard Peter's sermon in Jerusalem on the day of Pentecost (Acts 2:9). Among the most influential of all Christian theologians were the three called the Cappadocian Fathers, Gregory of Nazianzus, and two brothers, Basil of Caesarea and Gregory of Nyssa. Macrina the Younger, the sister of Basil and Gregory of Nyssa, was reportedly at least as accomplished a theologian as her brothers, but whatever she may have written has not survived. The Cappadocian synthesis of Biblical and classical learning, asceticism and culture, Nicene orthodoxy and philosophical vigour, were formative in the development of the Eastern Orthodox tradition of Christianity.

Gregory of Nazianzus was born about 329 into a socially important family. His father was bishop of Nazianzus in Cappadocia, but his mother was the more significant Christian influence on him. He loved literature and study, and pursued his education at Alexandria and Athens, among other places. He was an exceptional orator, teacher, and preacher, but personally he preferred the life of monastic retreat. Against his will he was cornered into ordination in about 361, and then snared into an appointment as bishop of a small Cappadocian village in about 371. In

379 the tiny Nicene Christian community in Constantinople, the capital of the Roman Empire, prevailed on him to come to them as their minister. He had to preach in a private house, since the Arians held all the church buildings. After a new Nicene emperor, Theodosius, took control of Constantinople at the end of 380, Gregory was finally installed in a church. In 381 he was recognized as bishop of Constantinople, but, with little energy for church politics, he resigned a few days later. He returned to look after the church at Nazianzus for two years, and spent most of the rest of his life withdrawn from the world. He died in 389 or 390. He wrote no treatises, only orations, poems, and letters. Of his 245 known letters, the three below proved to be the most important theologically. Letter 101 was adopted by the Ecumenical Council of Chalcedon in 451.

Apollinaris (315?–392), like the Cappadocians, championed the Nicene definition that Christ was truly God, but his zeal for that position led him to deny that Christ was fully human. Conflict with the Cappadocians and with the other mainstream Niceans therefore became inevitable. Apollinaris was born in Laodicea in southwestern Phrygia (near modern Denizli in Turkey), 18 kilometers west of Colossae on the Lycus River, in the Roman province of Asia. He was a man of great intellectual gifts, strong Christian commitment, personal courage, and political savvy. He maintained his loyalty to the Nicene position even when it was at its most unpopular, and suffered excommunication for his views at the hands of the bishop of Laodicea, who was an Arian.

By 363, Apollinaris was expressing the position that came to be known as Apollinarianism. In his view, since Christ was really God, and since God was too holy and perfect to be entirely merged into a fallen humanity, Christ could not be fully human. Had Christ really had a human mind, he would have been infected with spiritual weaknesses and the capacity for sin; his wisdom and moral discernment would have been subject to development; he would have been "a prey to filthy thoughts." His human mind and his divine mind would have been constantly at war. So Christ must have had, not a human mind, but the mind of God. Apollinaris therefore taught that the Logos or Word of God took the place of Christ's human mind. Who, then, was Jesus? He was not an amalgamation of divine and human natures, but he was simply of the single nature of God, fused, in the incarnation, with human flesh.

The details of Apollinaris' position and the arguments he used to support it can in some measure be inferred from Nazianzen's letters below, Nazianzen's hostility and selective quotation notwithstanding.

In about 376 Apollinaris and his followers separated from the Church, and his position was condemned by a synod in Rome in 377 and by the Ecumenical Council of Constantinople in 381. The Emperor began issuing edicts against his church in 383, but it continued in Antioch until 425. Apollinaris' ideas continued to be influential in Alexandria, and survived in some of the churches not in communion with Rome and Constantinople. Only a handful of his works have survived.

The letters below, which Gregory wrote to a priest or presbyter in Nazianzus named Cledonius, are usually dated to 382 or 383, when Apollinarianism, though condemned, remained active, public, and aggressive. Gregory wrote in Greek.

Questions on the reading

What makes Gregory think that Apollinarianism might be gaining adherents in the Church? What is at stake in this debate, and what repercussions does Gregory worry there might be for the Church if Apollinarianism were to prevail? Whom does Gregory address in the three epistles? What does he understand the doctrine of Apollinarianism to be? What does Gregory assume will be authoritative evidence and valid method in theology? Do the Apollinarians, as Gregory represents them, likely share his assumptions? Is it possible to judge how fair he is being to the Apollinarians? What are his theological objections to Apollinarianism? What is his own understanding of the person of Christ, and the relation of Christ's person to his work of redemption? What do you suppose might be the most important sentence in the entire set of three letters? What are Gregory's theological arguments in favour of his understanding? What is his theology of history?

Epistle 101
To Cledonius against Apollinaris

To our most reverend and God-beloved brother and fellow priest Cledonius, Gregory, greeting in the Lord.

I desire to learn what is this fashion of innovation in things concerning the Church, which allows anyone who likes, or the passer-by, as the Bible says, to tear asunder the flock[1] that has been well led, and to plunder it by larcenous attacks, or rather by piratical and fallacious teachings. For if our present assailants had any ground for condemning us in regard of the faith, it would not have been right for them, even in that case, to have ventured on such a course without giving us notice. They ought rather to have first persuaded us, or to have been willing to be persuaded by us (if at least any account is to be taken of us as fearing God, laboring for the faith, and helping the Church), and then, if at all, to innovate; but then perhaps there would be an excuse for their outrageous conduct. But since our faith has been proclaimed, both in writing and without writing, here and in distant parts, in times of danger and of safety, how comes it that some make such attempts, and that others keep silence?

The most grievous part of it is not (though this too is shocking) that the men instill their own heresy into simpler souls by means of those who are worse; but that they also tell lies about us and say that we share their opinions and sentiments; thus baiting their hooks, and by this cloak villainously fulfilling their will, and making our simplicity, which looked upon them as brothers and not as foes, into a support of their wickedness. And not only so, but they also assert, as I am told, that they have been received by the Western Synod, by which they were formerly condemned, as is well known to everyone. If, however, those who hold the views of Apollinaris have either now or formerly been received, let them prove it and we will be content. For it is evident that they can only have been so received as assenting to the orthodox faith, for this were an impossibility on any other terms. And they can surely prove it, either by the minutes of

---

Source: Gregory Nazianzus, "Letters on the Apollinarian Controversy" (=Letters 101, 102, 202), in E.R. Hardy, ed., *Christology of the Later Fathers* (Library of Christian Classics, vol. 3), Westminster Press, 1954, 215-232. Used by permission of Westminster John Knox Press.

the synod, or by letters of communion, for this is the regular custom of synods. But if it is mere words, and an invention of their own, devised for the sake of appearances and to give them weight with the multitude through the credit of the persons, teach them to hold their tongues, and confute them; for we believe that such a task is well suited to your manner of life and orthodoxy. Do not let the men deceive themselves and others with the assertion that the "Man of the Lord." as they call him, who is rather our Lord and God, is without human mind. For we do not sever the man from the Godhead, but we lay down as a dogma the unity and identity [of person], who of old was not man but God, and the only Son before all ages, unmingled with body or anything corporeal; but who in these last days has assumed humanity also for our salvation; passible in his flesh, impassible in his Godhead; circumscript in the body, uncircumscript in the Spirit; at once earthly and heavenly, tangible and intangible, comprehensible and incomprehensible; that by one and the same [Person], who was perfect human being and also God, the entire humanity fallen through sin might be created anew.

If anyone does not believe that holy Mary is the mother of God, he is severed from the Godhead. If anyone should assert that he passed through the Virgin as through a channel, and was not at once divinely and humanly formed in her (divinely, because without the intervention of a man; humanly, because in accordance with the laws of gestation), he is in like manner godless. If any assert that the humanity was formed and afterward was clothed with the Godhead, he too is to be condemned. For this were not a generation of God, but a shirking of generation. If any introduce the notion of two sons, one of God the Father, the other of the mother, and discredits the unity and identity, may he lose his part in the adoption promised to those who believe aright. For God and man are two natures, as also soul and body are; but there are not two sons or two gods. For neither in this life are there two personhoods; though Paul speaks in some such language of the inner and outer person.[2] And (if I am to speak concisely) the Saviour is made of [elements] which are distinct from one another (for the invisible is not the same with the visible, nor the timeless with that which is subject to time), yet he is not two [persons]. God forbid! For both [natures] are one by the combination, the deity being made human being, and the humanity deified or however one should express it. And I say different [elements], because it is the

151

reverse of what is the case in the Trinity; for there we acknowledge different [Persons] so as not to confound the Persons; but not different [elements], for the three are one and the same in Godhead.

If any should say that it wrought in him by grace as in a prophet, but was not and is not united with him in essence — let him be empty of the higher energy, or rather full of the opposite. If any worship not the Crucified, let him be anathema and be numbered among the deicides. If any assert that he was made perfect by works, or that after his baptism, or after his resurrection from the dead, he was counted worthy of an adoptive sonship, like those whom the Greeks interpolate as added to the ranks of the gods, let him be anathema. For that which has a beginning or a progress or is made perfect is not God, although the expressions may be used of his gradual manifestation. If any assert that he has now put off his holy flesh, and that his Godhead is stripped of the body, and deny that he is now with his body and will come again with it, let him not see the glory of his coming. For where is his body now, if not with him who assumed it? For it is not laid by in the sun, according to the babble of the Manichaeans, that it should be honored by a dishonor; nor was it poured forth into the air and dissolved, as is the nature of a voice or the flow of an odor, or the course of a lightning flash that never stands. Where in that case were his being handled after the resurrection, or his being seen hereafter by them that pierced him, for Godhead is in its nature invisible? Nay; he will come with his body — so I have learned — such as he was seen by his disciples in the Mount, or as he showed himself for a moment, when his Godhead overpowered the carnality. And as we say this to disarm suspicion, so we write the other to correct the novel teaching. If anyone assert that his flesh came down from heaven, and is not from hence, nor of us though above us, let him be anathema. For the words, "The second man is the Lord from heaven; and, as is the heavenly, such are they that are heavenly"; and, "No man hath ascended up into heaven save he which came down from heaven, even the Son of Man which is in heaven"[3]; and the like, are to be understood as said on account of the union with the heavenly; just as that "All things were made by Christ," and that "Christ dwelleth in your hearts" is said,[4] not of the visible nature which belongs to God, but of what is perceived by the mind, the names being mingled like the natures, and flowing into one another, according to the law of their intimate union.

If anyone has put his trust in him as a man without a human mind, he is really bereft of mind, and quite unworthy of salvation. For that which he has not assumed he has not healed; but that which is united to his Godhead is also saved. If only half Adam fell, then that which Christ assumes and saves may be half also; but if the whole of his nature fell, it must be united to the whole nature of Him that was begotten, and so be saved as a whole. Let them not, then, begrudge us our complete salvation, or clothe the Saviour only with bones and nerves and the portraiture of humanity. For if his humanity is without soul, even the Arians admit this, that they may attribute his Passion to the Godhead, as that which gives motion to the body is also that which suffers. But if he has soul, and yet is without a mind, how is he a human being, for a human being is not a mindless animal? And this would necessarily involve that while his form and tabernacle was human, his soul should be that of a horse or an ox, or some other of the brute creation. This then, would be what he saves; and I have been deceived by the truth, and led to boast of an honor which had been bestowed upon another. But if his humanity is intellectual and not without mind, let them cease to be thus really mindless.

But, says such a one, the Godhead took the place of the human intellect. How does this touch me? For Godhead joined to flesh alone is not a human being, nor to soul alone, nor to both apart from intellect, which is the most essential part of a human being. Keep, then, the whole human being, and mingle Godhead therewith, that you may benefit me in my completeness. But, he asserts, he could not contain two perfect [natures]. Not if you only look at him in a bodily fashion. For a bushel measure will not hold two bushels, nor will the space of one body hold two or more bodies. But if you will look at what is mental and incorporeal, remember that I in my one personality can contain soul and reason and mind and the Holy Spirit; and before me this world, by which I mean the system of things visible and invisible, contained Father, Son, and Holy Ghost. For such is the nature of intellectual existences, that they can mingle with one another and with bodies, incorporeally and invisibly. For many sounds are comprehended by one ear; and the eyes of many are occupied by the same visible objects, and the smell by odors; nor are the senses narrowed by each other, or crowded out, nor the objects of sense diminished by the multitude of the perceptions. But where is there mind of human being or angel so perfect in comparison of the Godhead that the presence of the greater must crowd out the other? The light is nothing compared with a river, that we must first do away with the lesser, and take the light from a house, or the moisture from the earth, to enable it to contain the greater and more perfect. For how shall one thing contain two completenesses, either the house, the sunbeam and the sun, or the earth, the moisture and the river? Here is matter for inquiry; for indeed the question is worthy of much consideration. Do they not know, then, that what is perfect by comparison with one thing may be imperfect by comparison with another, as a hill compared with a mountain, or a grain of mustard seed with a bean or any other of the larger seeds, although it may be called larger than any of the same kind? Or, if you like, an angel compared with God, or a human being with an angel. So our mind is perfect and commanding, but only in respect of soul and body; not absolutely perfect; and a servant and a subject of God, not a sharer of his princedom and honor. So Moses was a god to Pharaoh, but a servant of God, as it is written[5]; and the stars which illumine the night are hidden by the sun, so much that you could not even know of their existence by daylight; and a little torch brought near a great blaze is neither destroyed, nor seen, nor extinguished; but is all one blaze, the bigger one prevailing over the other.

But, it may be said, our mind is subject to condemnation. What, then, of our flesh? Is that not subject to condemnation? You must therefore either set aside the latter on account of sin, or admit the former on account of salvation. If he assumed the worse that he might sanctify it by his incarnation, may he not assume the better that it may be sanctified by his becoming human? If the clay was leavened and has become a new lump,[6] O ye wise men, shall not the image be leavened and mingled with God, being deified by his Godhead? And I will add this also: If the mind was utterly rejected, as prone to sin and subject to damnation, and for this reason he assumed a body but left out the mind, then there is an excuse for them who sin with the mind; for the witness of God — according to you — has shown the impossibility of healing it. Let me state the greater results. You, my good sir, dishonor my mind (you a Sarcolater [flesh worshipper], if I am an Anthropolater [person worshipper]) that you may tie God down to the flesh, since he cannot be otherwise tied; and therefore you take away the wall of partition. But what is my theory, who am but an ignorant man, and no philosopher?

Mind is mingled with mind, as nearer and more closely related, and through it with flesh, being a mediator between God and carnality.

Further let us see what is their account of the assumption of humanity, or the assumption of flesh, as they call it. If it was in order that God, otherwise incomprehensible, might be comprehended, and might converse with people through his flesh as through a veil, their mask and the drama which they represent is a pretty one, not to say that it was open to him to converse with us in other ways, as of old, in the burning bush and in the appearance of a man.[7] But if it was that he might destroy the condemnation by sanctifying like by like, then as he needed flesh for the sake of the flesh which had incurred condemnation, and soul for the sake of our soul, so, too, he needed mind for the sake of mind, which not only fell in Adam, but was the first to be affected, as the doctors say of illnesses. For that which received the command was that which failed to keep the command, and that which failed to keep it was that also which dared to transgress; and that which transgressed was that which stood most in need of salvation; and that which needed salvation was that which also he took upon him. Therefore, mind was taken upon him. This has now been demonstrated, whether they like it or no, by, to use their own expression, geometrical and necessary proofs. But you are acting as if, when a man's eye had been injured and his foot had been injured in consequence, you were to attend to the foot and leave the eye uncared for; or as if, when a painter had drawn something badly, you were to alter the picture, but to pass over the artist as if he had succeeded. But if they, overwhelmed by these arguments, take refuge in the proposition that it is possible for God to save humanity even apart from mind, why, I suppose that it would be possible for him to do so also apart from flesh by a mere act of will, just as he works all other things, and has wrought them without body. Take away, then, the flesh as well as the mind, that your monstrous folly may be complete. But they are deceived by the letter, and, therefore, they run to the flesh, because they do not know the custom of Scripture. We will teach them this also. For what need is there even to mention to those who know it the fact that everywhere in Scripture he is called "man," and "the Son of Man"?

If, however, they rely on the passage, "The Word was made flesh and dwelt among us," and because of this erase the noblest part of humanity (as cobblers do the thicker part of skins) that they may join together God and flesh, it is time for them to say that God is God only of flesh, and not of souls, because it is written, "As thou hast given him power over all flesh," and, "Unto thee shall all flesh come," and, "Let all flesh bless his holy Name," meaning every person.[8] Or, again, they must suppose that our fathers went down into Egypt without bodies and invisible, and that only the soul of Joseph was imprisoned by Pharaoh, because it is written, "They went down into Egypt with threescore and fifteen souls," and, "The iron entered into his soul,"[9] a thing which could not be bound. They who argue thus do not know that such expressions are used by synecdoche, declaring the whole by the part, as when Scripture says that the young ravens call upon God, to indicate the whole feathered race; or Pleiades, Hesperus, and Arcturus are mentioned, instead of all the stars and his providence over them.[10]

Moreover, in no other way was it possible for the love of God toward us to be manifested than by making mention of our flesh, and that for our sake he descended even to our lower part. For that flesh is less precious than soul, everyone who has a spark of sense will acknowledge. And so the passage, "The Word was made flesh," seems to me to be equivalent to that in which it is said that he was made sin, or a curse for us; not that the Lord was transformed into either of these — how could he be? But because by taking them upon him he took away our sins and bore our iniquities.[11] This, then, is sufficient to say at the present time for the sake of clearness and of being understood by the many. And I write it, not with any desire to compose a treatise, but only to check the progress of deceit; and if it is thought well, I will give a fuller account of these matters at greater length.

But there is a matter which is graver than these, a special point which it is necessary that I should not pass over. I would they were even cut off that trouble you,[12] and would reintroduce a second Judaism, and a second circumcision, and a second system of sacrifices. For if this be done, what hinders Christ also being born again to set them aside, and again being betrayed by Judas, and crucified and buried, and rising again, that all may be fulfilled in the same order, like the Greek system of cycles, in which the same revolutions of the stars bring round the same events? For what the method of selection is, in accordance with which some of the events are to occur and others to be omitted, let these wise men who glory in the multitude of their books show us.

But since, puffed up by their theory of the Trinity, they falsely accuse us of being unsound in the faith and entice the multitude, it is necessary that people should know that Apollinaris, while granting the name of Godhead to the Holy Ghost, did not preserve the power of the Godhead. For to make the Trinity consist of great, greater, and greatest, as of light, ray, and sun, the Spirit and the Son and the Father (as is clearly stated in his writings), is a ladder of Godhead not leading to heaven, but down from heaven. But we recognize God the Father and the Son and the Holy Ghost, and these not as bare titles, dividing inequalities of ranks or of power, but as there is one and the same title, so there is one nature and one substance in the Godhead.

But if anyone who thinks we have spoken rightly on this subject reproaches us with holding communion with heretics, let him prove that we are open to this charge, and we will either convince him or retire. But it is not safe to make any innovation before judgment is given, especially in a matter of such importance, and connected with so great issues. We have protested and continue to protest this before God and human beings. And not even now, be well assured, should we have written this if we had not seen that the Church was being torn asunder and divided, among their other tricks, by their present synagogue of vanity.[13] But if anyone when we say and protest this, either from some advantage he will thus gain, or through fear of people, or monstrous littleness of mind, or through some neglect of pastors and governors, or through love of novelty and proneness to innovations, rejects us as unworthy of credit, and attaches himself to such people, and divides the noble body of the Church, he shall bear his judgment, whoever he may be, and shall give account to God in the Day of Judgment. But if their long books, and their new psalters, contrary to that of David, and the grace of their meters, are taken for a third Testament, we too will compose psalms, and will write much in meter. For we also think we have the spirit of God, if indeed this is a gift of the Spirit, and not a human novelty. This I will that thou declare publicly, that we may not be held responsible, as overlooking such an evil, and as though this wicked doctrine received food and strength from our indifference.

Epistle 102
To Cledonius against Apollinaris

Forasmuch as many persons have come to Your Reverence seeking confirmation of their faith, and therefore you have affectionately asked me to put forth a brief definition and rule of my opinion, I therefore write to Your Reverence, what indeed you knew before, that I never have and never can honor anything above the Nicene faith, that of the holy Fathers who met there to destroy the Arian heresy; but am, and by God's help ever will be, of that faith; completely in detail that which was incompletely said by them concerning the Holy Ghost; for that question had not then been mooted, namely, that we are to believe that the Father, Son, and Holy Ghost are of one Godhead, thus confessing the Spirit also to be God. Receive then to communion those who think and teach thus, as I also do; but those who are otherwise-minded refuse, and hold them as strangers to God and the Catholic Church. And since a question has also been mooted concerning the divine assumption of humanity, or incarnation, state this also clearly to all concerning me, that I join in One the Son, who was begotten of the Father, and afterward of the Virgin Mary, and that I do not call him two sons, but worship him as one and the same in undivided Godhead and honor. But if anyone does not assent to this statement, either now or hereafter, he shall give account to God at the Day of Judgment.

Now, what we object and oppose to their mindless opinion about his mind is this, to put it shortly; for they are almost alone in the condition which they lay down, as it is through want of mind that they mutilate his mind. But, that they may not accuse us of having once accepted but of now repudiating the faith of their beloved Vitalius which he handed in in writing at the request of the blessed bishop Damasus of Rome, I will give a short explanation on this point also. For these men, when they are theologizing among their genuine disciples, and those who are initiated into their secrets, like the Manichaeans among those whom they call the "Elect," expose the full extent of their disease, and scarcely allow flesh at all to the Saviour. But when they are refuted and pressed with the common answers about the incarnation which the Scripture presents, they confess indeed the orthodox words, but they do violence to the sense; for they acknowledge the humanity to be neither without soul nor without reason nor without mind, nor imperfect, but they bring in the Godhead to supply the soul and reason and mind, as though it had mingled itself only with his flesh, and not with the other properties belonging to us human beings; although his sinlessness was far above us, and was the cleansing of our passions.

Thus, then, they interpret wrongly the words, "But we have the mind of Christ,"[1] and very absurdly, when they say that his Godhead is the mind of Christ, and not understanding the passage as we do, namely, that they who have purified their mind by the imitation of the mind which the Saviour took of us, and, as far as may be, have attained conformity with it, are said to have the mind of Christ; just as they might be testified to have the flesh of Christ who have trained their flesh, and in this respect have become of the same body and partakers of Christ; and so he says, "As we have borne the image of the earthly we shall also bear the image of the heavenly."[2] And so they declare that the perfect man is not he who has in all points tempted like as we are yet without sin[3]; but the mixture of God and flesh. For what, say they, can be more perfect than this?

They play the same trick with the word that describes the incarnation, viz., He was made man — explaining it to mean, not, He was in the human nature with which he surrounded himself, according to the Scripture, "He knew what was in man"; but teaching that it means, He consorted and conversed with people, and taking refuge in the expression which says that he was seen on earth and conversed with people.[4] And what can anyone contend further? They who take away the humanity and the interior image cleanse by their newly invented mask only our outside,[5] and that which is seen; so far in conflict with themselves that at one time, for the sake of the flesh, they explain all the rest in a gross and carnal manner (for it is from hence that they have derived their second Judaism and their silly thousand years' delight in paradise, and almost the idea that we shall resume again the same conditions after these same thousand years)[6]; and at another time they bring in his flesh as a phantom rather than a reality, as not having been subjected to any of our experiences, not even such as are free from sin; and use for this purpose the apostolic expression, understood and spoken in a sense which is not apostolic, that our Saviour "was made in the human likeness and found in fashion as a man,"[7] as though by these words was expressed, not the human form, but some delusive phantom and appearance.

Since, then, these expressions, rightly understood, make for orthodoxy, but wrongly interpreted are heretical, what is there to be surprised at if we received the words of Vitalius in the more orthodox sense, our desire that they should be so meant persuading us, though others are angry at the intention of his writings? This is, I think, the reason why Damasus himself, having been subsequently better informed, and at the same time learning that they hold by their former explanations, excommunicated them and overturned their written confession of faith with an anathema; as well as because he was vexed at the deceit which he had suffered from them through simplicity.

Since, then, they have been openly convicted of this, let them not be angry, but let them be ashamed of themselves; and let them not slander us, but abase themselves and wipe off from their portals that great and marvelous proclamation and boast of their orthodoxy, meeting all who go in at once with the question and distinction that we must worship, not a God-bearing man, but a flesh-bearing God. What could be more unreasonable than this, though these new heralds of truth think a great deal of the title? For though it has a certain sophistical grace through the quickness of its antithesis, and a sort of juggling quackery grateful to the uninstructed, yet it is the most absurd of absurdities and the most foolish of follies. For if one were to change the word man or flesh into God (the first would please us, the second them), and then were to use this wonderful antithesis, so divinely recognized, what conclusion should we arrive at? That we must worship, not a God-bearing flesh, but a man-bearing God. O monstrous absurdity! They proclaim to us today a wisdom hidden ever since the time of Christ — a thing worthy of our tears. For if the faith began thirty years ago, when nearly four hundred years had passed since Christ was manifested, vain all that time will have been our gospel, and vain our faith; in vain will the martyrs have borne their witness, and in vain have so many and so great prelates presided over the people; and grace is a matter of meters and not of the faith.

And who will not marvel at their learning, in that on their own authority they divide the things of Christ, and assign to his humanity such sayings as, he was born, he was tempted, he was hungry, he was thirsty, he was wearied, he was asleep[8]; but reckon to his divinity such as these: he was glorified by angels, he overcame the tempter, he fed the people in the wilderness, and he fed them in such a manner, and he walked upon the sea[9]; and say on the one hand that the "Where have ye laid Lazarus?" belongs to us, but the loud voice "Lazarus, come forth," and the raising him that had been four days dead,[10] is above our nature; and that while "He was in an agony,"[11] he was crucified, he was buried," belong to the veil, on the other hand, "He was confident,[12] he rose again, he ascended," belong to the inner treasure; and then they accuse us of introducing two natures, separate or conflicting, and of dividing the supernatural and wondrous union. They ought either not to do that of which they accuse us or not to accuse us of that which they do; so at least if they are resolved to be consistent and not to propound at once their own and their opponents' prinicples. Such is their want of reason; it conflicts both with itself and with the truth to such an extent that they are neither conscious nor ashamed of it when they fall out with themselves. Now, if anyone thinks that we write all this willingly and not upon compulsion, and that we are dissuading from unity, and not doing our utmost to promote it, let him know that he is very much mistaken, and has not made at all a good guess at our desires, for nothing is or ever has been more valuable in our eyes than peace, as the facts themselves prove; though their actions and brawlings against us altogether exclude unanimity.

Epistle 202
To Nectarius, Bishop of Constantinople

The care of God, which throughout the time before us guarded the Churches, seems to have utterly forsaken this present life. And my soul is immersed to such a degree by calamities that the private sufferings of my own life hardly seem to be worth reckoning among evils (though they are so numerous and great, that if they befell anyone else I should think them unbearable); but I can only look at the common sufferings of the churches; for if at the present crisis some pains be not taken to find a remedy for them, things will gradually get into an altogether desperate condition. Those who follow the heresy of Arius or Eudoxius (I cannot say who stirred them up to this folly) are making a display of their disease, as if they had attained some degree of confidence by collecting congregations as if by permission. And they of the Macedonian party have reached such a pitch of folly that they are arrogating to themselves the name of bishops, and are wandering about our districts babbling of Eleusius as to their ordinations. Our bosom evil, Eunomius, is no longer content with merely existing; but unless he can draw away everyone with him to his ruinous heresy, he thinks himself an injured man. All this, however, is endurable. The most grievous item of all in the woes of the Church is the boldness of the Apollinarians, whom Your Holiness has overlooked, I know not how, when providing themselves with authority to hold meetings on an equality with myself.

However, you being, as you are, thoroughly instructed by the grace of God in the divine mysteries on all points, are well informed, not only as to the advocacy of the true faith, but also as to all those arguments which have been devised by the heretics against the sound faith; and yet perhaps it will not be unseasonable that Your Excellency should hear from my littleness that a pamphlet by Apollinaris has come into my hands, the contents of which surpass all heretical pravity. For he asserts that the flesh which the only-begotten Son assumed in the incarnation for the remodeling of our nature was no new acquisition, but that that carnal nature was in the Son from the beginning. And he puts forward as a witness to this monstrous assertion a garbled quotation from the Gospels, namely, "No man hath ascended up into heaven save he which came down from heaven, even the Son of Man which is in heaven."[1] As though even before he came down he was the Son of Man, and when he came down he brought with him that flesh, which it appears he had in heaven, as though it had existed before the ages, and been joined with his essence. For he alleges another saying of an apostle, which he cuts off from the whole body of its context, that the second man is the Lord from heaven.[2] Then he assumes that that man who came down from above is without a mind, but that the Godhead of the only-begotten fulfills the function of mind, and is the third part of this human composite, inasmuch as soul and body are in it on its human side, but not mind, the place of which is taken by God the Word. This is not yet the most serious part of it; that which is most terrible of all is that he declares that the only-begotten God, the judge of all, the prince of life, the destroyer of death, is mortal, and underwent the Passion in his proper Godhead; and that in the three days' death of his body, his Godhead also was put to death with his body, and thus was raised again from the dead by the Father. It would be tedious to go through all the other propositions which he adds to these monstrous absurdities. Now, if they who hold such views have authority to meet, your wisdom approved in Christ must see that, inasmuch as we do not approve their views, any permission of assembly granted to them is nothing less than a declaration that their view is thought more true than ours. For if they are permitted to teach their view as godly men, and with all confidence to preach their doctrine, it is manifest that the doctrine of the Church has been condemned, as though the truth were on their side. For nature does not admit of two contrary doctrines on the same subject being both true. How then, could your noble and lofty mind submit to suspend your usual courage in regard to the correction of so great an evil? But even though there is no precedent for such a course, let your inimitable perfection in virtue stand up at a crisis like the present, and teach our most pious emperor that no gain will come from his zeal for the Church on other points if he allows such an evil to gain strength from freedom of speech for the subversion of sound faith.[3]

Notes

Epistle 101

[1]   Ps. 81 (80):12.

[2]   Rom. 7:22; II Cor. 4:16; Eph. 3:16.

[3]   I Cor. 15:47, 48; John 3:13.

[4]   John 1:3; Eph. 3:17.

[5]   Ex. 7:1; Num. 12:7 (Heb. 3:5).

[6]   I Cor. 5:7, mixed with Matt. 13:33, or Luke 13:21.

[7]   Ex. 3:2, and, e.g., Gen., ch. 18.

[8]   John 1:14; 17:2; Ps. 65 (64):2; 145 (144):21.

[9]   Acts 7:14 (Gen. 46:26); Ps. 105 (104):18.

[10]   Ps. 147 (146):9; Job 9:9.

[11]   John 1:14; II Cor. 5:21; Gal. 3:13; Isa. 53:4, 5 (LXX).

[12]   Gal. 5:12.

[13]   Ps. 26 (25):4 (LXX).

Epistle 102

1   I Cor. 2:16.

2   I Cor. 15:49.

3   Heb. 4:15.

4   John 2:25; Baruch 3:37.

5   Cf. Matt. 23:25, 26.

6   Cf. p. 222, n. 18.

7   Phil. 2:7, 8.

8   Matt. 4:2; Luke 4:2; John 19:28; 4:6; Mark 4:38.

9   Luke 2:14 or Mark 1:13; Mark 6:35-51 and parallels.

10   John 11:34, 43.

11   Luke 22:44.

12   Cf. Mark 6:50; John 16:33.

Epistle 202

1   John 3:13.

2   I Cor. 15:47.

3   As a result of this letter, or similar representations, a law of 388 (Codex Theodosianus 16.5.14) applied specially to Apollinarians the laws previously enacted against heretics generally.

11 Ambrose, *Letters 20 and 21* (385, Milan)

Ambrose was born in about 339 at Trier in Gaul, the youngest of three children. His family was wealthy and socially important; his father was the praetorian prefect of Gaul. The family was apparently Christian, like a growing minority of the Western aristocracy, but Ambrose was not baptized. It is not that infant baptism was uncommon. Cyprian, in his Letter 58, had argued passionately against the position that infants should not be baptized before the age of eight days, and about the same time Origen had claimed that infant baptism was an apostolic tradition. But it seems that among well-to-do Christians baptism was often deferred until adulthood, for reasons more guessed than known.

Not long after Ambrose was born his father died, and he was raised by his mother and his sister Marcellina, who was ten years older. Marcellina herself was a very committed Christian, and proved sympathetic to an ascetic movement which began around the time that Athanasius, the bishop of Alexandria, was beginning an exile in Rome (339). Living in the house of a well-to-do Christian family, he inspired his hosts and their visitors with stories of the Egyptian ascetics. He even had two Egyptian monks with him. His host's daughter soon committed herself to a lifetime of virginity, and several other daughters of the Roman Christian aristocracy followed her example. In 353 Marcellina received the virgin's veil from the Pope in a ceremony that Ambrose attended and always remembered. She was not, however, a nun living in a religious community according to a Rule; she continued to live at home. Later, as a bishop, Ambrose promoted the celibate life and supported the young and still controversial monastic movement.

Ambrose was educated at Rome in rhetoric, philosophy, science, Greek, and jurisprudence, practised law, and, in 370, was appointed consularis (governor) of an area in northern Italy called Aemilia and Liguria. In Milan, which was the most important city in the region, Niceans and Arians were in sharp conflict, and when the bishop died in 374 and a new bishop needed to be chosen, the battle-lines were drawn. A fracas broke out in the cathedral between the rival parties, and Ambrose decided that as governor he should intervene. He came to the cathedral and addressed the crowd. Then, according to a contemporary, a child's voice was heard to say, "Ambrose bishop." Ambrose was a Nicean, but the idea caught on even among the Arians, and Ambrose was elected. The Emperor, thrilled that the Niceans and Arians in Milan had finally agreed on something, released Ambrose from office. In the eight days from November 30 to December 7, 374, Ambrose was baptized, ordained through the various ecclesiastical orders from lector to presbyter, and consecrated bishop. He donated a large amount of his wealth to the Church and distributed most of the rest among the poor, and he began a crash course in Scripture and theology.

In his preaching Ambrose's classical education in the Latin and Greek writers and his reading in philosophy can often be discerned. He took an interest in liturgy, and introduced hymns into his services of worship. He wrote a treatise called *On the Duties of Ecclesiastics* which set moral and spiritual standards for the clergy. But what most distinguished his episcopacy was his outspoken policy of holding emperors accountable to the laws and standards of the Church. Here is one of the clearest differences which historians have seen between the Church in the western Empire and the Church in the eastern Empire. In the west, from the fourth century through the Middle Ages and down past the Reformation, Church authorities grew accustomed to challenging the power of the state and calling emperors, monarchs, and political officials to account. Eastern bishops, by contrast, learned to defer to the authority of the state.

The bishop in Milan was particularly well situated to influence emperors when in 379 Gratian, the young emperor for the western Empire, moved his court to Milan. Ambrose became his teacher, and he influenced him to legislate against heretics, to withdraw imperial financing from certain pagan cultic practices, and to have a pagan altar removed from the Roman senate. Gratian, however, was murdered in 383. The new emperor, Valentinian, was only eleven years old, and the imperial court in Milan now came under the influence of his mother, the empress Justina, a supporter of the Arian cause. In 386 a law was published permitting the Arians freedom of worship; imperial officials then told Ambrose to surrender one of the three large churches in Milan to the use of the Arians. Ambrose resisted. An imperial tribune came to Ambrose to arrange a commission to decide the matter. Ambrose refused to cooperate (Letter 21 below). Shortly thereafter, imperial troops seized one of the three basilicas. Letter 20 below tells this story.

Church and state conflicted again in 390. A new emperor, Theodosius I, lost his temper when rioters in Thessalonica killed one of his officials. In revenge he had his soldiers massacre 7,000 men, women, and children in the amphitheatre in the city. Ambrose excommunicated him and required him to do public penance. The emperor yielded.

Ambrose died in 397, and the episcopal see of Milan declined in importance. For two decades Ambrose had been the most influential ecclesiastic in the western Empire, ending the ambitions of western Arianism and paganism alike, setting precedents for the authority of bishops over emperors, and promoting the young monastic movement.

We are told that Ambrose was of short stature, with a narrow face, large expressive eyes, refined features, a black beard and mustache, and an aristocratic bearing.

Questions on the reading

What issue pits the emperor against the bishop? What social circumstances and political dynamics influence events? What is the role of personality? What are the goals and strategies of each side? In Letter 21, what tone does Ambrose take with the emperor? What is his understanding of the relationship of Church and state? In Letter 20, what is the chronology of the events recorded? What leverage does Ambrose have in this situation? How credible is Ambrose's version of events? In what ways might a narrative written by the empress differ? What, politically, does Ambrose win in his victory, and what does he lose?

$\wp$

Letter 21
To the most clement Emperor and the most blessed
Valentinian Augustus, Ambrose, Bishop (February 386)

Alleging that he was acting at your command, the tribune and notary Dalmatius came to me and asked that I choose judges just as Auxentius has done. Yet he has not indicated the names of those who have been demanded. But he adds that there will be a discussion in the consistory, and the judgment of your Piety will be the deciding factor.

To this I am making, as I think, a suitable response. No one should find that I am being insolent when I assert that your father of august memory not only gave his answer by word of mouth, but sanctioned by law this truth: In a matter of faith or of any Church regulation the decision should be given by him who is neither unsuited to the task nor disqualified by law. These are the words of his decree; in other words, he wished priests to make judgments regarding priests. In fact, if a bishop were accused of any charge and the case of his character needed to be examined, he wished these matters to belong to the judgment of bishops.

Who, then, has given your Clemency an insolent answer? One who wishes you to be like your father, or one who wishes you to be unlike him? Perhaps little importance is attached by some persons to the opinion of that greater emperor, although his faith was proved by his firm

Source: Ambrose, "Letter 21" (to the Emperor) and "Letter 20" (to his sister) in *Letters* , trans. Sister Mary Melchior Beyenke (Fathers of the Church vol. 26), N.Y.: Fathers of the Church Inc., 1954, 52-56, 365-375. Reprinted by permission of the Catholic University of America Press.

confession and his wisdom was declared by his development of a better commonwealth.

O most clement Emperor, when have you heard the laity judge a bishop in a matter of faith? Are we so bent down with flattery as to forget our priestly privileges and think that we should entrust to others that which God has given to us? If a bishop has to be instructed by a layman, what next? If so, the laity will dispute and the bishop will listen; and the bishop will learn from the laity! But if we examine the context of holy Scripture or of times past, who will deny that in a matter of faith, in a matter, I say, of faith, bishops usually judge Christian emperors; not emperors, bishops.

By God's favor you will reach a ripe old age, and then you will realize what kind of a bishop subjects his priestly power to the laity. By God's favor your father, a man of ripe old age, said: 'It does not belong to me to judge between bishops'; your Clemency now says: 'I must be the judge.' He, although baptized, thought he was unfit for the burden of such a judgment; your Clemency, who must still earn the sacrament of baptism, takes to yourself a judgment concerning faith, although you are unacquainted with the sacraments of that faith.

We can well imagine what sort of judges he [Auxentius] will choose, for he fears to reveal their names. Of course, let them come to the church, if there are any to come. Let them listen to the people, not so that each may sit in judgment, but that each may have proof of his disposition and choose whom he will follow. The matter concerns the bishop of that church; if the people decide after hearing him that he argues a better case, let them follow the faith he teaches. I shall not be jealous.

I will not mention the fact that the people have already passed judgment. I am silent about their demand from the father of your Clemency for the one whom they have. I am silent about the promise of the father of your Piety that there would be peace if the one chosen would assume the bishopric. I have kept faith in these promises.

If he boasts of the approval of some foreigners, let him be bishop there where there are people who think that he should be given the name of bishop. But I neither recognize him as a bishop nor know whence he comes.

When have we ever decided a matter on which you have declared your judgment? Nay, have you not even promulgated laws and not allowed anyone freedom of judgment? When you made such a provision for others, you also made it for yourself. An emperor passes laws which he first of all keeps. Do you want me to try to see whether those who have been chosen judges will begin to go contrary to your opinion, or at least excuse themselves on the grounds that they cannot act against so severe and rigid a law of the emperor?

This, then, is the action of an insolent individual, not of a well-meaning bishop. See, O Emperor, you are rescinding your own law in part. Would that you did so, not in part, but entirely, for I would not want your law to be above the law of God. God's law teaches us what we are to follow; human laws cannot teach us this. These alter the conduct of the timid; they are unable to inspire confidence.

What person will there be who reads that at one moment it has been decreed that one who opposes the emperor should be struck with the sword, and whoever does not hand over the temple of God is straightway slain; what person, I say, either singly or with a few could say to the emperor: 'Your law does not meet my approval'? If priests are not allowed this, are the laity permitted? And will he be the judge in a matter of faith who either hopes for favor or fears to give offence?

Shall I agree to choose laymen as judges, who, if they maintain the truth with faith, will be proscribed or killed, because a law passed about faith has so decreed? Shall I expose these men either to the denial of truth or to punishment?

Ambrose is not worth so much that he would throw away his priestly office for his own sake. The life of one man is not worth the dignity of all priests on whose advice I made these statements, since they suggested that we would perhaps surrender the triumph of Christ to some pagan or Jew, chosen by Auxentius, if we gave them judgment regarding Christ. What else do they rejoice to hear but the harm being done to Christ? What else can please them except that (God forbid!) Christ's divinity is being denied? Plainly, they agree completely with the Arians, who say that Christ is a creature, for heathens and Jews readily admit this.

This decree was made at the Synod of Ariminium and I rightfully despise that council, for I follow the rule of the Council of Nicaea from which neither death nor the sword can separate me. This is the creed which the parent of your Clemency, Theodosius most blessed emperor, follows and approves. This creed is held by the Gauls, it is held by the Spaniards, who keep it with pious profession of the Holy Spirit.

If there must be discussion, I have learned from my predecessor to have the discussion in church. If there has to be a conference about the faith, it should be a conference of bishops, as was done under Constantine, prince of august memory, who promulgated no laws until he had given free judgment to the bishops. This was also done under Constantius, emperor of august memory, heir of his father's dignity. Yet, what began well is ending otherwise. The bishops had subscribed at first to a definite creed. Then, when certain persons within the palace wished to pass judgment on the faith, they managed to alter the judgments of the bishops by surreptitious methods. The bishops at once called for resolute opinions. And, certainly, the greater number at Ariminium approved the creed of the Council of Nicaea and condemned the Arian decrees.

If Auxentius appeals to a synod to dispute the faith (please God it may not be necessary for so many bishops to be wearied on account of one man, for, even if he were an angel from heaven, he must not be esteemed above the peace of the Church), when I shall hear that the synod is gathering, I myself will not be missing. Pass the law if you want a struggle!

I would have come, O Emperor, to your Clemency's consistory to make these remarks in person if either the bishops or people had permitted me, but they said rather that discussions of the faith should be held in church in the presence of the people.

Would, O Emperor, that you had not sentenced me to go wherever I wished! I went out daily; no one guarded me. You should have dispatched me where you wished, me who offered myself for anything. Now I am told by the bishops: It makes little difference whether you willingly leave the altar of Christ or hand it over, for, when you leave it, you will be handing it over.

Would that it were clearly evident to me that the Church would not be handed over to the Arians! I would then willingly offer myself to the wishes of your Piety. But, if I am the only one guilty of making a disturbance, why is there the decree to invade all the other churches?

Would that there were the assurance that not one would harm the churches! I choose that you pass on me whatever sentence you wish.

Wherefore, O Emperor, receive with dignity my reason for being unable to come to the consistory. I have not learned to take my place in a consistory except to act in your behalf, and I am unable to dispute in the palace, neither seeking nor knowing the secrets of the palace.

I, Ambrose, the bishop, offer this notice to the most clement emperor and most blessed Augustus Valentinian.

Letter 20
Ambrose, Bishop, to Marcellina, his sister (Easter 386)

In most of your letters you make anxious inquiry about the church. Hear, then, what is going on: The day after I received your letter, in which you remarked that your dreams were troubling you, a great wave of serious disturbances began overwhelming us. This time it was not the Portian Basilica, that is, the one outside the walls, which was being demanded [by the Arians], but the new basilica, that is, the one inside the walls, the larger one.

First, the military authorities, imperial counts, came with their command to me to hand over the [new] basilica and also to see to it that the people caused no disturbance. I answered, as was proper, that a bishop could not hand over the temple of God.

On the following day in church this [statement of mine] was loudly approved by the people; then the praetorian prefect arrived there and began to urge us to give up the Portian Basilica. The people protested again, whereupon he left, saying that he would make a report of matters to the emperor.

The following day, the Lord's day, after the lessons and sermon, I dismissed the catechumens and then went on giving an exposition of the Creed to several candidates for baptism in the baptistries of the basilica. There I was informed that some of the people were flocking over to the Portian Basilica since they had learned that officers had been sent from the palace and were hanging up the imperial banners. Yet I stayed at my duty and began to celebrate Mass.

While I was offering [Mass] I learned that a certain Castulus, whom the Arians declared to be a priest, had been seized by the people as they encountered him in the public square. I began to weep very bitterly and to pray God precisely at the Offertory that there would be no blood shed in a case involving the Church, or, at least, that it would be my blood which would be poured out, not alone for the salvation of my people but also for the unbelievers themselves. To be brief, I dispatched priests and deacons and rescued the man from harm.

Very severe penalties were decreed then and there, first on the entire class of merchants. Consequently, during the holy days of the last week [of Lent], when the bonds of debtors are customarily loosed, chains rattled and were put upon the necks of innocent people, and they were taxed 200 pounds' weight of gold [to be paid] in three days' time. People said they would give that much, or double, if asked, provided that they might practice their faith. The prisons, too, were packed with tradesmen.

All the palace officials, the clerks, the agents of affairs, the attendants of various counts were ordered to avoid going out on the pretext that they were forbidden to take part in the rebellion. Men of high rank were threatened with many dire consequences unless they effected the surrender of the basilica. The persecution spread, and, had they opened their doors, the people seemed on the verge of breaking forth into every sort of abuse.

To effect a speedy surrender of the basilica I myself was approached by counts and tribunes who said that the emperor was using his rights inasmuch as all property was under his jurisdiction. I answered that if he were asking for what was mine — my estate, my money, or anything of this sort — I would not resist, even though all my property belongs to the poor; but sacred objects are not subject to the jurisdiction even of the emperor. If he wants my patrimony, come take it; my person, I am here; do you want to drag me off to prison, or to death? The pleasure is mine, I will not shelter myself with a throng of people, nor cling to the altars, begging for my life. Instead, I will more gladly be sacrificed before the altars.

Actually, in my heart I was frightened, since I knew that armed men had been sent to seize the basilica of the church; [I feared] that in defending the basilica bloodshed would occur and turn to the harm of the whole city. I kept praying that I would not live to see the ruin of this great city or, possibly, of all Italy. I dreaded the ill-will that would arise from the spilling of blood; I offered my own throat. Some tribunes of the Goths were there; I assailed them, saying: 'Is this why the Roman state has taken you in, to make you agents of a public riot? Where will you go if these lands are destroyed?'

I was told to quiet the people. I retorted that it was in my power to arouse them, but to quell them rested with God. Then I said that if I was considered the trouble-maker I should be punished, or banished to any lonely spot on earth they wished. After these words, they went off, and I spent the entire day in the old basilica. Then I went home to sleep, so that, if anyone wanted to arrest me, he might find me ready.

Before dawn, when I set foot out of doors, the basilica had been surrounded and was being occupied by soldiers. The soldiers were said to have told the emperor that if he wished to leave he would be given the opportunity; too, they would escort him if they saw him joining the Catholics; otherwise, they would join the meeting called by Ambrose.

No one of the Arians dared appear, for there were none among the citizens; they consisted of a few who belonged to the imperial household and several Goths. Just as formerly they had a wagon for a dwelling, so now the church is their wagon. Wherever that woman goes, she takes along with her all her retinue.

From the groaning populace I understood that the basilica was surrounded. But, while the lessons were being read, I was informed that even the new basilica was filled with the populace; the crowd seemed to be greater than when they were all free to go there, and they were clamoring for a reader. In short, the soldiers themselves, who appeared to be besieging the basilica, after learning that I had ordered them kept from membership in our communion, began coming over to our meeting. Some of the women were deeply troubled when they saw them and one rushed out. But the soldiers declared they had come to pray, not to fight. The people broke into some kind of shouting, With what restraint, with what steadfastness, with what reliance on God did they keep begging that we go to that basilica! It was said that in that basilica, too, the people were demanding my presence.

Then I began the following discourse: Brethren, you have heard the Book of Job being read which we follow during this solemn service and season. Even the Devil knew from experience that this book would be made known where all the power of his temptation is revealed and set forth. On that account he hurled himself today with greater strength. But, thanks be to our God who so confirmed you in faith and patience. I mounted the pulpit to praise one man, Job; I have found all of you to be Jobs whom I admire. In each of you Job has lived again, in each the patience and virtue of that holy man has shone again. For, what more timely could be said by Christians than what the Holy Spirit has said in you today? We beg, O Augustus, we do not battle. We are not afraid, but we are begging. It befits Christians to hope for the tranquility of peace and not to check the steadfastness of faith and truth when faced with danger of death. The Lord is our Head who will save those who hope in Him.

But let us come to the lessons before us. You see, permission is granted to the Devil to be a tempter in order that the good may be tried. The Devil envies the progress of the good; he tempts them in various ways. He tempted Job in his possessions; he tempted him in his children; he tempted him in pain of body. The strong man is tempted in his own body, the weak man in another's. And he wanted to take from me the riches which I have in you, and he desired to scatter this inheritance of your tranquility. He longed to snatch you away, too, my very good children, for whom I daily renew the Sacrifice. He was trying to drag you into the ruins of public disorder. I have, therefore, experienced two kinds of temptations. And perhaps because the Lord God knows that I am weak, He still has not given him [the Devil] power over my body. Although I make it my will and make the offering, He judges me still unequal to this struggle, and He tries me with various labors. And Job did not begin but ended with this struggle.

Moreover, Job was tried by accumulated tidings of evils; he was even tried by his wife who said: 'Speak a word against God, and die.' You see what great disturbances are suddenly at hand — Goths, armed men, heathens, fining of merchants, punishment of saints. You see what is asked when this command is given: Hand over the basilica — that is:

'Speak a word against God, and die,' do not merely speak a word opposing God, but make yourself an opponent of God. The order is: Hand over the altars of God.

We are hard-pressed by the royal edicts, but we are strengthened by the words of Scripture, which answered: 'You have spoken like one of the senseless.' And that was no slight temptation, because we know that those temptations are more severe which are brought about through women. Indeed, through Eve Adam was deceived, and thus did it come about that he departed from the divine commands. When he learned his mistake and was conscious of the sin within himself, he wished to hide but could not. And so God said to him: 'Adam, where art thou?' that is, what were you before? Where now have you begun to stay? Where did I put you? Whither have you wandered? You realize that you are naked because you have lost the robes of good faith. Those are leaves with which you now seek to cover yourself. You have repudiated the fruit, wishing to hide under the leaves of the law, but you are betrayed. You desired to leave the Lord your God for one woman, and you are fleeing One whom formerly you wished to behold. With one woman you have preferred to hide yourself, to abandon the Mirror of the world, the abode of paradise, the grace of Christ.'

Why should I tell of how Jezabel severely persecuted Elias, and Herodias caused John the Baptist to be put to death? Individual women persecuted individual men, but in so far as my merits are far less, so are these trials of mine heavier. My strength is weaker, my danger greater. Women's fortune changes, their hatreds are replaced by others, their contrivances vary, they are following their elders and making a pretext [of protecting] the king from harm. What reason is there for such serious trials against a mere worm, except that they are persecuting not me but the Church?

Then the command is given: 'Hand over the basilica.' I answer: 'It is not lawful for me to hand it over, nor is it expedient for you, O Emperor, to receive it. If you cannot rightly violate the house of a private individual, do you think that the house of God can be appropriated?' It is alleged that all things are permitted the emperor, that everything is his. To this I reply: 'Do not burden yourself with thinking that you have imperial power over the things which are divine. Do not exalt yourself, but, if you wish to be emperor for a long time, be subject to God. Scripture says:

"What things are God's to God, what are Caesar's to Caesar." Palaces belong to the emperor, churches to the bishop. You have been given authority over public edifices, not over sacred ones.' Again it is said the order came from the emperor: 'I, too, ought to have a basilica.' I answered: 'It is not lawful for you to have one. What have you to do with an adulteress? She is an adulteress who is not joined to Christ by lawful union!'

While I was treating of these matters, word was brought to me that the royal hangings had been gathered up, the basilica was filling with people, and they were demanding my presence. At once I turned my discourse in that direction, saying: How lofty and deep are the sayings of the Holy Spirit! As you remember, brethren, we responded with great sorrow of soul to the words read at Matins: 'O God, the heathen have invaded thine inheritance.' In reality, the heathen have invaded, and even more than the heathen have invaded. For the Goths have invaded, and men of different nations; they invaded with arms and surrounded and seized the basilica. We lamented this, being ignorant of your greatness, but our want of wisdom drew forth this [lament].

The heathen have invaded, and truly they have invaded your inheritance, for those who invaded as heathen have become Christians. Those who came to invade the inheritance became co-heirs of God. I have as defenders those whom I thought to be enemies; I possess as allies those whom I thought to be adversaries. That is fulfilled which David the Prophet sang of the Lord Jesus: 'His abode is in peace,' and 'There he has broken the sides of the bows, the shield, the sword and the war!' Whose task is this, whose work but Yours, O Lord Jesus? You saw armed men coming to Your temple, people groaning for this reason and coming in crowds that they might not seem to be handing over God's basilica, and, on the other hand, the soldiers were under orders to do violence. Death was before my eyes, but that amid these events madness should be given no right You put Yourself in our midst, O Lord, and made both one. You quieted the armed men, saying, no doubt: 'If you rush to arms, if those shut up in my temple are disturbed, "What profit will be from my blood?"' Thanks be to You, Christ! Not a legate or messenger, but 'Thou, O Lord, hast made safe thy people.' Thou hast tossed away my sackcloth, and thou hast girt me with gladness.'

These things I said and marveled that the feeling of the emperor could have grown gentle through the zeal of the soldiers, the entreaty of the counts, and the prayers of the people. Meanwhile the message came to me that an envoy had been sent to bring me a decree. I withdrew a little and he acquainted me with the decree. 'What,' he said, 'is your idea in acting contrary to the emperor's wish?' 'I do not know his wish,' I answered, 'nor am I certain of what I have done in disobedience.' 'Why,' he asked, 'did you assign priests to the basilica? If you are a usurper, I want to know how to prepare myself against you.' I replied, saying that I had done nothing to harm the church, that when I had heard the basilica was besieged by soldiers, I only gave free vent to my lament, and when many urged me to go there I stated: 'I cannot hand over the basilica, yet I cannot wage a fight.' And after I learned that the royal hangings had been taken away when the people demanded that I go there, I sent some priests. I was unwilling to go myself, but I told them: In Christ I believe that the emperor himself will join us.

If these seem to be the acts of a usurper, I have weapons, but only in the name of Christ. I can offer my life. Why does he delay striking if he thinks I am a usurper. Under the Old Testament imperial power was bestowed by priests, not despotically claimed, and it is commonly said that emperors aspired to the priesthood rather than priests to the imperial power. Christ fled lest He be made a king. We have a power of our own. The power of the priest is weakness. He [St. Paul] said: 'When I am weak, then I am strong.' He should take care not to make himself a usurper, he against whom God has not raised up an adversary. Maximus does not say that I am a usurper of Valentinian, though he complained that through the intervention of my delegation he was unable to come to Italy. I said, too, that bishops were never usurpers but often had suffered from usurpers.

That whole day was spent in sorrow on our part. The royal hangings were torn by children in their play. I could not return home because soldiers were stationed around the basilica, keeping it under guard. We recited the Psalms with the brethren in the smaller chapel of the church.

The next day the Book of Jonah was read according to custom, and when it was finished I began this sermon: Brethren, a book has been read in which it is prophesied that sinners shall return to penance. It is understood to mean that they may hope for the future in the present. I added that the just man had been willing to receive even blame, so as not to see or prophesy destruction for the city. And because that sentence was mournful, he grew sad when the gourd withered. God said to the Prophet: 'Are you sad over the gourd?' Jonah answered: 'I am sad.' The Lord said that if he was grieving because the gourd had withered, how much greater should his care be for the salvation of so many people! And, in fact, he did sway with the destruction which had been prepared for all the city.

Word came promptly that the emperor had ordered the soldiers to withdraw from the basilica, and fines which had been levied on the merchants were being returned to them. What, then, was the joy of all the people! What cheering from the whole crowd! What thanksgiving! It was the day on which the Lord had delivered Himself for us, the day when penance in the Church is ended. Soldiers vied with one another in spreading the good news; rushing to the altars, and kissing them, they gave token of peace. Then I knew that God had smitten the early worm so that the whole city might be saved.

These events took place, and would that they were now at an end! But the words of the emperor, full of turmoil, point to greater disturbances. I am called a usurper; even worse than a usurper. For when the counts begged the emperor to give in to the Church, and said that they did this at the request of the soldiers, he answered: 'If Ambrose ordered you, you will give me to him in chains.' After such a speech, just think what is coming! All were horrified at this statement, but some of his men are urging him on.

Finally, too, Calligonus, the grand chamberlain, dared to address me in this fashion: 'While I live, do you treat Valentinian with contempt? I will take your life!' I answered: 'May God grant you to fulfill what you threaten, for I shall suffer what bishops suffer, and you will act as eunuchs act.' May God turn them from the Church and direct their weapons all on me, and slake their thirst with my blood.

12 John Chrysostom, *Homilies on the Gospel of St. John*, number 62 (John 11:1-29) (391?, Antioch)

Christian antiquity gave John the title "Chrysostom", "the one with the golden mouth", because he was the greatest preacher in the early Church. But his eloquence was not only a great asset, but also a great liability.

John was born between 344 and 354 at Antioch, where he spent most of his life. Antioch, in northern Syria (modern Antakya, Turkey), was the fourth city of the Empire, after Rome, Constantinople, and Alexandria. It was almost a sea-port, being just a few kilometers up-river from Seleucia on the Mediterranean. It was a military headquarters for the imperial defence of the Euphrates frontier. Its main street was a broad Roman avenue two miles long with colonnades on both sides. Like Alexandria, Antioch originated with Alexander the Great, who conquered much of the territory around the eastern Mediterranean in the late fourth century B.C.E. He sent colonists from Athens to settle it, and the Athenians brought with them the traditions of their city-state, such as philosophy, rhetoric, religious festivals, and Olympic contests. Antioch liked to think of itself as a kind of Athens in Asia. In the fourth century, Antiochene Christianity developed a school of Biblical exegesis that opposed the allegorical methods of the Alexandrians. Antiochenes analyzed Scripture grammatically, sought the meaning intended by the text, and investigated Biblical history. In this way they laid a foundation for most modern Biblical scholarship.

John's family was well to do though not socially prestigious. His father died when he was an infant, and he received his early Christian orientation and education from his mother. He then continued with higher studies under good classical teachers, including one of the most distinguished teachers of rhetoric. He was baptized in 368. His intellectual gifts caught the attention of the bishop, who taught him the Scriptures and mentored him in the Christian life. John retreated from the world for several years and lived an austere ascetic life. His health afflicted, he returned to Antioch, where he was ordained deacon in 381, and presbyter in 386. From 386 to 397 he preached in the principal church in Antioch, often three times a week. He was apparently the first to preach not from the altar but from the deacon's pulpit, in order to be closer to the people. His preaching attracted large crowds and excited considerable applause.

Where Origen, consistently with the Alexandrian school, interpreted Scripture allegorically, John, consistently with the school of Antioch, interpreted it historically. Then, working from his exegesis, he sought the spiritual truth of the passage, and applied it to the Christian life. In doing so he often critiqued the social ethos and practices of his community, and he characteristically summoned his audience to commit themselves to higher standards of Christian morality. He particularly targeted the wealthy on account of their luxurious living and their indifference to the poor; wealth itself, he thought, was usually a sign of unjust gain. He sometimes used violently disparaging language concerning the Jews, who had a vigorous community in Antioch and whose theology and services of worship were, in Chrysostom's view, rather too appealing to many Christians. Thus Chrysostom has won an unhappy place in the ugly history of Christian anti-semitism. He is also known as one of the most anti-feminist of early Christian leaders, although he appears to have mellowed in this respect as he advanced in years.

In 398, most unwillingly, he was made bishop of Constantinople. Chrysostom, transparent, impulsive, uncompromising, and tactless, was scarcely suited to the most politicized ecclesiastical office in the world. The Empress Eudoxia took umbrage at his attacks on wealth and luxury, his clergy were grievously provoked by his attempts to reform their moral and spiritual lives, and his brother bishops wished that he would learn to mind his own business. He was deposed by a synod in 403, but the deposition was quashed by another synod. On Easter eve 404, soldiers raided his church and attacked the faithful, and at Pentecost the Emperor sent him into exile in Armenia. There he continued to attract a large following, so in 407 the emperor had him marched through severe weather into a still more remote exile. He died on the way.

Chrysostom's literary legacy is the largest of any Greek Christian of the first six centuries, and it is attested by a huge number of manuscripts. He left hundreds of sermons. He likely did not preach from a script, and it is thought that the most authentic copies of his sermons are actually transcriptions or paraphrases taken down by stenographers. His works enjoyed considerable popularity in the Greek East, in the Western Middle Ages, and in the Protestant Reformation. A good biography of him was written within a year or two of his death by a Bithynian historian named Palladius. In the following reading, footnoted Scripture references are supplied by the translator.

Questions on the reading

How is the homily structured? What initially interests Chrysostom in this passage? What questions does he ask of it? What other questions might he have asked of the passage, and why does he not raise them? What differences of interpretation does he decide to explain? How does he decide among these differences of interpretation? When he comes to applying this passage to Christian faith and lifestyle, what pastoral and social issues does he identify? What can we know about Chrysostom's social setting from this homily? What is his attitude towards women; death; grief; social custom? What is his theology of Scripture; human nature; the ways of God; the Christian life? Is he sexist? What might be "Antiochene" about Chrysostom's approach? How much of his training in rhetoric and the classics can be discerned in this document?

Chrysostom, Homily on John 11:1–29

'Now a certain man was sick, Lazarus of Bethany, the village of Mary and her sister Martha. Now it was Mary who anointed the Lord with ointment.'[1]

Many are scandalized when they see those who are pleasing to God enduring some terrible suffering, for example, falling into sickness or poverty or some such thing. They do not know that to have these sufferings is the privilege of those especially dear to God. For Lazarus was one of Christ's friends, and he was sick. Indeed, the messengers sent to Him stated this when they said: 'Behold, he whom thou lovest is sick.'

However, let us look at the account of his affliction from its beginning. 'A certain man was sick,' the Evangelist stated, 'Lazarus of Bethany.' It was not at random or by chance that he mentioned where Lazarus was from, but for a reason that will be explained later. Meanwhile, let us consider the text before us now. To aid us to identify Lazarus, the Evangelist mentioned the latter's sisters and noted besides the privilege Mary was to enjoy later, by saying: 'Now it was Mary who anointed the Lord with ointment.'

With regard to this some are in doubt. They ask: 'How was it that Christ allowed a woman to do such a thing?'

In the first place, they must understand this: that she was not the sinner mentioned in the gospel of Matthew,[2] or the one in the gospel of Luke,[3] for she was a different person. Those others, indeed, were notorious sinners, reeking with many vices, while she was devout and zealous. And I say this for she used to show much concern for the hospitable reception of Christ.

Now, the Evangelist pointed out both that the sisters loved Christ, and that He allowed Lazarus to die. But why was it that they did not leave their sick brother and go to Him, as the centurion and the royal official did, but sent messengers to Him? They had the highest confidence

Source: John Chrysostom, "Homily 62" (on John 11:1-29), in *Sermons on the Gospel of John*, trans. Sister Thomas Aquinas Goggin (Fathers of the Church, vol. 41), N.Y.: Fathers of the Church Inc., 1960, 165-179. Reprinted by permission of the Catholic University of America Press.

in Christ and were on terms of great familiarity with Him. But they were weak women, and were restrained also by their grief, for they made it clear later that they did not act in this way through any lack of respect. It is obvious, therefore, that Mary and that sinner were not the same person.

'But why did Christ receive that sinner?' you will ask.

That He might free her from her sinfulness; that He might show His mercy; that you might learn that there is no disease too powerful for His goodness. Do not, then, consider only the fact that He received her; rather, reflect on that other aspect of the incident: how she became a changed person.

And why did the Evangelist tell us this story[4] in detail? Or rather, what did he wish to teach us when he said: 'Now Jesus loved Martha and her sister, and Lazarus'? That we ought not to complain and bear it hard if those who are exemplary people and friends of God become sick.

'Behold, he whom thou lovest is sick.' They wished to arouse Christ's grief, for they were as yet looking on Him as Man. This is evident from what they said: 'If thou hadst been here, he would not have died'; and also from the fact that they did not say: 'Behold, Lazarus is sick,' but: 'Behold, he whom thou lovest is sick.'

What, then, did Christ reply? 'This sickness is not unto death but for the glory of God, that through it the Son of God may be glorified.' See how once again He spoke of His glory and the Father's as one. For, after saying 'the glory of God,' He added: 'that the Son of God may be glorified.'

'This sickness is not unto death.' Since He intended to remain where He was for two days, He sent them back meanwhile to give this message. At this point the sisters are worthy of admiration, for the fact that, though they heard 'is not unto death,' yet saw him die, they did not lose confidence because the outcome was just the opposite, but even so came to Him and did not conclude that He had deceived them.

However, the word 'that' here is used not in a causal sense, but with the idea of result.[5] For the sickness developed from another cause, but He used it for the glory of God. When He had said this, 'He remained two days.' Why did He remain? In order that Lazarus might breathe his last and be buried, that no one might be able to claim that Christ revived a man who was not yet dead; that it was a coma, that it was a faint, that it was a seizure, but not death. And it was for this reason that He remained so long a time, so that corruption of the body might begin and the statement might be made: 'He is already decayed.'

'Afterwards He said to His disciples, "Let us go into Judea."' Why in the world is it that though He nowhere else gave them notice beforehand [of moving from one place to another], in this instance He did so? They had been extremely fearful and, because they felt that way, He warned them of His intention lest it disturb them by it unexpectedness. But what did the disciples reply?

'Just now the Jews were seeking to stone thee, and dost thou go there again?' They were fearful, then, in His behalf, but more so for their own sake, because they had not yet been 'made perfect.'6 Therefore Thomas, quaking with fear, said: 'Let us also go, that we may die with him,' for he was weaker than the rest, and more lacking in faith.

However, see how Jesus encouraged them by what He said. 'Are there not twelve hours in the day?' He meant either: 'The one who is not conscious of having done any wrong will suffer no dreadful punishment, while the one who does evil deeds will suffer it (so that we ought not to be afraid for we have done nothing worthy of death)'; or else: 'The one who can see the light of this world walks in safety. And if the one who sees the light of this world is safe, much more is this true of the one who is in My company if that one does not separate from Me.'

After uttering these words of encouragement, He went on to mention the reason that made it necessary for them to make the journey thither,7 and He pointed out that they were not going to go to Jerusalem, but to Bethany. 'Lazarus, our friend, sleeps. But I go that I may wake him from sleep'; that is 'I am not going for the same reason as before, to dispute and contend once more with the Jews, but to arouse our friend from sleep.'

'His disciples said, "Lord, if he sleeps, he will be safe."' Moreover, they did not say this undesignedly, but in the desire to prevent His going there. They meant: 'You say that he sleeps? Well, then, there is no urgent need for Your departure.' Yet, it was for this reason that He said 'Our friend,' namely, to show that the journey was necessary.

Therefore, since they were somewhat reluctant, He then said: 'He is dead.' He had uttered the first statement as He did, because He did not want to be boastful, but when they did not understand, He added: 'He is dead; and I rejoice on your account.' Why in the world 'on your account'?

'Because I have spoken of his death beforehand, when I was not there; and because when I raise him up there will be no possibility for doubt of what I have done.'

Do you see how imperfect His disciples were as yet and that they did not comprehend His power as they should have? And the fears that insinuated themselves were the cause of this, since they disturbed and confused their souls. Moreover, when He said: 'He sleeps,' He continued: 'I go that I may wake him.' On the contrary, when He declared: 'He is dead,' He did not now add: 'I go that I may raise him up.' For He did not wish to make known ahead of time by His words what He intended to affirm by His deeds. This was to teach us always to avoid vainglory and that we ought not to make promises too freely.

However, if He did this when He was appealed to in the case of the centurion (for He said: 'I will come and cure him'), He did so in order to show the faith of the centurion.[8]

Now, someone may say: 'How is it that the disciples conceived the idea that it was literally sleep He meant and did not understand that Lazarus was dead — I mean because He said: "I go that I may wake him"? And I say this for it was stupid if they thought that He was traveling fifteen stadia to wake him from sleep.'

In reply we should say this: 'They supposed that this was a riddle like many things He said.' Accordingly, they all feared the hostility of the Jews, and Thomas was more fearful than all the rest. Therefore he said: 'Let us also go, that we may die with him.'

Some maintain that Thomas himself wished to die, also, but this is not so, for the statement was rather one that proceeded from fear. However, he was not reproved, for Christ still was making allowance for his weakness. Later, in fact, he became strongest of all and even swept all before him. It is indeed a wonderful thing that we see him who was so weak before the crucifixion becoming most fervent of all after the crucifixion, and after he came to believe in the Resurrection. So great is the power of Christ. For, the same man who did not dare to go into Bethany in company with Christ traversed almost the whole world, though he could no longer see Christ, and freely moved about in the midst of murderous people who even wanted to kill him.

'But if Bethany was fifteen stadia distant, and this is but two miles,[9] how was Lazarus dead for four days?'

He remained two days and on the day before these two the messenger had come,[10] that is, on the very day of Lazarus' death. Then, on the fourth day Jesus arrived in Bethany. Now, He waited to be summoned, and did not go uninvited, lest someone might hold in question what was to happen. Further, not even the beloved sisters came, but others were sent.

'Now Bethany was some fifteen stadia distant.' From this it is evident that it was likely that many people from Jerusalem were present there. In fact, the Evangelist immediately added that many of the Jews were comforting them. How could they offer comfort to those who were loved by Christ, despite the fact that they had agreed that, if anyone should confess Christ, he would be put out of the synagogue?

They were there either because of the grave misfortune that had occurred, or out of respect for the noble ladies or, at any rate, they were not of evil intent; and many of them, to be sure, believed in Christ. Further, the Evangelist mentioned these details to confirm the fact that Lazarus was really dead.

But why in the world was it that the one who came to meet Christ was not accompanied by her sister? She wished to meet Him by herself and to inform Him of what had happened. And when He had inspired her with fair hopes, then she went off and called Mary and the latter went to meet Him, still sunk in the depths of woe. Do you perceive how ardent her love of Him was? She it was of whom He said: 'Mary has chosen the best part.'[11]

'How is it, then,' you will ask, 'that Martha seems more fervent?'

She was not more fervent, for it was not Mary who heard [His words about the resurrection] since Martha was the weaker. Indeed, though she had heard such sublime words, she said afterwards: 'He is already decayed, for he is dead four days.' Mary, on the contrary, though she had listened to no instruction said nothing of the kind, but merely declared at once, with faith: 'Master, if thou hadst been here, my brother would not have died.'

Do you perceive how much true wisdom the women possessed, even if their understanding was weak? For on seeing Christ they did not immediately begin to lament or to cry or moan, as we are accustomed to do when we see some of our close friends coming in to us in time of sorrow. On the contrary, they at once expressed admiration of their Master. And so they both believed in Christ, but not as was fitting. For they did not yet understand clearly either that He was God or that He performed these miracles by His own power and authority, though He had instructed them regarding both these facts.

Moreover, it is evident from what they said that they did not know this: 'If thou hadst been here, our brother would not have died.' And this is likewise clear because they[12] added: Whatever thou shalt ask of God, God will give it to thee,' as if speaking of some exemplary and highly esteemed person. But notice, too, what Christ said. 'Thy brother shall rise.'

That reply answered for the moment the words: 'Whatever thou shalt ask,' for He did not say: 'I am making a petition that he will rise,' but what? 'Thy brother shall rise.' Therefore, if He had said: 'O woman, are you still casting your gaze down to earth? I do not need help from anyone else, but I do everything of myself,' it would have been very confusing and might have offended the woman. However, by now saying merely: 'He will rise,' He made the statement with the moderation which the situation required, and by His next words He hinted at what I have just now said. For when she declared: 'I know that he will rise on the last day,' He more clearly gave evidence of His own authority by saying: 'I am the resurrection and the life.' He made it plain that He did not need anyone to help Him, if He was in truth the life, for if He needed someone how could He Himself be the resurrection and the life? However, He did not yet say this explicitly, but merely hinted at it.

Again, because she said: 'Whatever thou shalt ask,' He Himself replied in turn: 'He who believes in me, even if he die, shall live,' to point out that it is He Himself who dispenses favors and it is necessary to ask them of Him. 'And whoever lives and believes in me, shall never die.' Do you perceive how He conducted her thoughts heavenward? For it was not merely restoring Lazarus to life that was His object here, but it was also necessary for her and those who were with her to learn of the resurrection. Therefore, before actually bringing the dead man to life, it was by His words that He instructed them in true wisdom. But if He is Himself the resurrection and the life, He is not restricted by place, and since He is present everywhere He can heal everywhere. Therefore, if they had spoken as the centurion did: 'Only say the word, and my servant will be healed,'[13] He would have done this. But since they called Him to them and thought He ought to have come, for this reason He condescended to their wishes and came to the place, so as to raise them up from their lowly opinion of Him.

Nevertheless, though He condescended to them, He continued to show that He was able to heal, even when absent, and that is the reason why He delayed. For the favor would not have been so evident, if given at once and if the fetid odor had not preceded it. Furthermore, how did Martha know about the future resurrection? She had often heard Christ speaking of the resurrection; nevertheless she now had a great desire to see it take place.

Yet, see how confused she still was. For after hearing: 'I am the resurrection and the life,' she did not say, in keeping with this: 'Raise him up from the dead.' On the contrary, what did she say? 'I believe that thou art the Christ, the Son of God.'

What, then, did Christ reply to her? 'Whoever believes in me, even if he die, shall live' — He was referring to the death of the body. 'And whoever lives and believes in me shall never die' — referring to the death of the soul. 'Therefore, since I am the resurrection do not be upset if Lazarus is already dead, but have faith. For actually this is not death.'

He was, for the moment, offering her consolation for what had happened, and holding out hope to her, both by declaring: 'He shall rise,' and by saying: 'I am the resurrection,' and: 'After coming to life if he should die again, it would be no suffering. Hence, thou oughtest not to shudder at this kind of death.'

Now, what He meant is something like this: 'Neither is Lazarus dead, nor wilt thou be. Dost thou believe this?'

She replied: 'I believe that thou art the Christ, the Son of God, who hast come into the world.' It seems to me that the woman did not grasp the meaning of what was said. However, she did understand that it was something great, though she did not altogether understand it. That was why, when asked one thing, she replied another. Meanwhile, she gained enough profit so that she brought her grief to an end.

Such, indeed, is the power of Christ's words. That is why, when Martha had gone forth first, Mary followed. For her regard for the Master was not overcome by her strong feeling of grief when she was in His presence. So that, besides being loving, the minds of the women were truly virtuous.

At present, on the contrary, along with the rest of our vices there is one disorder especially prevalent among women. They make a show of their mourning and lamentation: baring their arms, tearing their hair, making scratches down their cheeks. Moreover, some do this because of grief, others for show and vain display. Still others through depravity both bare their arms and do these other things to attract the gaze of men.

What are you doing, O woman? Tell me, do you who are a member of Christ shamelessly strip yourself in the middle of the market-place, when men are present there? Do you tear your hair, and rend your garments, and utter loud cries, and gather a chorus around you, and act like a mad woman, and do you think you are not offensive to God? What great insanity is this?

Will not the heathen ridicule you? Will they not think that our teachings are myths? For they will say: 'There is no resurrection; the Christian teachings are jokes, lies, and tricks. The women among them, in fact, lament as if no one exists after this life. They pay no attention to the words inscribed in their books. And as they show that all those doctrines are mere fancies. For, if they believed that he who has died has not come to an end, but is transferred to a better life, they would not mourn him as one who no longer exists; they would not mutilate themselves so; they would not utter such words, completely lacking in faith, as "I will never see you again; I will never have you back again." All their teachings are fables. Moreover, if the most important one of their blessings is so thoroughly disbelieved, how much more must this be true of the rest of their piety.'

Pagans do not thus play the woman; many among them have lived according to the precepts of true wisdom. For example, a pagan woman on hearing that her son had fallen in battle, at once asked: 'But how are the fortunes of the city getting on?'[14] Furthermore, another true philosopher, who was crowned with a garland, took off the garland when he heard that his son had fallen in behalf of his native land, and asked which of his two sons it was. When he had learned the one who had fallen, he at once donned the garland again.[15]

Many, too, have given up sons and daughters to be sacrificed, to honor demons. Further, the Spartan women even exhort their sons either to bring their shield safely back from war or else to be carried back on it, dead.

Therefore, I am ashamed because the pagans practice such true wisdom, while we act so basely. They who know nothing of the resurrection perform the actions that should be performed by those who know about it, while those who do know about it act like those who are ignorant of it. Besides, many frequently do through human respect what they will not do for God's sake. The wealthier women, indeed, do not tear their hair or expose their arms; yet this is itself altogether blameworthy, not because they do not expose them, but because they act in this way, not through piety, but in order not to seem to disgrace themselves. So, then, human respect prevails over grief, while the fear of God does not prevail over it. Yet, is this not deserving of the utmost condemnation? In that case, then, poor women ought to do for the sake of the fear of God what wealthy women do on account of their wealth. However, actually it is just the opposite: the wealthy practice virtue for the motive of vainglory, while the poor act disgracefully because of their ignoble spirit.

What is worse than this discrepancy? We perform all our actions for human considerations; we perform all our actions with material ends in view. Moreover, we utter things full of stupidity and a great deal of nonsense. The Lord said: 'Blessed are they who mourn,'[16] meaning: 'who mourn for their sins,' yet no one mourns with that kind of sorrow or cares about the loss of his soul. But we were not enjoined to do this other thing and we do it.

'What, then,' you will ask, 'is a man not allowed to weep, though he is human?'

I do not forbid this, but I do forbid tearing yourself to pieces; I do forbid weeping without restraint. I am not brutal or cruel; I know that human nature is tried [by the death of dear ones] and misses their companionship and daily converse with them. It is impossible not to show grief. Christ also showed it, for He wept because of Lazarus. Follow His example yourself: weep, but gently, with decorum, with the fear of God. If you weep in this way, you do so, not as if you were without faith in the resurrection, but as one finding the separation hard to bear.

Besides, we also weep for those who are going away from home, or who are going on a journey, but we do not do this as if we were in despair. Weep in this way, then, at the death of a dear one, as if you were bidding farewell to one setting out on a journey. I am telling you this, not as an impersonal rule of conduct, but in consideration of your human nature. For, if the dead man is a sinner who has committed many offenses against God, you ought to weep, or, rather, not only to weep (for that is no help to him), but you ought to do what can give him assistance, namely, give alms and offer sacrifices. Furthermore, you ought to rejoice for this advantage, namely, that the opportunity to do evil deeds has been taken away from him.

On the contrary, if he was a just man, you ought to be still happier, because his fate now rests secure and he is free from uncertainty for the time to come. If he is a young man, you ought to be happy because he has been quickly freed from the evils of this life; if he is old, because he has departed this life after having received in its fullness what seems to be desirable. However, neglecting to consider these truths, you urge on your maid-servants to tear themselves to pieces, as if by this means honoring the departed, while actually it is a mark of the greatest dishonor. Truly, honor for the dead does not consist in lamentations and moanings, but in singing hymns and psalms and living a noble life. For the man who has departed this life will go on his way in the company of the angels, even if no one is present at his funeral; while he who has been corrupt will gain no profit, even if he has the entire city sending him off to the grave.

Do you wish to honor the departed? Honor him in other ways; namely, by giving alms, performing good works, taking part in the divine services. What good is done him by copious weeping? Moreover,

I have heard also of another serious fault. I have heard that many women, forsooth, attract lovers by their mournful cries, gaining for themselves the reputation of loving their husbands because of the vehemence of their wailings. Oh, what devilish scheming! Oh, what diabolic trickery! What advantage for us who are but earth and ashes, for us who are but flesh and blood?

Let us look heavenward; let us reflect on spiritual considerations. How shall we be able to refute the heathen? How shall we be able to exhort them if we do such things? How shall we preach to them of the resurrection? How shall we discuss with them the rest of the Christian doctrines? How shall we ourselves live in security? Do you not know that death may be caused by grief? Darkening the soul's spiritual vision not only prevents if from perceiving what it should, but even causes it much harm. By showing excessive grief, therefore, we offend God and help neither ourselves nor the departed.

By restraining our grief, on the contrary, we both please God and conduct ourselves becomingly in people's eyes. For, if we ourselves do not succumb unrestrainedy to grief, He will quickly take away the portion of grief we feel; whereas, if we give way to excessive grief, He will permit us to become entirely possessed by it. If we give thanks for it, we shall not be disheartened.

'Yet how is it possible for a man not to grieve,' you will ask, 'when he has lost his son, or his daughter, or his wife?'

I am not saying; 'Do not grieve,' but: 'Do not give way to unrestrained grief.' For, if we reflect that it is God who has taken him away, that it was a mortal husband or son we had, we shall quickly feel consoled. Excessive grief indicates that those who give way to it are seeking for something that is above and beyond nature. You were born a human being, and therefore mortal; why, then, do you repine because something has happened in accordance with nature? You do not repine, do you, because you are nourished by eating food? You do not seek to maintain your life without this, do you? Act thus, also, in regard to death, and do not try to obtain immortality in the present life, though you are but mortal.

This doctrine has now been once and for all defined. Do not give way to excessive grief, do not tear yourself to pieces, but be resigned to the lot decreed for us all in common. Grieve, rather, for your sins. This is in truth the best kind of sorrow; this is the soundest practice of Christian teachings.

Let us, then, give way to this grief continually that we may obtain joy in the life to come, by the grace and mercy of our Lord Jesus Christ. Glory be to Him forever and ever. Amen.

Notes

[1]   John 11.1-2.

[2]   At the house of Simon the leper; cf. Matt. 26.6-13.

[3]   Cf. Luke 7.36-50.

[4]   That is, of the raising of Lazarus from the dead.

[5]   That is, 'that the Son of God may be glorified.'

[6]   Cf. John 17.23.

[7]   Into Judea.

[8]   Matt. 8.7.

[9]   A stade was a measure of distance equivalent to about one-eighth of a Roman mile.

[10]   To say that Lazarus was ill.

[11]   Luke 10.42.

[12]   Actually, it was Martha alone who said it.

[13]   Matt. 8.8.

[14]   Cf. Plutarch, *Moralia* 241C 7.

[15]   Xenophon. That is, he calmly went on with what he had been doing. Cf. Diogenes Laertius 26, *Xenophon* 54.

[16]   Matt. 5.5.

13 Paulinus of Nola, *Letter 29* (400, Nola, in Campania)

P aulinus is surely one of the lesser lights of the early Church, but through his letters we can observe the piety, values, and lifestyle of the upper-class, cultured Latins who embraced the monastic movement when it came to the West in the second half of the fourth century. Perhaps we see in him, too, a forerunner of the Christianity of the western Middle Ages. Among the most representative of medieval personages were the monk, the noble landowner, and the bishop, and Paulinus was all three. Moreover, one of the most characteristic institutions of medieval religion was the pilgrimage centre housing the relics of a local saint, and Paulinus devoted 36 years of his life as the guardian of the shrine of a Catholic martyr called St. Felix of Nola.

Paulinus (Meropius Pontius Paulinus) was born in about the year 354 into a wealthy noble family which owned large estates in what are now France, Italy, and Spain. The estate where he grew up was near Bordeaux. He took a good classical education, trained as a lawyer, served a public office or two, was admitted to the Roman senate, and, beginning in 381, served for two or three years as governor of Campania (the area around Naples). One year while he was there he travelled to Nola, thirty kilometers east of Naples, to assist in the celebration of the feast day of St. Felix of Nola, a third- or fourth-century martyr. He was deeply moved by the holiness of the place and by the stories of the saint's miracles, and the experience, he later reflected, must have planted the seed of his Christian salvation. After his term as governor concluded, he returned home and lived the agreeable life of a cultured nobleman, reading books and writing poems. But his interest in Christianity grew, and he made a point of meeting Martin of Tours, who had introduced monasticism into Gaul in 360. Travelling in Spain he met and married a wealthy Christian woman named Therasia, and they spent a few years alternating between their properties in Spain and Gaul.

Paulinus' comfortable worldliness was shattered first by the death of their infant son, and then the violent death of his brother, in which, for a while, he was apparently a suspect. Partly through the persuasions of his wife, he made a decision to follow Christ, and was baptized, about 389. Presently, his wife and he began selling off their property, and giving the proceeds to the poor. The news caused a sensation in Rome. At Barcelona in Spain, in December 394, the Christian community insisted that he be ordained. Inspired by the burgeoning monastic movement, he and his wife decided in 395 to become monks. They sold their possessions (or most of them), moved to Nola, donned the distinctive dress of monks (apparently a goat-haired cloak with a rope cincture), lived next to St. Felix' tomb, and gave themselves to a life of a simple diet, sexual abstinence, study, and prayer — but not, apparently, much physical labour, apart from gardening. They also had the property developed as a pilgrimage centre. They repaired the basilica around Felix' grave, and then they built a grand new one beside it, featuring a cloister for the monks, a shelter for pilgrims, a hospital for the sick, and rooms for guests.

Paulinus maintained a correspondence with distinguished Latin Christians like Augustine and Ambrose. He also turned his taste for poetry from pagan to Christian themes, and he became one of the first two Latin Christian poets. He never failed to write a poem for St. Felix once a year on his feast day of January 14. In 409 he was made bishop of Nola. He died in 431.

Melania the Elder, whose life Paulinus discusses in the letter below, may have been his wife's sister. She was born about 342 into an affluent family of noble line. She had returned to Italy from Jerusalem when Paulinus wrote this letter; later, in 408, as barbarians were invading Italy, she returned to Jerusalem, where she died in 410. The letter is addressed to Sulpicius Severus (360?-420?), who, like Paulinus, had been a lawyer in Aquitaine, and who began the ascetic life about the same time, but in southern Gaul instead of Italy.

Questions on the reading

What appears to be the relationship between Paulinus and Severus? How does the relationship influence what Paulinus writes? What are Paulinus' interests? How does he understand the Christian life; holiness? Does he have Pelagian tendencies? How does he seem to understand the Christian's relation to the wider world? What impression do you have of his personality? How does he know Melania? What prompts him to write about her? What impresses him about her? What are his attitudes towards gender? Why does he cite Scriptural precedents for writing a narrative of a holy person? What does he know about Melania, and what does he think it is important to say about her? What kind of person is she, in Paulinus' eyes? What demonstrates her holiness? In what ways might she be representative of a late fourth-century Latin aristocratic piety?

Paulinus, Letter 29

Paulinus greets his loving brother Severus.

1. In your letter which spoke of the burden I bear, your uncontrolled love called forth my rebuke. But that love is tempered by your kind gifts, which are suited and well-directed to my profit. The cloaks woven from camel's hair[1] were a gift necessary for this sinner, who needs to utter the

Source: St. Paulinus of Nola, "Letter 29" (on Melania), in P.G. Walsh, *Letters of St. Paulinus of Nola*, vol.2 (Ancient Christian Writers, vol. 36), Westminster, MD: The Newman Press, 1968, 101-118.

prayers and wear the dress of lamentation, so that when I am prostrate in the sight of the Most High their profitable itch may remind me, as I am pricked with their sharp bristles, to be pricked also with dismay by my sins; and as the garments chafe me outwardly, to be likewise chafed in spirit.

There are many other profitable ways in which they help to fashion faith as recorded by saints of old. I think of Elias when sent on an errand, and of John who was sent before Christ. The first was girdled with a prickly belt of hair; the second, as Scripture says, was clothed in a shaggy covering of camel's hair.[2] I remember also *David and all his meekness*, in which *he sacrificed a contrite and humbled heart to God, made haircloth his garment*, and *covered his soul in fasting*,[3] so that he could invest it with the repletion of the spirit.

So we learn that such fasting, by which we abstain from all that is forbidden by God's law, is the clothing of the soul. We know this from the stripping of our first parents, who were made naked once they ceased to fast from the forbidden food.[4] Now the prophet himself instructs us with what kind of fasting he has protected his soul from the nakedness which brings confusion,[5] when he says to the Lord: *I have restrained my feet from every evil way, that I may keep Thy word.*[6]

2. The hair of this gift of yours also impresses on my mind the camel of the Gospel, which *passes more easily through the eye of a needle than a rich man enters the kingdom of heaven.*[7] This makes me think of the riches now remaining with me only in my sins. And because I cannot aim at the virtues like those of the men of God, I desire that there should at least accrue to me the grace of the publican[8] who with afflicted heart accused himself before God and repeatedly beating his bruised breast did not dare to raise to heaven eyes bent down through shame at his guilt. The foulness of his sins was like the camel's hump. But so effectively did he contract himself into the necessary humility, level out his reformed soul, and direct his way, that he obtained a hearing from God and squeezed through the eye of the needle, that is, along the path of the Word or of the cross, which leads to life by the narrow strait.[9]

For, as Scripture says, *the prayer of him that humbleth himself pierces the clouds.*[10] On the other hand, the Pharisee, so rich in his boastful spirit, presented an account of the good works which he owed

— for by the law of good works he did owe them — on the grounds that he had performed voluntary works beyond what was necessary. And because he proclaimed his own merits and accused another's, so that he did not so much entreat God as accost Him, he could not gain admittance there because the entrance is too narrow for those who are fat. Portly boasting could not be given entry where pinched humility betook itself and entered, because it was more pinched than the pinched emaciation of a sorrowful heart.

3. May your prayers intercede for me, so that the needle of the Lord's cross may be threaded with the word of salvation, and repair my soul which is extensively worn and haphazardly pinned with the thorns[11] of feeling. For I think that the faith and word of Christ's cross are the needle by which the clothing of our life is repaired, by which our mind is pricked, and by which we are sewn on God Himself through the intercession of the Mediator Himself. The eye of the needle, too, lies in Christ, for through Him and in Him lies the path to life desired by many but attainable by few; on that path the humility of wickedness enters more easily than the pride of righteousness.

So I owe you greater gratitude for being my spiritual physician, since even your bodily gifts to me are spiritually useful; for you have sent these cloaks to me to incite me to prayer and to the practice of humility, as if you were sending a bag of dung to the barren fig tree.[12] I think that this parable reveals the perennial profit of loving humility, which fertilises the barren soul so that it should not become complacent like the Pharisee with an empty show of pride, or be like a tree which yields no fruit yet blossoms with unproductive foliage.

The blessed Job teaches us how good and useful such dung is for cultivating salvation, for after he sat on a dunghill he ceased to be tempted.[13] He had exhausted the hatred of the tempter by his perfect humility, which can rise more easily than be thrust down. For by sitting in the dirt it cannot fall further, but can rise up from there through Him who *raises up the needy from the earth, and lifts up the poor out of the dunghill,*[14] and relegates the proud to the dung because, as Scripture says, every proud person is unclean in the sight of God.[15] So those who accuse their own wickedness are more righteous in God's sight than those who proclaim their own justice. The Pharisee accused himself with his self-praise, whereas the publican defended himself with his self-accusation.

4. So let us not flatter ourselves because of our works, but rather always *commend our spirit into His hands*, for *with Him is the fountain of light.*[16] Let us seek from him an understanding of our journey, for *by the Lord are a person's steps directed.*[17] But even if we shall be able through His help to perform His commands, we must even so confess our uselessness, for we cannot enter an account of the service we owe if we are only carrying out His commands.

He whose love makes no voluntary addition to the necessary task he must perform is an unprofitable and wicked servant. He will have no reason to hope for reward if he has discharged only the duties of his state. Therefore, as I often write to you, even if we fulfil His commands, we must always fear and say to the Lord: *Enter not into judgment with Thy servant, for in Thy sight no person living shall be justified.*[18] Whilst even humble confession will be able to gain us admission before God as people without self-esteem, useful and industrious service will fail to commend us, for we shall be branded as idlers.

The people of Ninive are a further proof of the great cure which the sinner finds in the mercy of God, provided he does not spare himself. For they were reconciled to God by their decision to repent, and so deserved to escape the threatened destruction, because they anticipated God's sentence with their own, and punished themselves with voluntary lamentation.[19]

5. I cannot worthily repay you in words or deeds, but with the sole quality in which I equal you, that love which is my sole endowment, I have sent you a tunic. Kindly accept it (for I have worn it) as a shirt obtained from the foulness of a dunghill; for it suits your blameless life, being woven from soft lambswool which soothes the skin with its touch.

But let me mention an additional value and grace which it possesses, so that it may be approved as more worthy of your use. It is a pledge to me of the blessing of the holy Melania, famous amongst the holy women of God. So the tunic seemed more worthily yours, for your faith has greater affinity with her than has my blood. Yet I confess that though I earmarked it for you at the very moment I received it, I disregarded this intention to the extent of wearing it first. I knew that by thus wronging you I would visit you more effectively than if I honoured you with the tunic all new and unworn. I also wished to snatch a prior blessing from the garment which was now yours, so that I might boast that I shared your clothing; for I was putting on the shirt which with God's kindness you will wear, as if you had already worn it.

6. But the Lord conferred a further grace as a result of your gifts and letter. Our brother Victor arrived here about the very time when I welcomed that holy lady who was returning from Jerusalem after twenty-five years. What a woman she is, if one can call so virile a Christian a woman! What am I to do now? Fear of being unbearably tedious forbids me to add more to the volumes written about her; yet the worth of her person, or rather God's grace in her seems to demand that I should not exclude with hasty omission a mention of this great soul. Just as voyagers, seeing some notable spot on the shore, do not pass by, but briefly draw in their sails, or lift their oars, and linger to feast their eyes in gazing, so I must alter the course of my words to tell you about her for a moment. In this way I may be seen to make some return for that book of yours, so splendid in its matter and style, if I describe the woman who is a soldier for Christ with the virtues of Martin, though she is of the weaker sex. She is a noble-woman who has made herself nobler than her consular grandfathers by her contempt for mere bodily nobility.

7. I think that I should begin to proclaim her praiseworthy holiness by praising her ancestry, for this, too, has a bearing on the grace which God has heaped on her. The most learned Luke attests that this order of topics is adopted not from the practice of rhetoricians but from the example of the Gospels. Luke began his description of the merits of blessed John the Baptist with his illustrious ancestry. He would not have you think that he mentioned the noble father of the Lord's forerunner as a mere historical detail. He links up the revered distinction of John's ancient nobility and gives the genealogy of both parents. When he says that *the priest Zachary was of the course of Abia*,[20] in my opinion he does it to demonstrate his high merit from that very fact. He appends the name Abia because of Zachary's office, which was undoubtedly a distinction amongst the Jews, for it was because he was descended from Abia that he obtained and held that honoured priesthood. Finally, he adds: *And his wife was of the daughters of Aaron*.[21]

You notice that the evangelist, by mentioning the birth of these holy persons, has pronounced on their merit, so that before proclaiming their own deserving acts he set down their ancestral names. *And his wife*, he says, *was of the daughters of Aaron.* The merit of the priest is increased by mention of the nobility of his marriage. Before praising Zachary's life, he first praised his lineage, so that he might emerge more worthy of respect because his inbred holiness accorded with that of his holy parents as if it were some inherited righteousness. Zachary recalled the name of Aaron, outstanding amongst priests' names, because by his office he succeeded to Aaron's distinction and through his wife he continued his race.

Again, Elizabeth, who with her husband drew the harmonious yoke of truth along life's path, was to be chosen to bear her child by means of an angel, of whom it was written: *Behold, I shall send an angel before thy face.*[22] And she was to show herself all the worthier to have a priest as husband and John, ranked before the prophets, as her son, because not only her righteous life but also her privileged family made her suitable to receive God's gifts.

But apart from John's origin, which flowed forth form a divine source, two of the evangelists start their account of the birth of the Lord Himself, by which He deigned to be the Son of man, by recounting His ancestors from the beginning.[23] Each writer, with equal faith and grandeur, records differing courses of His body's blood; for it was right that the only-begotten Son of God, Firstborn of the whole creation, Head of the whole body, should hold the primacy also in distinction of bodily race, and that the one Son of God in heaven, born before all ages by a beginning which cannot fathomed, should likewise claim for Himself on earth the crown of splendid titles, being on the witness of the two authors the famed Offspring of kings and priests.

So it is our own procedure, not that of outsiders, that I shall clearly follow if I proclaim the worldly as well as the spiritual nobility of this maidservant of God; for it is clear that the Lord conferred this distinction also on the glory of His work, so that the world which glories in such honors might be confounded. So to despise the world she employed the attributes which the vain employ to despise God. Moreover, as the exemplar of salvation she wielded greater authority before the eyes of the proud. Here was a woman of higher rank who for love of Christ had sublimely lowered herself to practise humility, so that as a strong member of the weak sex she might arraign idle men, and as a rich woman embracing poverty and a noblewoman embracing humility she might confound the haughty of both sexes.

8. Her grandfather was the consul Marcellinus, and the pomp of her family and opulence of wealth ensured that she married whilst still a young girl. Soon she became a mother, but that transitory happiness she enjoyed only briefly so that she might not love earthly things too long. For quite apart from the bereavements which she mourned in company with her surviving husband after labour vainly ended in premature births, her griefs so accumulated that she lost two sons and her husband in a year; only a baby boy was left to provide remembrance of, rather than solace for, her loved ones.

But since the Lord brings forth from the seeds of our ills the sources of heavenly blessings, through the loss of her human love she conceived a love of God. She was made wretched to become blessed; she was afflicted to be healed. For the Lord says: *I will strike and I will heal.*[24] So great is the love of our highest Father that even His anger springs from mercy, and He punishes to spare. For example, the blessed Paul was blinded to be enlightened; the persecutor fell that the apostle might rise; on a journey he found the true journey, and on the path of impiety he recognized the patch to peace.[25]

In the same way the good Lord, who ever up to this moment, as He has witnessed, *performed the work of His Father*[26] with the same outpouring of His love even on us His least ones, laid hold of this holy woman, too, with fatherly love, not because He considered her unfaithful, but to make her perfect. In His mercy He assailed her with trials to crown her with patience, for *He scourgeth every son whom He receiveth.*[27] So after accompanying her three dead in tearful processon, robbed of both husband and sons, she arrived in Rome with her one child who stimulated rather than allayed her tears. For he either experienced grief before his proper time, and could already bewail the death of others before being able to know his own life, or he was inappropriately happy in the ignorance of childhood, and smiled in pathetic joking while his mother wept.

9. She was taught by these proofs not to bound herself with this frail world and to put her hope only in God, the sole Person whom we cannot lose involuntarily. So she clad her son and herself in the knowledge of salvation, so that she loved her child by neglecting him and kept him by relinquishing him. By commending him to the Lord she was to possess him in absence more firmly than she would have embraced him in person if she had entrusted him to herself.

In her situation she imitated so far as she could the faithful vow of the barren Anna.[28] For disastrous fertility had made her very like a barren woman; and because she was afraid, now that her fertility was nullified, to become as Anna had been before she attained the fruitfulness she deserved, she dedicated to God a different gift but with similar love. Whereas Anna wished to conceive a child, Melania was troubled about the dear one she had borne. Anna wished to begin being a mother; Melania, not to cease being one.

You may regard the two cases as dissimilar, because Melania's son, unlike Samuel, is not set in the temple to serve the Lord, but rather enjoys the riches and distinctions of the world; but you should nonetheless realise that love and faith are equally balanced on both sides. For Melania has paid to God through her own person what the glorious Anna paid through her son. The dedication of Samuel to God was subsequently compensated by several children;[29] but Melania's only son was the sum of her childbearing, the end of her labour. When Anna consigned her firstborn to a position in the temple, she had other dear ones at home to console her, as well as the fact that she was not far separated from her son though he was consecrated, and that she paid a return visit annually to the temple. But once Melania had torn her one son from her breast and set him in Christ's bosom so that the Lord Himself might nourish him, she bestowed no subsequent personal care on him, for she thought it a sin of distrust to give her own attention to one whom she had entrusted to Christ.

The extent of her faith in this gesture can be gauged from this: though she had crowds of very influential and affectionate relatives at Rome, she thought it right to entrust her child to none of them for the proverbial rearing, tutoring, and protecting. So convinced was she that he had been taken up by Christ, she deserved to keep him because she did not wish to enjoy him, and she also has deserved to see him again now, because of that loving faith with which, once she left him with God, she had not longed for him in this world.

So He who can grant to believers more than they hope for *has done great things for her.*[30] He has allowed her to see her son even here, as He granted Solomon, for electing to follow Wisdom, all the other wealth which he had not sought, and precisely because he had not sought it. God rewarded his right understanding, by which he had preferred the highest things to the lowest, by adding the lesser to the greater. So Solomon deserved to become the owner of all his wealth because he had elected to seek out the highest things. This is the example which warns us to be wise when we are taught to choose. For if we prefer the lesser to the greater and the lowest to the highest (that is, earthly to heavenly things), as punishment for our foolish desires we shall be deprived of both highest and lowest blessings. Quite justly we shall not get the things we did not desire, and we must rightly be robbed of the things our disastrous love of which causes us to neglect the better choice.

Like Melania, father Abraham got back his one son whom he had offered to God, because when the demand was made he readily offered the child.[31] The Lord is content with the perfect sacrifice of heartfelt love, so the angel's hand intervened to stay the father's right arm as it was poised for the blow. The angel snatched up the victim and in its place set a hastily furnished sheep, so that God should not lose His offering, nor the father his son. There was this further reason, that the mystery to be fulfilled in Christ and rehearsed in Isaac (so far as that image of God could rehearse it) could be given shape through a ram. For the lamb which was to be later sacrificed in Egypt to typify the Saviour[32] was thus already anticipated by a beast of its own species — the ram which replaced Isaac as victim to prefigure Christ. So the ram was found for Abraham, since the highest sacrament was not his due, but it was killed for Him for whom the fulfilment of the sacrament was being preserved.

10. Melania had many struggles, too, with the hatefilled dragon during her training for this service, because the envy of the spiteful enemy did not allow her to depart without difficulty and in peace. The devil attempted, through the utmost pressure of her noble relatives, whom he equipped to detain her, to block her design and prevent her

from going. But she was lent strength superior to the power of the tempters. She gladly threw off the bonds of human love with the ropes of the ship, as all wept. She joined unwearied battle with the waves of the sea, so that she could conquer these as well as the billows of the world, and sailed away. Abandoning worldly life and her own country, she chose to bestow her spiritual gift at Jerusalem, and to dwell there in pilgrimage from her body. She became an exile from her fellow citizens, but a citizen amongst the saints. With wisdom and sanctity she chose to be a servant in this world of thrall so as to be able to reign in the world of freedom.

11. Of her many divine virtues I shall recount just one, so that from this you can assess all her achievements. During the notorious reign of Valens, when the rage of the Arians assailed the church of the living God using that king of impiety as their lackey, Melania was the leader or companion of all who stood fast for the faith. She gave refuge to fugitives or accompanied those arrested. But after she had hidden those who were the objects of greater hatred from the heretics because of their notable faith, and those who helped to conceal them had incurred loathing, the torches of the devil fired the serious discord.

She was ordered to be haled forth for holding the state law in contempt and to suffer the fate awaiting her hidden protégés unless she agreed to produce them. She advanced fearlessly, desirous of suffering, and rejoicing at the unjust proclamation. Though she had not anticipated arrest, she flew along before her would-be escort to the judge's tribunal. His respect for the woman before him troubled him, and his surprise at her bold faith caused him to drop his heretical rage.

About the same time she fed five thousand monks, who lay in hiding, for three days with her own bread, so that by her hand the Lord Jesus again fed in the desert the same number as of old.[33] But now His kindness was all the greater as the hidden monks were being accorded less freedom and affection than that former five thousand who had voluntarily assembled before the Lord in freedom and in peace.

But Melania did not fear arrest. Untroubled she provided the assistance which was forbidden. She wished to obtain no recognition or glory from her work, but the scale of her assistance brought fame, and she was renowned by as many attestations before men as the number whom she fed in league with God. Let us assess the extent of her merit.

Abdias is famed in the history of the Kings[34] for hiding a hundred men of God from the anger of an equally impious king, and feeding them; are we to doubt, then, that Melania, who bettered that total countless times over, has brought forth fruit a hundredfold?

12. I shall now hasten over her other achievement and days, and in imitation of her journey I shall embark on the crossing on which she made her return, so that I may conclude my words more speedily by recounting her arrival here.

In this event I witnessed the great grace of God. She put in at Naples, which lies a short distance away from the town of Nola where I live. There she was met in welcome by her children and grandchildren, and then she hastened to Nola to enjoy my humble hospitality. She came to me here surrounded by a solicitous retinue of her very wealthy dear ones. In that journey of mother and children I beheld the glory of the Lord. She sat on a tiny thin horse, worth less than any ass; and they attended her on the journey, their trappings emphasizing the extraordinary contrast. For they had all the pomp of this world with which honoured and wealthy senators could be invested. The Appian Way[35] groaned and gleamed with swaying coaches, decorated horses, ladies' carriages all gilded, and numerous smaller vehicles.

Yet the grace of Christian humility outshone such vain brilliance. The rich marvelled at this poor saint whilst our poverty mocked them. I beheld the world in a turmoil fit for God's eyes, crimson silk and gilded trappings playing servant to old black rags. I blessed the Lord who exalts the humble, lends them wisdom, and fills them with good things, whilst the rich He sends empty away.[36]

Yet on that day I was astounded at the spirit of poverty shown by those rich people towards their mother's welfare, for they took pride more in her holy poverty than in their own conspicuous wealth. God's glory seemed to ensure that I beheld the riches of my sister in poverty now possessed by her children, so that she was already obtaining a reward for her faith by beholding her victory over the utter emptiness of this world, when at close quarters she saw all that she had left for Christ, all that she had continued unremittingly to despise.

Those silk-clad children of hers, though accustomed to the splendour of a toga or a dress according to their sex, took joy in touching that thick tunic of hers, with its hard threads like broom, and her cheap cloak. They longed to have their woollen garments, so valuable with their golden embroidery, trodden down beneath her feet or worn away with the rubbing of her rags. For they thought that they were cleansed from the pollution of their riches if they succeeded in gathering some of the dirt from her tawdry clothing or her feet.

13. We have a cottage here raised off the ground, which runs quite a distance along to the dining hall, and has a colonnade separating it from the guest rooms. God in His kindness seemed to make this bigger, and it afforded modest but not too constricted accommodation not only for the numerous holy ladies who accompanied Melania, but also for the bands of rich people as well, The ringing choirs of boys and maidens in the cottage made the near-by roof of our patron Saint Felix resound.

Nor did the other type of guests, however different their manner of life, protest, though they were dwelling in the same lodging. Even in them there was a pious sobriety emulating our disciplined silence, so that if they declined to watch and sing with us because they were overcome with sleep and mental indolence, they did not dare to register dissent for the voices at worship. They were calmed by that fear of the faithful which restrained the hubbub of their secular anxieties, and made them join, if only under their breath, with the peaceful voices as they sang the Psalms.[37]

But I hasten to return to the perfect dove of the Lord. Be sure that there is such divine strength in that weak woman's body that she finds refreshment in fasting, repose in prayer, bread in the Word, clothing in rags. Her hard couch (for she lies on the ground on a cloak and quilt) becomes soft as she studies, for her pleasure in reading reduces the hardship of that stiff bed. That holy soul is at rest when she is awake for the Lord.

Up to now the daughter of Sion has possessed her, and longs for her; but now the daughter of Babylon possesses and admires her. For now even Rome herself in the greater number of her population is the daughter of Sion rather than of Babylon. So Rome admires Melania, as she dwells in the shadow of humility and the light of truth, as she offers incentives to faith among the rich and the consolations of poverty among the poor. Yet now that she is amongst the crowds of Rome, she yearns for her silence and obscurity at Jerusalem, and cries: *Woe is me that my sojourning is prolonged!* Has my journey been postponed that I might now *dwell with the inhabitants of Cedar?*[38] (For I have discovered that Cedar in Hebrew means darkness.)

So I think she is to be felicitated on the virtues I have mentioned provided that she is fearful about her present abode, and as long as so outstanding a soul bestows more on Rome than she draws from it. She must *sit on the rivers of Babylon yet remember Sion.*[39] She must keep the instrument of her body above all the ambushes and attractions of hostile Babylon, secure in the steady course of her committed life, which we may call the willows always thriving on true moisture. So she may flourish unceasingly, and with the enduring constancy of faith and the grace of virtue, *her leaf will not fall off.*[40] Just as on the journey of this life she is a model, so at its end her praise will be sung.

14. My brother, I could not allow Melania to go in ignorance of you. So that she might savour more fully the grace of God in you, I made you plain to her through your own words rather than mine, for with my own lips I declaimed to her your life of our Martin. She is most interested in such historical works.

In the same manner I portrayed you both to the revered and most learned bishop Nicetas, who arrived from Dacia, a figure rightly admired by the Romans, and also to very many holy men abiding in God's truth. I did this not so much to tell of you as to boast of myself, for it is my boast that I have your love and affection, and your life accords with your tongue in attesting that you are the servant of truth. *May the Lord grant me to find mercy of the Lord on that day*[41] through the grace which He Himself creates, so that as I am now refreshed in the bowels of your charity, I may likewise be saved from the fires I deserve by the cooling finger of your inheritance. For I hope that in His kindness the Lord will judge me favourably because you are righteous and because I have great love for you, even though I am unworthy, and cannot presume to hope for a share in your crown.

Notes

1   Such garments of goat or camel's hair, worn in imitation of John the Baptist, were the regular clothing of fourth-century monks in both the Eastern and

Western worlds. In Letter 29 Paulinus acknowledges a gift from Severus of garments of camel's hair.

2   Cf. 2 Chronicles 1:8; Matt. 3:4.

3   Psalm 131:1, 50:19, 68:11ff.

4   Cf. Gen. 3:7.

5   Cf. Ezekiel 16:7.

6   Psalm 118:101.

7   Matt. 19:24.

8   Cf. Luke 18:23.

9   Cf. Matt. 7:14.

10   Eccli. 35:21.

11   For the use of thorns to fasten up clothing, cf. Virgil *Aeneid* 3:594; Tacitus, *Germania* 17.

12   Cf. Luke 13:8.

13   Cf. Job 2:8.

14   Psalm 112:7.

15   Cf. Proverbs 16:5.

16   Psalm 30:6, 35:10.

17   Psalm 36:23.

18   Psalm 142:2.

19   Cf. Jonah 3:4–10.

20   Luke 1:5.

21   Luke 1:5.

22   Matt. 11:10.

23   Cf. Matt. 1:1ff.; Luke 3:23ff.

24   Deut. 32:39.

25   Cf. Acts 9:8.

26   John 9:4.

27   Heb. 12:6.

28   Cf. I Kings 1:11.

29   Cf. I Kings 2:21.

30   Luke 1:49.

31   Cf. Gen. 22.

32   Cf. Exodus 12:3.

33 Cf. Matt. 14:21.

34 Cf. 1 Chronicles 18:4.

35 The Appian Way actually ran from Rome to Capua and then to Beneventum; the Via Poplilia joined Nola to this road.

36 Cf. Luke 1:53.

37 This passage provides interesting evidence of congregational singing at vigils. Augustine, *Confessions* 9:15, mentions that this had been introduced at Milan by Ambrose in 386 on the pattern of monastic practice in the East, where Basil had initiated it about 372.

38 Psalm 119:5.

39 Psalm 136:1.

40 Psalm 1:3.

41 2 Tim. 1:18.

Augustine of Hippo, *Letter 211*
(420?, North Africa)

No one in the early Church, and indeed no one in the ancient world, is better known to us than Augustine. It is not just that he wrote an enormous number of works or that he changed the course of Western Christianity and culture. We know him with some intimacy because he disclosed his inner spiritual and intellectual and emotional life to the world, most notably in the *Confessions.* He was born in 354 in Thagaste in northern Numidia (now Souk-Ahras in northeastern Algeria) into a middle-class family. His mother, a Christian with a possessive personality, devoutly desired his conversion. His father, a pagan, provided for his classical education, which was as good as North Africa had to offer. As with many adolescents and post-adolescents, sex was a chronic issue. A mistress helped. Also like many adolescents and post-adolescents he went seeking the meaning of life. He tried Latin philosophy, a dualistic and ascetic Persian religion called Manicheism, and an adaptation of Plato's religious thought called neoplatonism. None satisfied. Meanwhile, in 384 he had won a plum appointment as public orator in Milan, the western capital of the Roman Empire. His social standing was rising, and he dismissed his mistress. But at Milan he began listening intently to the sermons and conversation of the bishop, Ambrose. Here was a far more cultured and intellectually vigorous Christianity than he had known, and it touched greater depths than neoplatonism could reach. Step by step he was led to conversion — or, at least, a decision — in August 386, and he was baptized at Easter 387. His mother died in October.

Augustine cared greatly for friendship all his life — when he was a boy, as he recalled in his *Confessions*, he was often led astray by his friends — and in the months before and after his baptism he felt strongly drawn to a life in Christian community. He learned about Antony, who had created a community of monastic cells in Egypt earlier in the century, and he visited Christian house communities in Rome. Preparing for his baptism, he lived with relatives and friends in a cultured spiritual retreat at a place called Cassiciacum, forty miles northeast of Milan in the shadow of the Italian Alps. Now in 388 he established a Christian community in his parents' home in Thagaste, with a routine of Scripture reading, prayer, study, conversation, and friendship.

In 391, investigating possibilities for another Christian house community, he visited Hippo Regius (now Annaba, on the Mediterranean coast of Algeria), the most important sea-port in North Africa after Carthage, 100 kilometers north of Thagaste. Without warning and quite unwillingly, he found himself conscripted into ordination. Soon he began regular preaching in the Catholic church in town. The bishop gave him a piece of Church property for a new Christian house community. In 395 or 396 Augustine himself became bishop of Hippo, and he lived in the bishop's residence with a community of clergy. His life as a bishop was study and prayer, adjudicating lawsuits, preaching and teaching, writing theological and controversial works, engaging in Church politics, and, in partnership with the bishop of Carthage, reforming the Church. He also established other monasteries at Hippo, including one for women. He died in 430.

Letter 211 below is not formally addressed, but in one manuscript a scribe has added the notation that it was "to the consecrated virgins". Where the women lived or when the letter was written we do not know. It was written in Latin. A large portion of the letter, from the sentence beginning, "These are the rules..." to the end, circulated as an independent work in scores of medieval manuscripts, sometimes with male gender language and sometimes with female gender language. It became incorporated into a document, or set of documents, known as the Rule of St. Augustine, perhaps the oldest rule in the western Church. Through the centuries it was adopted or adapted by several religious orders as their Rule for living the monastic life. It is not known whether the Rule first existed as part of this letter or whether it pre-existed the letter and was appended to it. Most scholars seem to favour the latter alternative. If the Rule did pre-exist the letter, it is not known whether the Rule for Men came before the Rule for Women or vice versa. There is little dispute — some, but not very much — that Augustine wrote the letter itself, that is, the first four paragraphs of the document below. The authorship of the Rule is more controversial, and depends partly on analyzing some 43 manuscripts dating from the sixth to the sixteenth centuries. The majority opinion seems to be that Augustine's authorship is, on the whole, probable. The modern translator has supplied the Biblical citations.

Questions on the reading

To whom is this letter addressed? What has prompted Augustine to write this letter? What theological, administrative, or pastoral principles shape his response? In the part that is the Rule, what does the author understand to be the primary purpose of Christian community life? (For instance, asceticism; witness and service to the world; Christian friendship; intimacy with God?) Can specifically cultural dimensions in the author's understanding of community be distinguished from specifically theological dimensions? What resources might Augustine have used in framing the Rule? Is this a relatively lenient and liberal Rule, or a relatively austere and severe one? (What criteria of leniency or severity would you apply to answer this question?) Is this a life for a spiritual élite, or a model for the life of all Christians? How realistic or otherwise is the author about the dynamics of community? What is the author's understanding of sexuality? Do you think that the Rule was originally attached to the first four paragraphs?

211. Letter of Aurelius Augustine to the consecrated virgins (c. 423)

As severity is ready to punish the sins which it discovers, so charity does not wish to discover anything to punish. That was the reason which kept me from coming to you when you were expecting my presence, which would not have been a joy added to your peace, but an increase of your strife. For how could I have overlooked your quarrel or left it unpunished if it had burst out in my presence as violently as it did in my absence; when it was not visible to my eyes, yet assailed my ears with your clamor? Perhaps your rebellion might have been even worse in my presence which I was obliged to withhold from you, since you were demanding something that was not good for you, and that would have formed a most dangerous precedent against sound discipline; thus, I should not have found you such as I wished and you would have found me such as you did not wish.

When the Apostle writes to the Corinthians, he says: 'I call God to witness upon my soul that to spare you I came not any more to Corinth; not because we exercise dominion over your faith but we are helpers of your joy.'[1] I also spared myself lest 'I have sorrow upon sorrow,'[2] and rather than show my face among you I chose to pour out my heart to God for you and to plead the cause of your great peril, not in words before you, but in tears before God, that He may not turn to sorrow the joy I am wont to feel on your account. Even in the midst of the great scandals which abound everywhere in this world I oftentimes comfort myself with the thought of your numerous community, your chaste love, your holy conversation, and the grace of God which has been given more generously to you that you might not only despise carnal marriage, but might also choose the fellowship of dwelling together in a house in unity,[3] that you may have one soul and one heart[4] toward God.

When I think upon these good things among you, these gifts of God, my heart is accustomed to find some kind of rest amid the many storms arising from other evils by which it is shaken. 'You did run well;

Source: Augustine, "Letter 211: To a convent of consecrated virgins", trans. Sister Wilfrid Parsons (Fathers of the Church, vol. 32), Fathers of the Church Inc., 1956, 38-50. Reprinted by permission of the Catholic University of America Press.

who hath bewitched you? This persuasion is not from God who hath called you. A little leaven'[5] — I hate to repeat the rest; this, rather, I desire and pray for and urge that the same leaven may be changed for the better that the whole lump may not be changed for the worse, as had almost happened. If, then, you have put forth new growth of sound wisdom, 'Pray that ye enter not into temptation,'[6] that you enter not again into 'contentions, envying, animosities, dissensions, detractions, seditions, whisperings.'[7] For we have not planted and watered[8] the Lord's garden in you only to reap these thorns[9] from you. But if your weakness still stirs up a storm, pray that you may be delivered from temptation.[10] Those among you who trouble you, whoever they may be, will incur judgment unless they amend their lives.

Think what a misfortune it is that in the midst of our rejoicing over those born of God in unity we should have to bewail internal schism in the monastery. Stand firm in your good purpose and you will not want to change your Superior, who has persevered in that monastery for so many years, during which you have increased in numbers and in age, and who has borne you as another — not in her womb, but in her heart. All of you at your entrance found her there, either serving under the holy Superior, my sister, or winning approval as actual Superior herself when she received you. Under her you have been trained, under her you have received the veil, under her your numbers have multiplied, yet you make all this disturbance to force us to change her for you — when you ought to grieve if we wanted to change her for you. She is the one you have known, she is the one to whom you came, she is the one you have had for so many years of your increase. You have not received any new Superior except your spiritual director, and if it is because of him that you are seeking a change, through envy for him that you have thus rebelled against your Mother, why have you not rather demanded that he should be changed for you? If you shrink from doing this, for I know what respect and affection you have for him in Christ, why should you not shrink even more from attacking her? For the beginnings of your director's terms of authority have been thrown into such disorder that he should be the one to desert you sooner than be subject to the invidious criticism of having it said that you would not have asked for another Superior if you had not begun to have him for spiritual director. May God, then, calm and pacify your minds; may the work of the Devil make no headway among you, but may 'the peace of Christ rule in you hearts.'[11] Do not rush to destruction in your acute regret, either because you are vexed at not having the accomplishment of what you want, or because you are ashamed of wanting what you ought not; rather, by repenting renew your courage, and let it not be the repentance of the traitor Judas,[12] but the tears of the shepherd Peter.[13]

These are the rules which we prescribe for the observance of those of you who have been admitted to the monastery. In the first place, as you are gathered into one community, see that you dwell together in unity in the house and that you have 'one heart and one soul' toward God; that you do not call anything your own, but that you have all things in common. Let your Superior distribute food and clothing to each one of you, not equally to all, because you are not all of the same bodily strength, but to each one according to her need. It is thus that you read in the Acts of the Apostles that 'all things were common unto them, and distribution was made to everyone according as he had need.'[14] Let those who had something in the world before they entered the monastery be entirely willing for it to become common property, but let those who had nothing not seek in the monastery for what they could not have had outside. However, if they are sickly, let them receive what is needful, even if their poverty could not procure them those necessities when they were outside, but they are not to think themselves fortunate merely because they now have food and raiment such as they could not have provided outside.

Let them not go about with their heads in the air because they associate with those whom they would not have dared to approach outside, but let them lift up their hearts, not seeking earthly goods; otherwise, monasteries might begin to be useful to the rich but not to the poor, if in them the rich are humbled but the poor puffed up. Again, those who seemed to be something in the world should not look down with scorn on their Sisters who have come to that holy community from poor circumstances, they should strive to take greater pride in the company of their poor Sisters than in the important position of their wealthy parents. Let them not have a high opinion of themselves if they have made some contribution from their resources to the common life, lest they become more proud of their wealth because they are sharing it with the monastery than they would be if they were enjoying it in the world. Every other kind of wrong-doing operates to further evil deeds, but pride hides itself even in good deeds to spoil them. What good does it do to distribute one's goods by giving them to the poor and to become poor oneself, if the wretched soul becomes prouder by despising wealth than it had been by possessing it? Live then, all of you, in unity and harmony; honor God in each other, for you have become His temples.[15]

Be instant in prayer[16] at the hours and times appointed. Let no one do anything in the oratory but that for which it was made and from which it takes its name, so that if some of the Sisters have time and wish to pray even outside the appointed hours, those who wish to do something else there may not be a hindrance to them. When you pray to God in psalms and hymns, meditate in your heart on what you utter with your voice, and do not sing anything that is not noted to be sung; what is not noted to be sung is not to be sung.

Subdue your flesh by fasting and abstinence from food and drink as far as your health allows. When a Sister is not able to fast, she should not for that reason take any food outside the time of meals, unless she is sick. From the time when you come to the table until you rise from it, listen without noise or argument to what is read according to custom; let it not be only your mouth that takes food, but let your ears also drink in the word of God.

If those who are weak in health as a result of their former mode of living are treated differently in the matter of food, this ought not to be irksome or to seem unfair to others whom another kind of life has made more robust. They are not to think the former more fortunate because they have food which the latter do not enjoy, but they are rather to congratulate themselves on being in good health as the others are not. And if those who have come to the monastery from a more luxurious manner of life are given something in the way of food, clothing, bedding and covering, which is not given to the others who are stronger and therefore more fortunate, these latter to whom it is not given should reflect how great a step the former have taken in coming down from their worldly life to this one, although they have not been able to attain to the asceticism of those who are stronger in body. And they should not be troubled at seeing these others receive more than they do, not as a mark of honor but as a form of concession; otherwise there might arise in the monastery that hateful reversal whereby, as far as it can be done, the rich become toilers and the poor enjoy luxury. Certainly, in the case of the sick, as they must of necessity take less food in order not to grow worse, so, after the illness they must be treated in a manner to speed their recovery, even if they came from the lowest state of poverty in the world, just as if their recent illness were to confer on them what the rich have because of their former state. But when they have recovered their former strength, let them return to their own more fortunate mode of life, which is more fitting for the handmaids of God in proportion as it has fewer wants, and let them not want to retain, when they are well, the dispensations which necessity required when they were ill. Let those who have been more courageous in bearing austerity esteem themselves the richer, for it is better to need less that to have more.

Let your garb be inconspicuous; do not aim at winning favor by your garments, but by your conduct. Do not wear such thin head-covering that your hairnets show underneath. Do no let any part of your hair be uncovered or go out of doors with it either flying carelessly or arranged fastidiously. When you go abroad, walk together; when you have arrived at the place to which you were going, stop together. In walking, in standing, in your costume, in all your movement, let there be nothing that could rouse passion in anyone, but let all accord with your sacred character. If your eyes glance at anyone, let them rest upon no one, for you are not forbidden to look at men when you go out, but to desire them or to wish to be desired by them. It is not by touch alone, but also by feeling and sight, that a woman desires and is desired. Do not claim to have chaste minds if you have unchaste eyes, because the unchaste eye is the messenger of the unchaste heart; and when unchaste hearts reveal themselves to each other by a mutual glance, even though the tongue is silent, and when they take pleasure in each other's passion according to the lust of the flesh, chastity flees from the character though the body remain untouched by impure violation. The virgin who fastens her glance upon a man and loves to have his fastened on her must not think she is unseen by others. When she does so she is indeed seen, and by those of whom she is not thinking. But suppose she does escape notice and is observed by no human being, what will she do about that Observer from above from whose notice nothing can escape?[17] Or are we to think that He does not see because His seeing is accomplished with equal patience and wisdom? Therefore, let the holy woman fear to displease Him so as to avoid the desire of wrongfully pleasing a man; let her reflect that He sees everything, and thus she will avoid the desire of gazing sinfully upon a man. In this matter fear of Him is recommended to us by the passage: 'One that fixeth the eye is an abomination to the Lord.'[18] So, then, when you are together in church or in any place where men are present, keep mutual guard over your chastity, for God who dwells in you[19] guards you in that way even from yourselves.

If you notice in any of your number this roving glance of which I speak, warn her at once that beginnings may go no further, but may be remedied at once. But if, after the warning, you see her doing the same thing again on any other day, let whoever has discovered her report her as one wounded and in need of treatment; but let her first be pointed out to a second or a third that she may be convicted out of the mouth of two or three witnesses[20] and may be disciplined with proper severity. Do not consider yourselves mean when you report thus, for, indeed, you are not without guilt if through your silence you allow your Sisters to perish when you are able to correct them by reporting them. If your Sister through fear of the knife were trying to hide a sore which she had on her body, would not silence on your part be cruelty and notification kindness? How much greater, then, is your obligation to point out one in whose heart a deadly infection may lurk! But before she is pointed out to the others through whom she is to be convicted if she denies her guilt, she ought to be named to the Superior, so that by a secret correction she may escape being made known to others. If, however, she denies her guilt, her lie is to be confronted with others, so that in the presence of all she may be not merely charged by one, but convicted by two or three witnesses. When convicted, she is to be subjected to some corrective discipline at the discretion of the Superior or the spiritual director. If she refuses to submit and does not leave of her own accord, she is to be expelled from your community. This is not an act of cruelty, but of kindness — to prevent her from destroying many companions by her deadly contagion. What I have said about custody of the eyes is to be observed, with love for person and hatred for the sin, in discovering, preventing, reporting, convicting and punishing other offenses. But if any Sister is so far gone in sin that she is secretly receiving letters or keepsakes of any kind from a man, she is to be spared and prayed for if she confesses it voluntarily, but if she is caught and her guilt is proved, she is to receive a more serious punishment at the discretion of the Superior or the spiritual director or even the bishop.

Have your clothing kept under the care of one or two or as many as may be needed to shake out the garments in order to preserve them from moths; and just as you receive food from one storeroom so you must be clothed from one wardrobe. Whenever something is offered you to wear in accord with the season, do not be concerned, if that is possible, whether each one of you receives back what she had given up, or something else which another had worn, so long as no one is refused what she needs. If strife and murmurings arise among you from this source, when one complains that she has received something worse than she had previously worn, and thinks she is slighted in being dressed as another of her Sisters was, let this prove how far you are from that inward 'holy attire'[21] of the heart when you quarrel about the attire of the body. However, if your weakness is indulged so far that you receive back the dress which you had put off, let what you take off still be kept in one place under community care. Thus, no one will work at anything for her own use, whether it be clothing or bedding or underclothing or covering or head-dress, but let all your work be done for the common good, with greater zeal and more constant eagerness than if you were making things for your own use. For the charity of which it is written that 'she seeketh not her own'[22] is understood in the sense of preferring the general good to personal good. And so, the more care you take to promote the general good rather than your own, the more progress in perfection you will know that you have made, so that in all things of which passing necessity makes use the 'charity which endureth'[23] may superabound. It follows, then, that whatever any man or woman bestows upon the inmates of the monastery, either to daughters or to persons bound to them by any other tie of kinship, whether it be clothing or anything else rated among necessities, it is not to be received in secret, but is to be left to the disposal of the Superior to put it in the common stock or to give it to anyone who needs it. If anyone conceals what has been given her, let her be judged guilty of theft.

Let your clothes be washed, either by yourselves or by laundresses, at the discretion of the Superior, so that excessive craving for clean clothing may not sully your soul with inward filth. The washing of the body, also, and the use of baths is not to be too frequent, but may be allowed at the usual interval of time, that is, once a month. In the case of illness, however, where there is urgent need of bathing the body, let it not be postponed too long, but let it be done without objection for medical reasons. If the patient herself objects, she must do what health requires to be done at the bidding of the Superior. If she wishes it and it is not good for her, there should be no yielding to her caprice, for there are times when something agreeable is believed to be beneficial whereas it is hurtful. Finally, if a handmaid of God has a hidden pain in her body and tells what ails her, she should be believed without reserve, but when it is not certain whether something pleasant would be good for her, a doctor should be consulted. If they go to the baths or wherever they have to go, let there be not less than three. The one who is under the necessity of going somewhere shall not go with the companions of her choice, but with those whom the Superior shall ordain. The care of the sick, whether they are convalescent or suffering from some weakness not accompanied by fever, should be entrusted to someone who may procure from the storeroom what she sees needful for each. Moreover, those who have charge of the storeroom or of the wardrobe or of the library should serve their Sisters without grumbling. Books are to be applied for at a stated hour each day; those who apply outside that time are not to receive them. But in the case of clothing and shoes, when required for someone in need, those who have charge of them should not delay to give what is asked.

You should either have no quarrels or put an end to them as speedily as possible, lest anger grow into hatred, turn a mote into a beam,[24] and make the soul a murderer. The saying of Scripture, 'Whoever hateth his brother is a murderer,'[25] does not apply to men alone; the female sex, too, has received this teaching as well as the male sex, which God created first. Whoever has injured another, either by reviling her or taunting her or accusing her of wrong-doing, should remember to make amends as quickly as possible, so as to heal the hurt she has caused, and the injured Sister must forgive without reserve. If the injury has been mutual, they will be obliged to make mutual amends because of your prayers, which must be more holy in proportion to their frequency. The Sister who is often tempted to anger but quickly begs pardon of the one she knows she has injured is better than the one who is slower to anger, but less easily moved to ask pardon. She who refuses to forgive her Sister should not hope to feel the effect of prayer, but the one who is never willing to ask pardon or who does not ask it sincerely has no place in the monastery even if she is not actually expelled. Refrain, therefore, from harsh words; if any slip from your mouth, do not be ashamed to utter healing words from the same mouth that caused the wounds. However, when the duty of the discipline obliges you to speak sharply in order to restrain the younger members, you have no obligation to ask their pardon even if you feel that you have gone too far in your words; otherwise, by a too great regard for humility toward those who ought to be subject to you, you might undermine the authority needed to control them. You should, however, ask pardon of the Lord of all who knows how great is your kindness and love even for those whom you rebuke, perhaps with undue severity. The love between you, however, ought not to be earthly but spiritual, for the things which shameless women do even to other women in low jokes and games are to be avoided not only by widows and chaste handmaids of Christ, living under a holy rule of life, but also entirely by married women and maidens destined for marriage.

Let your Superior be obeyed as a mother, with due respect, lest God be offended in her person; and even more readily should you obey the priest who has charge of you all. It will be the particular responsibility of the Superior to see to the observance of all these regulations; and if anything is not observed she is not to neglect or overlook the lapse, but to take pains to amend and correct it. In matters that exceed her authority she is to refer to the priest who watches over you. Let her esteem herself happy not in having power to rule, but in having charity to serve.[26] Let her be set over you in honor before men; before God let her be beneath your feet. Toward all let her show herself an example of good works.[27] Let her rebuke the unquiet, comfort the feeble-minded, support the weak, be patient toward all;[28] let her maintain her authority with good will, but impose it with fear. And, however necessary both may be, let her seek to be loved by you rather than feared, always bearing in mind that she will have to give an account of you to God. Thus, by your ready obedience you will show consideration not only for yourselves but also for her, because, as between you, the one who is in the higher position runs the greater risk.

May the Lord grant you to observe all these regulations with love, as souls whose affections are set on spiritual beauty, whose good conduct is fragrant with the good odor of Christ,[29] not as bondswomen under the law, but as free women established under grace.[30] Now, in order that you may look at yourselves in this book as in a mirror, and that you may not omit anything through forgetfulness, let it be read to you once a week, and when you find yourselves practising what is written, give thanks to the Lord, the giver of all good gifts; but, when any one of you sees that she falls short in any point, let her feel sorrow for the past and take precautions for the future, praying that her trespass may be forgiven and that she may not be led into temptation.[31]

Notes

[1]   2 Cor. 1.23.

[2]   2 Cor. 2.3; Phil. 2.27.

[3]   Ps. 132.1.

[4]   Acts 4.32.

[5]   Gal. 5.7-9; 3.1; 1 Cor. 5.6.

[6]   Matt. 7.41; Mark 14.38; Luke 22.46.

[7]   2 Cor. 12.20.

[8]   1 Cor. 3.6-8.

[9]   Jer. 12.13.

[10]   Ps. 17.30.

[11]   Cf. Col. 3.15

[12]   Matt. 27.3-5.

[13]   Matt. 26.75; Mark 14.72; Luke 22.62.

[14]   Acts 4.32,35.

[15]   1 Cor. 3.16; 2 Cor. 6.16.

[16]   Col. 4.2.

[17]   Prov. 24.12.

[18]   Prov. 27.20 (Septuagint).

[19]   1 Cor. 3.16; 2 Cor. 6.16.

[20]   Deut. 19.15; Matt. 18.16; 2 Cor. 13.1.

21   Titus 2.3.

22   1 Cor. 13.5.

23   Eph. 3.19; 1 Cor. 13.8.

24   Matt. 7. 3-5; Luke 6.41-42.

25   1 John 3.15.

26   Dan. 11.4; Gal. 5.13.

27   Titus 2.7.

28   1 Thess. 5.14.

29   2 Cor. 2.15.

30   Rom. 6.14,15.

31   Matt. 6.12,13; Luke 11.4.

15   Patrick, *Confession* (450?, Ireland)

St. George may be questionable, but there really was a St. Patrick. Two writings are commonly agreed to be written by him. One is an *Epistle to the Soldiers of Coroticus*, in which he demands the return of a group of his Christian converts. The other is this *Confession*, so-called. Several other writings have been unconvincingly ascribed to him.

The earliest biographies of Patrick were written many decades later by Irish authors called Muirchu and Tirechan, but modern historians have little confidence in them. Still less are they inclined to rely on later medieval traditions that developed around Patrick. The best sources for his life are his own writings.

From the *Confession* it appears that Patrick came from Britain, and it can be inferred that he lived near enough the Irish Sea or one of the firths on the west coast of Scotland that he could be kidnapped by Irish pirates. Numerous sites have been proposed, mainly in north or south Wales, but also in Scotland. It is usually supposed that he was British in race. The British were a Celtic people; they were displaced by the Anglo-Saxons in the fifth century, but their descendants can be found today in Wales and in Brittany (in France).

As a bishop in Ireland Patrick may have been based in the area around Armagh. The diocese of Armagh in the Church of Ireland has always claimed Patrick as its founder, and for centuries the archbishop of Armagh has been the primate or chief bishop of the Church of Ireland.

When Patrick may have lived is a matter of controversy. In his *Epistle to Coroticus* he describes the Franks as a pagan people; they became Christian in 496. The authors of early chronicles called the Irish Annals, which listed important events year by year, recorded the beginning of the mission of someone named Patrick for the year 432, but they also recorded the death of what seems to be another Patrick in 493. The annalists recorded the death of several of Patrick's disciples for the years between 480 and 549. Prosper of Aquitaine, a contemporary, wrote that in 431 (or 430) Palladius was appointed "first bishop to the Irish believing in Christ"; Palladius was Patrick's predecessor. Irish sea raids are known to have been frequent in the first half of the fifth century. Inventive scholars have also tried to determine his dates by deciding which Latin translation of Scripture he used, where he might have found a creed such as the one he wrote in section 4 of the *Confession*, when his father might have been served as both a *decurion* (alderman) and a deacon, where he might have derived his Latin style and vocabulary, and who Coroticus was. Perhaps a majority of scholars are content with the year 432 as the beginning of Patrick's mission, and from that they work back to a birthdate around 390, and forward to a date of death around 460. Very little in the interpretation of the document, however, depends on its date.

Patrick's Latin, compared to classical Latin, appears decadent and undisciplined. It may be that his Latin represents an ordinary spoken Latin, in contrast to the literary Latin of cultured writers; and it is also not unlikely that Latin was Patrick's second language, after British. When Patrick's meaning is unclear in the original, as it often is, translators usually leave it unclear in their translation.

There are several manuscripts of the *Confession*. There is reason to believe that they all derive ultimately from a single manuscript that existed in the seventh century. The pre-history of that manuscript cannot be known. In the following document, quotation marks around Scriptural citations have been supplied by the translator.

Questions on the reading

To whom does Patrick appear to be writing, and what is his purpose? How do his intended audience and his agenda shape what he writes?

What is ambiguous about what Patrick says in the text? To what extent can we know the events that happened, where they happened, and in what order they happened? What can be said about Patrick's personality? Is it possible to gauge his sincerity and honesty? How does Patrick understand himself? Does he think of himself as a figure of Jesus? or Paul? How is Patrick being interpreted by his opponents? How has conflict arisen? He calls himself uneducated; how uneducated is he, and what is his purpose in saying so? What can be said about Patrick's faith and his theological position? If he is really writing in the middle of the fifth century, is there any evidence that he has been touched by the controversies around Pelagianism and Eutycheanism? What is his eschatology (e.g., his understanding of Christ's second coming)? What is his purpose in stating his creed in chapter four? How does he use Scripture, and why does he use it the way he does? Do his quotations from Scripture ever seem to be unusual? What is Ireland like in Patrick's day? What has been his ministry there? What is his approach to evangelism?

Patrick's Confession

I am Patrick, a sinner, most unlearned, the least of all the faithful, and utterly despised by many. My father was Calpornius, a deacon, son of Potitus, a priest, of the village Bannavem Taburniae; he had a country seat nearby, and there I was taken captive.

I was then about sixteen years of age. I did not know the true God. I was taken into captivity to Ireland with many thousands of people — and deservedly so, because we turned away from God, and did not keep His commandments, and did not obey our priests, who used to remind us of our salvation. And the Lord "brought over us the wrath of His anger

Source: Patrick, *Confession*, in Ludwig Bieler, ed., *The Works of St. Patrick* (Ancient Christian Writers, vol. 17), Westminster, MD: The Newman Press, 1953, 21-40.

and scattered us among many nations," even "unto the utmost part of the earth," where now my littleness is placed among strangers.

2. And there "the Lord opened the sense of my unbelief" that I might at last remember my sins and "be converted with all my heart to the Lord my God," who "had regard for my abjection," and mercy on my youth and ignorance, and watched over me before I knew Him, and before I was able to distinguish between good and evil, and guarded me, and comforted me as would a father his son.

3. Hence I cannot be silent — "nor, indeed, is it expedient" — about the great benefits and the great grace which the Lord has deigned to bestow upon me "in the land of my captivity;" for this we can give to God in return after having been chastened by Him, "to exalt and praise His wonders before every nation that is anywhere under the heaven."

4. Because there is no other God, nor ever was, nor will be, than God the Father unbegotten, without beginning, from whom is all beginning, the Lord of the universe, as we have been taught; and His son Jesus Christ, whom we declare to have always been with the Father, spiritually and ineffably begotten by the Father before the beginning of the world, before all beginning; and by Him are made all things visible and invisible. He was made man, and, having defeated death, was received into heaven by the Father; "and He hath given Him all power over all names in heaven, on earth, and under the earth, and every tongue shall confess to Him that Jesus Christ is Lord and God," in whom we believe, and whose advent we expect soon to be, "judge of the living and of the dead," who will render to every man according to his deeds; and "He has poured forth upon us abundantly the Holy Spirit," "the gift and pledge" of immortality, who makes those who believe and obey "sons of God and joint heirs with Christ;" and Him do we confess and adore, one God in the Trinity of the Holy Name.

5. For He Himself has said through the Prophet: "Call upon me in the day of thy trouble, and I will deliver thee, and thou shalt glorify me." And again He says: "It is honourable to reveal and confess the works of God."

6. Although I am imperfect in many things, I nevertheless wish that my brethren and kinsmen should know what sort of person I am, so that they may understand my heart's desire.

7. I know well "the testimony of my Lord," who in the Psalm declares: "Thou wilt destroy them that speak a lie." And again He says: "The mouth that belieth killeth the soul." And the same Lord says in the Gospel: "Every idle word that men shall speak, they shall render an account for it on the day of judgment."

8. And so I should dread exceedingly, "with fear and trembling," this sentence on that day when no one will be able to escape or hide, but we all, without exception, shall have "to give an account" even of our smallest sins "before the judgment seat" of the Lord Christ.

9. For this reason I long had in mind to write, but hesitated until now; I was afraid of exposing myself to people's talk, because I have not studied like the others, who thoroughly imbibed law and Sacred Scripture, and never had to change from the language of their childhood days, but were able to make it still more perfect. In our case, what I had to say had to be translated into a tongue foreign to me, as can be easily proved from the savour of my writing, which betrays how little instruction and training I have had in the art of words; for, so says Scripture, "by the tongue will be discovered the wise man, and understanding, and knowledge, and the teaching of truth."

10. But of what help is an excuse, however true, especially if combined with presumption, since now, in my old age, I strive for something that I did not acquire in youth? It was my sins that prevented me from fixing in my mind what before I had barely read through. But who believes me, though I should repeat what I started out with?

As a youth, nay, almost as a boy not able to speak, I was taken captive, before I knew what to pursue and what to avoid. Hence to-day I blush and fear exceeding to reveal my lack of education; for I am unable to tell my story to those versed in the art of concise writing — in such a way, I mean, as my spirit and mind long to do, and so that the sense of my words expresses what I feel.

11. But if indeed it had been given to me as it was given to others, then I would not be silent "because of my desire of thanksgiving;" and if perhaps some people think me arrogant for doing so in spite of my lack of knowledge and my slow tongue, it is, after all, written: "The stammering tongues shall quickly learn to speak peace."

How much more should we earnestly strive to do this, we, who are, so Scripture says, "a letter of Christ for salvation unto the utmost part of the earth," and, though not an eloquent one, yet . . . "written in your hearts, not with ink, but with the spirit of the living God!" And again the Spirit witnesses that "even rusticity was created by the Highest."

12. Whence I, once rustic, exiled, unlearned, who does not know how to provide for the future, this at least I know most certainly that before I was humiliated I was like a stone lying in the deep mire; and He that is mighty came and in His mercy lifted me up, and raised me aloft, and placed me on the top of the wall. And therefore I ought to cry out aloud and so also render something to the Lord for His great benefits here and in eternity — benefits which the human mind is unable to appraise.

13. Wherefore, then, be astonished, "ye great and little that fear God," and you men of letters on your estates, listen and pore over this. Who was it that roused up me, the fool that I am, from the midst of those who in human eyes are wise, and expert in law, and powerful in word and in everything? And He inspired me — me, the outcast of this world — before others, to be the man (if only I could!) who, "with fear and reverence and without blame," should faithfully serve the people to whom the love of Christ conveyed and gave me for the duration of my life, if I should be worthy; yes indeed, to serve them humbly and sincerely.

14. In the light, therefore, of our faith in the Trinity I must make this choice, regardless of danger I must make known the gift of God and everlasting consolation, without fear and frankly I must spread everywhere the name of God so that after my decease I may leave a bequest to my brethren and sons whom I have baptised in the Lord — so many thousands of people.

15. And I was not worthy, nor was I such that the Lord should grant this to His servant; that after my misfortunes and so great difficulties, after my captivity, after the lapse of so many years, He should give me so great a grace in behalf of that nation — a thing which once, in my youth, I never expected nor thought of.

16. But after I came to Ireland — every day I had to tend sheep, and many times a day I prayed — the love of God and His fear came to me more and more, and my faith was strengthened. And my spirit was

moved so that in a single day I would say as many as a hundred prayers, and almost as many in the night, and this even when I was staying in the woods and on the mountain; and I used to get up for prayer before daylight, through snow, through frost, through rain, and I felt no harm, and there was no sloth in me — as I now see, because the spirit within me was then fervent.

17. And there one night I heard in my sleep a voice saying to me: "It is well that you fast, soon you will go to your own country." And again, after a short while, I heard a voice saying to me: "See, your ship is ready." And it was not near, but at a distance of perhaps two hundred miles, and I had never been there, nor did I know a living soul there; and then I took to flight, and I left the man with whom I had stayed for six years. And I went in the strength of God who directed my way to my good, and I feared nothing until I came to that ship.

18. And the day that I arrived the ship was set afloat, and I said that I was able to pay for my passage with them. But the captain was not pleased, and with indignation he answered harshly: "It is of no use for you to ask us to go along with us." And when I heard this, I left them in order to return to the hut where I was staying. And as I went, I began to pray; and before I had ended my prayer, I heard one of them shouting behind me, "Come, hurry, we shall take you on in good faith; make friends with us in whatever way you like." And so on that day I refused to suck their breasts for fear of God, but rather hoped they would come to the faith of Jesus Christ, because they were pagans. And thus I had my way with them, and we set sail at once.

19. And after three days we reached land, and for twenty-eight days we travelled through deserted country. And they lacked food, and hunger overcame them; and the next day the captain said to me: "Tell me, Christian: you say that your God is great and all-powerful; why, then, do you not pray for us? As you can see, we are suffering from hunger; it is unlikely indeed that we shall ever see a human being again."

I said to them full of confidence: "Be truly converted with all your heart to the Lord my God, because nothing is impossible for Him, that this day He may send you food on your way until you be satisfied; for He has abundance everywhere." And, with the help of God, so it came to pass: suddenly a herd of pigs appeared on the road before our eyes, and they killed many of them; and there they stopped for two nights and fully recovered their strength, and their hounds received their fill, for many of them had grown weak and were half-dead along the way. And from that day they had plenty of food. They also found wild honey, and offered some of it to me, and one of them said: "This we offer in sacrifice." Thanks be to God, I tasted none of it.

20. That same night, when I was asleep, Satan assailed me violently, a thing I shall remember "as long as I shall be in this body." And he fell upon me like a huge rock, and I could not stir a limb. But whence came it into my mind, ignorant as I am, to call upon Helias? And meanwhile I saw the sun rise in the sky, and while I was shouting "Helias! Helias!" with all my might, suddenly the splendour of that sun fell on me and immediately freed me of all misery. And I believe that I was sustained by Christ my Lord, and that His Spirit was even then crying out in my behalf, and I hope it will be so "on the day of my tribulation," as is written in the Gospel: "On that day," the Lord declares, "it is not you that speak, but the Spirit of your Father that speaketh in you."

21. And once again, after many years, I fell into captivity. On that first night I stayed with them. I heard a divine message saying to me: "Two months will you be with them." And so it came to pass: on the sixtieth night thereafter "the Lord delivered me out to their hands."

22. Also on our way God gave us food and fire and dry weather every day, until, on the tenth day, we met people. As I said above, we travelled twenty-eight days through deserted country, and the night that we met people we had no food left.

23. And again after a few years I was in Britain with my people, who received me as their son, and sincerely besought me that now at last, having suffered so many hardships, I should not leave them and go elsewhere.

And there I saw in the night the vision of a man, whose name was Victoricus, coming as it were from Ireland, with countless letters. And he gave me one of them, and I read the opening words of the letter, which were, "The voice of the Irish"; and as I read the beginning of the letter I thought that at the same moment I heard their voice — they were those beside the Wood of Voclut, which is near the Western Sea — and thus did they cry out as "with one mouth:" "We ask thee, boy, come and walk among us once more."

And I was quite broken in heart, and could read no further, and so I woke up. Thanks be to God, after many years the Lord gave to them according to their cry.

24. And another night — whether within me, or beside me, "I know not, God knoweth" — they called me most unmistakably with words which I heard but could not understand, except that at the end of the prayer He spoke thus: "He that has laid down His life for thee, it is He that speaketh in thee"; and so I awoke full of joy.

25. And again I saw Him praying in me, and I was as it were within my body, and I heard Him above me, that is, over "the inward man," and there He prayed mightily with groanings. And all the time I was astonished, and wondered, and thought with myself who it could be that prayed in me. But at the end of the prayer He spoke, saying that He was the Spirit; and so I woke up, and remembered the Apostle saying: "The Spirit helpeth the infirmities of our prayer. For we know not what we should pray for as we ought; but the Spirit Himself asketh for us with unspeakable groanings, which cannot be expressed in words;" and again: "The Lord our advocate asketh for us."

26. And when I was attacked by a number of my seniors who came forth and brought up my sins against my laborious episcopate, on that day indeed was I struck so that I might have fallen now and for eternity; but the Lord graciously spared the stranger and sojourner for His name and came mightily to my help in this affliction. Verily, not slight was the shame and blame that fell upon me! I ask God that "it may not be reckoned to them as sin."

27. As cause for proceeding against me they found — after thirty years! — a confession I had made before I was a deacon. In the anxiety of my troubled mind I confided to my dearest friend what I had done in my boyhood one day, nay, in one hour, because I was not yet strong. "I know not, God knoweth" — whether I was then fifteen years old; and I did not believe in the living God, nor did I so from my childhood, but lived in death and unbelief until I was severely chastised and really humiliated, by hunger and nakedness, and that daily.

28. On the other hand, I did not go to Ireland of my own accord, not until I had nearly perished; but this was rather for my good, for thus was I purged by the Lord; and He made me fit so that I might be now what was once far from me — that I should care and labour for the salvation of others, whereas then I did not even care about myself.

29. On that day, then, when I was rejected by those referred to and mentioned above, in that night I saw a vision of the night. There was a writing without honour against my face, and at the same time I heard God's voice saying to me: "We have seen with displeasure the face of Deisignatus" (thus revealing his name). He did not say, "Thou hast seen," but, "We have seen," as if He included Himself, as He sayeth: "He who toucheth you toucheth as it were the apple of my eye."

30. Therefore "I give Him thanks who hath strengthened me" in everything, as He did not frustrate the journey upon which I had decided, and the work which I had learned from Christ my Lord; but I rather felt after this no little strength, and my trust was proved right before God and people.

31. And so I say boldly, my conscience does not blame me now or in the future: God is my witness that I have not lied in the account which I have given you.

32. But the more am I sorry for my dearest friend that we had to hear what he said. To him I had confided my very soul! And I was told by some of the brethren before that defence — at which I was not present, nor was I in Britain, nor was it suggested by me — that he would stand up for me in my absence. He had even said to me in person: "Look, you should be raised to the rank of bishop!" — of which I was not worthy. But whence did it come to him afterwards that he let me down before all, good and evil, and publicly, in a matter in which he had favoured me before spontaneously and gladly — and not he alone, but the Lord, who "is greater than all?"

33. Enough of this. I must not, however, hide God's gift which He bestowed upon me "in the land of my captivity;" because then I earnestly sought Him, and there I found Him, and He saved me from all evil because — so I believe — "of His Spirit that dwelleth" in me. Again, boldly said. But God knows it, had this been said to me by a man, I had perhaps remained silent for the love Christ.

34. Hence, then, I give unwearied thanks to God, who kept me faithful "in the day of my temptation," so that today I can confidently offer Him my soul as a living sacrifice — to Christ my Lord, who "saved me out of all my troubles." Thus I can say: "Who am I, O Lord, and to what hast Thou called me," Thou who didst assist me with such divine

power that to-day "I" constantly "exalt" and magnify Thy name "among the heathens" wherever I may be, and not only in good days but also in tribulations? So indeed I must accept with equanimity whatever befalls me, be it good or evil, and always give thanks to God, who taught me to trust in Him always without hesitation, and who must have heard my prayer so that I, however ignorant I was, "in the last days" dared to undertake such a holy and wonderful work — thus imitating somehow those who, as the Lord once foretold, would preach His Gospel "for a testimony to all nations" before "the end of the world." So we have seen it, and so it has been fulfilled: indeed, we are witnesses that the Gospel has been preached unto those parts beyond which there lives nobody.

35. Now, it would be tedious to give a detailed account of all my labours or even a part of them. Let me tell you briefly how the merciful God often freed me from slavery and from twelve dangers in which my life was at stake — not to mention numerous plots, which I cannot express in words; for I do not want to bore my readers. But God is my witness, who knows all things even before they come to pass, as He used to forewarn even me, poor wretch that I am, of many things by a divine message.

36. "How came I by this wisdom," which was not in me, who neither "knew the number of my days" nor knew what God was? Whence was given to me afterwards the gift so great, so salutary — to know God and to love Him, although at the price of leaving my country and my parents?

37. And many gifts were offered to me in sorrow and tears, and I offended the donors, much against the wishes of some of my seniors; but, guided by God, in no way did I agree with them or acquiesce. It was not grace of my own, but God, who is strong in me and resists them all — as He had done when I came to the people of Ireland to preach the Gospel, and to suffer insult from the unbelievers, "hearing the reproach of my going abroad," and many persecutions even unto bonds, and to give my free birth for the benefit of others; and, should I be worthy, I am prepared to give even my life without hesitation and most gladly for His name, and it is there that I wish to spend it until I die, if the Lord would grant it to me.

38. For I am very much God's debtor, who gave me such great grace that many people were reborn in God through me and afterwards confirmed, and that clerics were ordained for them everywhere, for a

people just coming to the faith, whom the Lord took from the utmost parts of the earth, as He once had promised through His prophets: "To Thee the gentiles shall come from the ends of the earth and shall say: "How false are the idols that our fathers got for themselves, and there is no profit in them"; and again: I have set Thee as a light among the gentiles, that Thou mayest be for salvation unto the utmost part of the earth."

39. And there I wish to wait for His promise who surely never deceives, as He promised in the Gospel: "They shall come from the east and the west, and shall sit down with Abraham and Isaac and Jacob" — as we believe the faithful will come from all the world.

40. For that reason, therefore, we ought to fish well and diligently, as the Lord exhorts in advance and teaches, saying: "Come ye after me, and I will make you to be fishers of people." And again He says through the prophets: "Behold, I send many fishers and hunters, saith God, and so on." Hence it was most necessary to spread our nets so that a great multitude and throng might be caught for God, and that there be clerics everywhere to baptise and exhort a people in need and want, as the Lord in the Gospel states, exhorts, and teaches, saying: "Going therefore now, teach ye all nations, baptising them in the name of the Father, and the Son, and the Holy Spirit, teaching them to observe all things whatsoever I have commanded you: and behold I am with you all days even to the consummation of the world." And again He says: "Go ye therefore into the whole world, and preach the Gospel to every creature. He that believeth and is baptised shall be saved; but he that believeth not shall be condemned." And again: "This Gospel of the kingdom shall be preached in the whole world for a testimony to all nations, and then shall come the end." And so too the Lord announces through the prophet, and says: "And it shall come to pass, in the last days, saith the Lord, I will pour out of my Spirit upon all flesh; and your sons and your daughters shall prophesy, and your young men shall see visions, and your old men shall dream dreams. And upon my servants indeed, and upon my handmaids will I pour out in those days of my Spirit, and they shall prophesy." And in Hosea He saith: "I will call that which was not my people, my people; . . . and her that had not obtained mercy, one that hath obtained mercy. And it shall be in the place where it was said: 'You are not my people,' there they shall be called the sons of the living God."

41. Hence, how did it come to pass in Ireland that those who never had a knowledge of God, but until now always worshipped idols and things impure, have now been made a people of the Lord, and are called sons of God, that the sons and daughters of the kings of the Irish are seen to be monks and virgins of Christ?

42. Among others, a blessed Irishwoman of noble birth, beautiful, full-grown, whom I had baptised, came to us after some days for a particular reason: she told us that she had received a message from a messenger of God, and he admonished her to be a virgin of Christ and draw near to God. Thanks be to God, on the sixth day after this she most laudably and eagerly chose what all virgins of Christ do. Not that their fathers agree with them; no — they often even suffer persecution and undeserved reproaches from their parents; and yet their number is ever increasing. How many have been reborn there so as to be of our kind, I do not know — not to mention widows and those who practice continence.

But greatest is the suffering of those women who live in slavery. All the time they have to endure terror and threats. But the Lord gave His grace to many of His maidens; for, though they are forbidden to do so, they follow Him bravely.

43. Wherefore, then, even if I wished to leave them and go to Britain — and how I would have loved to go to my country and my parents, and also to Gaul in order to visit the brethren and to see the face of the saints of my Lord! God knows it that I much desired it; but I am bound by the Spirit, who gives evidence against me if I do this, telling me that I shall be guilty; and I am afraid of losing the labour which I have begun — nay, not I, but Christ the Lord who bade me come here and stay with them for the rest of my life, if the Lord will, and will guard me from every evil way that I may not sin before Him.

44. This, I presume, I ought to do, but I do not trust myself "as long as I am in this body of death," for strong is he who daily strives to turn me away from the faith and the purity of true religion to which I have devoted myself to the end of my life to Christ my Lord. But the hostile flesh is ever dragging us unto death, that is, towards the forbidden satisfaction of one's desires; and I know that in part I did not lead a perfect life as did the other faithful; but I acknowledge it to my Lord, and do not blush before Him, because I lie not: from the time I came to know

Him in my youth, the love of God and the fear of Him have grown in me, and up to now, thanks to the grace of God, I have kept the faith.

45. And let those who will, laugh and scorn — I shall not be silent; nor shall I hide the signs and wonders which the Lord has shown me many years before they came to pass, as He knows everything even "before the times of the world."

46. Hence I ought unceasingly to give thanks to God who often pardoned my folly and my carelessness, and on more than one occasion spared His great wrath on me, who was chosen to be His helper and who was slow to do as was shown me and as the Spirit suggested. And the Lord had mercy on me thousands and thousands of times because He saw that I was ready, but that I did not know what to do in the circumstances. For many tried to prevent this my mission; they would even talk to each other behind by back and say: "Why does this fellow throw himself into danger among enemies who have no knowledge of God?" It was not malice, but it did not appeal to them because — and to this I own myself — of my rusticity. And I did not realise at once the grace that was then in me; now I understand that I should have done so before.

47. Now I have given a simple account to my brethren and fellow servants who have believed me because of what I said and still say in order to strengthen and confirm your faith. Would that you, too, would strive for greater things and do better! This will be my glory, for "a wise son is the glory of his father."

48. You know, and so does God, how I have lived among you from my youth in the true faith and in sincerity of heart. Likewise, as regards the heathen among whom I live, I have been faithful to them, and so I shall be. God knows it, I have overreached none of them, nor would I think of doing so, for the sake of God and His Church, for fear of raising persecution against them and all of us, and for fear that through me the name of the Lord be blasphemed; for it is written: "Woe to the one through whom the name of the Lord is blasphemed."

49. "For although I be rude in all things," nevertheless I have tried somehow to keep myself safe, and that, too, for my Christian brethren, and the virgins of Christ, and the pious women who of their own accord made me gifts and laid on the altar some of their ornaments; and I gave

them back to them, and they were offended that I did so. But I did it for the hope of lasting success — in order to preserve myself cautiously in everything so that they might not seize upon me or the ministry of my service, under the pretext of dishonesty, and that I would not even in the smallest matter give the infidels an opportunity to defame and defile.

50. When I baptised so many thousands of people, did I perhaps expect from any of them as much as half a screpall? "Tell me, and I will restore it to you." Or when the Lord ordained clerics everywhere through my unworthy person and I conferred the ministry upon them free, if I asked any of them as much as the price of my shoes, "speak against me and I will return it to you."

51. On the contrary, I spent money for you that they might receive me; and I went to you and everywhere for your sake in many dangers, even to the farthest districts, beyond which there lived nobody and where nobody had ever come to baptise, or to ordain clergy, or to confirm the people. With the grace of the Lord, I did everything lovingly and gladly for your salvation.

52. All the while I used to give presents to the kings, besides the fees I paid to their sons who travel with me. Even so they laid hands on me and my companions, and on that day they eagerly wished to kill me; but my time had not yet come. And everything they found with us they took away, and me they put in irons; and on the fourteenth day the Lord delivered me from their power, and our belongings were returned to us because of God and our dear friends whom we had seen before.

53. You know how much I paid to those who administered justice in all those districts to which I came frequently. I think I distributed among them not less than the price of fifteen men, so that you might enjoy me, and I might always enjoy you in God. I am not sorry for it — indeed it is not enough for me; I still spend and shall spend more. God has power to grant me afterwards "that I myself may be spent for your souls."

54. Indeed, "I call God to witness upon my soul that I lie not;" neither, I hope, am I writing to you in order to make this an occasion of flattery or covetousness, nor because I look for honour from any of you. Sufficient is the honour that is not yet seen but is anticipated in the heart. "Faithful is He that promised; He never lieth."

55. But I see myself exalted even in the present world beyond measure by the Lord, and I was not worthy nor such that He should grant me this. I know perfectly well, though not by my own judgment, that poverty and misfortune becomes me better than riches and pleasures. For Christ the Lord, too, was poor for our sakes; and I, unhappy wretch that I am, have no wealth even if I wished for it. Daily I expect murder, fraud, or captivity, or whatever it may be; "but I fear none of these things" because of the promises of heaven. I have cast myself into the hands of God Almighty, who rules everywhere, as the prophet says: "Cast thy thought upon God, and He shall sustain thee."

56. So, now "I commend my soul to my faithful" God, "for whom I am an ambassador" in all my wretchedness; but God "accepteth no person," and chose me for this office — to be, although among His least, one of His ministers.

57. Hence let me "render unto Him for all He has done to me." But what can I say or what can I promise to my Lord, as I can do nothing that He has not given me? May He "search the hearts and reins;" for greatly and exceedingly do I wish, and ready I was, that He should give me His chalice to drink, as He gave it also to the others who loved Him.

58. Wherefore may God never permit it to happen to me that I should lose His people which He purchased in the utmost parts of the world. I pray to God to give me perseverance and to deign that I be a faithful witness to Him to the end of my life for my God.

59. And if ever I have done any good for my God whom I love, I beg Him to grant me that I may shed my blood with those exiles and captives for His name, even though I should be denied a grave, or my body be woefully torn to pieces limb by limb by hounds or wild beasts, or the fowls of the air devour it. I am firmly convinced that if this should happen to me, I would have gained my soul together with my body, because on that day without doubt we shall rise in the brightness of the sun, that is, in the glory of Christ Jesus our Redeemer, as children of the living God and "joint heirs with Christ," "to be made conformable to His image;" for "of Him, and by Him, and in Him" we shall reign.

60. For this sun which we see rises daily for us because He commands so, but it will never reign, nor will its splendour last; what is more, those wretches who adore it will be miserably punished. Not so we, who

believe in, and worship, the true sun — Christ — who will never perish, nor will he "who doeth His will;" but he "will abide for ever as Christ abideth for ever," who reigns with God the Father Almighty and the Holy Spirit before time, and now, and in all eternity. Amen.

61. Behold, again and again would I set forth the words of my confession. I testify in truth and in joy of heart "before God and His holy angels" that I never had any reason except the Gospel and its promises why I should ever return to the people from whom once before I barely escaped.

62. I pray those who believe and fear God, whosoever deigns to look at or receive this writing which Patrick, a sinner, unlearned, has composed in Ireland, that no one should ever say that it was my ignorance if I did or showed forth anything however small according to God's good pleasure; but let this be your conclusion and let it so be thought, that — as is the perfect truth — it was the gift of God. This is my confession before I die.

16 Pope Leo I, *Letter 28 ("The Tome")* (449, Rome)

There were two general approaches to Christology, or the doctrine of Christ, by the beginning of the fifth century. One was the school of Antioch, which in its Biblical exegesis interpreted the New Testament primarily as an historical record. In its Christology it typically emphasized the character and work of the historical Jesus, and sought to protect the Biblical truth that, in Christ, God shared our human nature. The other approach was connected with Alexandria, where exegetes interpreted Biblical characters, places, and events as allegorical figures of eternal truths about God. In their Christology Alexandrians were less interested in recognizing Christ as our human brother, and thought of Jesus as a kind of figure of the glory of God. Antiochenes sometimes took such great care to safeguard Christ's humanity that they could be accused of dividing Christ into two beings, divine and human. Alexandrians sometimes took such great care to affirm Christ's divinity that they could be accused of dissolving his human personality into it.

Dividing Christ, the error to which the Antiochene position tended, came to be connected in the 420s with a bishop named Nestorius, and was condemned in 431 at the Ecumenical Council of Ephesus. Confounding the two natures of Christ into one, the error to which the Alexandrian position tended, came to be connected in the 440s with a certain Eutyches, the shrewd head of a large monastery in Constantinople. It is with Eutyches' heresy that Leo's *Tome* below was connected.

The *Tome* emerged out of the debate about Eutyches. Among Eutyches' opponents was the bishop of Constantinople, Flavian, who convened a synod in 448 which condemned him. Eutyches sent appeals to several dioceses, including Rome. In due course Pope Leo wrote Flavian the letter below, in which he agreed with the condemnation of Eutyches. Nevertheless, Eutyches was initially vindicated. At what history has called "the Robbers' Council", convened by the Emperor Theodosius II at Ephesus in 449, and chaired by the bishop of Alexandria, Leo's letter was not read, the bishops were bullied into vindicating Eutyches, and Flavian was beaten and sent into exile to die. It looked like the moment of victory for an extreme Alexandrianism in the Christian Church. Then, in one of history's most momentous accidents, Theodosius II was thrown by his horse and died. His sister Pulcheria, an Antiochene who desired good relations with the papacy, took the throne, and in 451 convened a new council at Chalcedon, in Asia Minor near Constantinople. This council accepted Leo's *Tome,* and thus received Leo's dyophysite or two-nature position. It also exonerated the martyred Flavian, condemned Eutyches, and excommunicated and exiled the bishop of Alexandria. Three monophysite or one-nature churches have never accepted Chalcedon: the Coptic in Egypt, the Jacobite in Syria, and the Armenian.

Leo's life before his election as bishop of Rome is obscure. He was born probably at some point in the years before or after 400. It is thought that he was from Tuscany, in what is now west central Italy. He served in the administration of two popes before becoming pope himself in 440. He is called "the Great"; he consolidated and expanded the pope's jurisdiction in the western Empire, strengthened the papal administration, fought heresy, and assumed political and diplomatic leadership as the Emperor's influence in European affairs waned. He wrote clearly and preached eloquently. He much preferred custom to innovation. We have 96 of his sermons and 123 of his letters. His *Tome* is particularly well attested; not only was it copied into several papal collections, but it was also included in the official Acts of the Council of Chalcedon. Leo died in 461.

Four things were required in an orthodox, catholic doctrine of Christ, said the sixteenth-century English theologian Richard Hooker: his perfect Godhead, his perfect humanity, the conjunction of both without separation, and the conjunction of both without confusion. The first was defined by the Council of Nicea in 325 against Arius; the second by the Council of Constantinople in 381 against Apollinaris; the third by the Council of Ephesus in 431 against Nestorius; the fourth by the Council of Chalcedon in 451 against Eutyches. Chalcedon declared that Christ was "of one substance with the Father as touching the Godhead, the same of one substance with us as touching the humanity,. . . without confusion, without change, without division, without separation; the distinction of natures being in no way abolished because of the union but rather the characteristic property of each nature being preserved and concurring into one person and one subsistence [hypostasis]."

In the text below, the translator has supplied quotation marks around passages that are (or appear to be) quotations from Scripture. Some other passages without quotation marks may echo Scripture as well.

Questions on the reading

What has prompted Leo's letter? What motives and principles have animated his reply? What is his doctrine of Christ? How does he support it in his arguments? What attitude does he take towards Flavian, bishop of Constantinople? What authority does Leo understand himself to have in this dispute? What is Leo's information about Eutyches? Do his doctrinal views influence his judgment concerning Eutyches? or vice versa? What Christian doctrines are at stake in this dispute; what sides are being taken? How does Leo make use of Scripture, and how might his opponents be using Scripture against him? The letter has been described as "the ordinary person's doctrine of the Incarnation," more straightforward than speculative: is it so? Alexandrians thought that Leo was really proclaiming two Christs, a human and a divine, divided from each other; were they correct? Apart from the doctrinal controversy itself, what kinds of divisions do there appear to be in the Church? What do the different sides have in common theologically and ecclesiastically?

165. Bishop Leo, to his most glorious and clement son Leo, Augustus (August 17, 458)[1]

Venerable Emperor, I recall my promise[2] that a fuller letter from my humble self would be sent to you in the interests of the faith, about which I know that your Clemency is dutifully solicitous. With God's help, now that I have a sure opportunity, I am fulfilling my promise, so that you may not lack instruction, useful (in my judgment) for your Piety's holy zeal. Although I am aware that your Clemency does not lack human instruction and that, from the abundance of the Holy Spirit, you have imbibed the purest doctrine, it is my duty to make clear what you know and to preach what you believe, in order that the fire which Christ at His coming cast on the earth,[3] being aroused by the impulse of frequent meditation, may so heat up as to glow, may so burn as to give light. The heresy of Eutyches attempted to overcast the Eastern world with enormous clouds and tried to blind the eyes of the unskilled to that light which, as the Gospel says, 'shines in the darkness, and the darkness grasped it not.'[4] Although the heresy itself collapsed in its own blindness, that which failed in the author is now sprouting anew among his disciples.

Two enemies (the one shortly after the other) attacked the Catholic faith, which is one and true; nothing can be added to or subtracted from it. The first of these to rise was Nestorius; then came Eutyches. They[5] sought to introduce into God's Church two heresies, the one contrary to the other. As a result, both were rightly condemned by the advocates of truth, for the teachings of both men, false in different ways, were utterly foolish and blasphemous. Nestorius believed that the blessed Virgin Mary was the mother of the man only and not of God; that is, in his opinion, the divine Person was different from the human Person. He did not think there was one Christ existing in the Word of God and the flesh, but taught that one was the son of man and the other the Son of God, each separate and distinct from the other. For this he was condemned. The truth is that, while that essence of the unchangeable Word remained (which is timeless and co-eternal with the Father and the Holy Spirit), the Word was made flesh in the womb of the Virgin in such a way that,

---

Source: Leo the Great, "The Tome", trans. Brother Edmund Hunt (Fathers of the Church, vol. 34), Fathers of the Church Inc., 1957, 262-274. Reprinted by permission of the Catholic University of America Press.

by an ineffable mystery, through one conception and one birth the same Virgin and Handmaid was also the Mother of the Lord, according to the reality of both natures. Elizabeth also realized this and said, as Luke the Evangelist relates: 'And how have I deserved that the mother of my Lord should come to me?'[6] Eutyches is likewise crushed by the same condemnation. Wallowing about in the impious errors of old heretics, he picked out the third teaching of Apollinaris;[7] that is, in denying the reality of the human flesh and soul, he stated that the whole of our Lord Jesus Christ is of one nature, as if the very divinity of the Word had changed Itself into the flesh and soul. By this view, to be conceived and born, to take food and grow, to be crucified and to die, to be buried and to rise again, and to ascend into heaven and to sit at the right hand of the Father, whence He will come to judge the living and the dead — all these pertained only to His divine nature, which in fact did none of these in Itself apart from the reality of the flesh. For the nature of the only-begotten Son is the nature of the Father, is the nature of the Holy Spirit — at once incapable of suffering, unchangeable, the undivided unity and consubstantial equality of the eternal Trinity. Hence, if any Eutychian departs from the error of Apollinaris in order to avoid having a non-sentient God feel and be mortal, yet dares to proclaim that there is but one nature of the Word Incarnate, that is, the Word and the flesh, he has obviously veered over into the madness of Valentinus and Mani.[8] And he believes that the man Christ Jesus, the Mediator between God and human beings, did all these things by trickery; that is, He had no human body, but to the eyes of the beholders there was an imaginary appearance of a body.

Since the Catholic faith of old detested these impious lies, and the views of the blessed Fathers, in accord throughout the entire world, have already condemned such sacrilegious statements, there is no doubt that we preach and defend the same faith which the holy Council of Nicaea established. It stated: 'We believe in one God, the Father Almighty, the Maker of things visible and invisible, and in our one Lord, Jesus Christ, the Son of God, the Only-begotten of the Father, that is, from the substance of the Father, God from God, light from light, true God from true God, begotten not made, being of one substance with the Father (which they call in Greek '*homoousion*'), by whom all things were made, whether in heaven or on earth, who for us and for our salvation

251

came down and was made flesh; and being made man, suffered, and arose on the third day; He ascended into heaven and will come to judge the living and the dead; and in the Holy Spirit.'[9] In this profession of faith is most clearly contained what we also profess and believe concerning the Incarnation of the Lord. To restore salvation to the human race, He did not bring from heaven with Him the real flesh containing our weakness, but He assumed the flesh in the womb of His Virgin Mother.

Whoever, then, are so blinded and so estranged from the light as to deny the reality of human flesh in the Word of God from the moment of the Incarnation on, ought to show what right they have for using the title of Christians. They should show by what process of reasoning they are in agreement with the Gospel of truth in their claim that, when the blessed Virgin gave birth, there was produced either flesh without divinity or divinity without the flesh. As it is impossible to deny that, according to the Evangelist's words, 'The Word was made flesh and dwelt among us,'[10] so it is impossible to deny that, according to the teaching of blessed Paul the Apostle, 'God was in Christ, reconciling the world to himself.'[11] What reconciliation could there be in which God might again be made propitious to the human race if the Mediator between God and human beings did not take upon Himself the cause of all people? How, indeed, might anyone fulfill the reality of a mediator unless he shared in the nature of God, equal to the Father, and also in our servile nature, so that the bonds of death, brought about by the lie of one person, might be loosed by the death of One who alone was in no way subject to death? The outpouring[12] of Christ's blood for sinners was so rich in value that, if all the enslaved believed in their Redeemer, none of them would be held by the chains of the Devil. For, as the Apostle says: 'Where the offense has abounded, grace has abounded yet more.'[13] And since those born under the sentence of original sin have received the power of rebirth unto justification, the gift of freedom became stronger than the debt of slavery.

Consequently, what hope do they leave themselves in the refuge of this mystery who deny the reality of the human body in our Saviour? Let them say by what sacrifice they have become reconciled; let them say by what blood they have been redeemed. Who is there, as the Apostle says, that 'has delivered himself up for us an offering and a sacrifice to God to ascend in fragrant odor'?[14] Or what sacrifice was ever more holy than that which the true and eternal Priest placed upon the altar of the cross by the immolation of His own flesh? Although the death of many holy people was precious in the sight of the Lord,[15] the redemption of the world was not effected by the killing of any of these guiltless persons. The just received, did not give, crowns; and from the courage of the faithful came examples of patience, not the gifts of justification. Indeed, their individual deaths affected them individually, and none gave up life to pay another's debt. For among the sons of men only one stood out, our Lord Jesus Christ, who was truly the spotless Lamb, in whose person all were crucified, all died, all were buried, all were even raised from the dead. He Himself said about them: 'And I, if I be lifted up from the earth, will draw all things to myself.'[16] Indeed, true faith, justifying the impious and making just people, being drawn to Him who shares in their human nature, receives salvation in Him in whom alone one finds oneself without guilt. And it can freely boast, through God's grace, of the power of Him who in the lowliness of our flesh attacked the enemy of the human race and who turned over His victory to those in whose body He triumphed.

It is true, therefore, that there is in one Lord Jesus Christ, the true Son of God and man, one person of the Word and the flesh, and without separation and division they perform their acts in common. Still, we must understand the character of the acts themselves and must note, by the contemplation of pure faith, to which acts the lowliness of the flesh is elevated, to which acts the height of Divinity bends down; what the flesh does not perform apart from the Word, what the Word apart from the flesh does not effect. Without the power of the Word the Virgin would not conceive and not give birth, and without the reality of the flesh the infant would not lie wrapped in swaddling clothes. Without the power of the Word the Magi would not adore the boy pointed out to them by the guiding star, and without the reality of the flesh there would be no command to transfer the boy into Egypt and remove Him from Herod's persecution. Without the power of the Word the voice of the Father sent from heaven would not say: 'This is my beloved Son, in whom I am well pleased.'[17] And without the reality of flesh John would not exclaim: 'Behold the lamb of God, behold him who takes away the sin of the world.'[18] Without the power of the Word there would be no curing of the infirm, no restoration of life to the dead, and without the reality of flesh there would be no need for Him to eat when hungry, to sleep when tired. Finally, without the power of the Word the Lord would not claim to be equal to the Father, and without the reality of flesh He would not say that the Father was greater than He. For, both are accepted and defended by the Catholic faith, which, according to the profession of the blessed Apostle Peter, believes in one Christ, the Son of the living God, both man and the Word.[19] Hence it is true that, from that beginning when 'the Word was made flesh'[20] in the womb of the Virgin, there never existed any division between the two natures, and, during the entire growth of His body, His acts were at all times the work of one person. Yet, those very acts which were performed by one person are not confused, in our thinking, by any mixing of them; we decide from the character of the acts what is pertinent to each nature.

Consequently, let those hypocrites (who with blinded minds are unwilling to accept the light of truth) say in which nature Christ, the Lord of Majesty, was affixed to the wood of the cross, which lay in the tomb, and which flesh arose on the third day after the stone of the tomb was rolled back; and in which nature, after the Resurrection, He upbraided some of His unbelieving disciples and blamed the hesitation of the doubting when He said: 'Feel me and see; for a spirit does not have flesh and bones, as you see I have';[21] and to the Apostle Thomas: 'Put thy hand into my side, and see my hands and feet; and be not unbelieving, but believing.'[22] So, by this display of His body He already destroyed the lies of heretics. And thus the universal Church, imbued with the teachings of Christ, did not doubt that it should believe what the Apostles undertook to preach. And if in the presence of so great a light of truth heretical obstinacy does not abandon its darkness, let them show from what source they promise themselves hope of eternal life, which no one can attain without the help of the man Jesus Christ, the Mediator between God and human beings. As the blessed Apostle Peter says: 'There is no other name under heaven given to people by which they must be saved.'[23] There is no redemption of captive humanity except in the blood of Him 'who gave himself a ransom for all,'[24] and, as the blessed Apostle Paul says: 'Who thought he was by nature God, did not consider being equal to God a thing to be clung to, but emptied himself, taking the nature of a slave and being made like unto people. And appearing in the form of man, he humbled himself, becoming obedient to death, even to death on the cross. Therefore God also has exalted him and has bestowed upon him the name that is above every name, so that at the name of Jesus every knee should bend of those in heaven, on earth and under the earth, and every tongue should confess that the Lord Jesus Christ is in the glory of God the Father.'[25]

Although, then, the Lord Jesus Christ is one and there is really one and the same person in Him, composed of true divinity and true humanity, the exaltation with which God exalted Him (as the Teacher of the Gentiles says) and gave to Him a name superior to every other name — this exaltation, as we know, took place in that same nature which needed enrichment by the increase of so great a glorification. Indeed, in His nature as God the Son was equal to the Father; and there was no distinction of essence between the Father and the Only-begotten, no difference in majesty; and through the mystery of the Incarnation the Word did not lose anything which the Father might restore to Him as a gift. But the servile form, through which the non-sentient God fulfilled the mystery of great and fatherly concern, is human lowliness, which was carried up to the glory of divine power. The divinity and humanity were bound together in so great a unity from the very time of conception by the Virgin that divine acts were not done without the man and human acts were not done without God. For that reason, just as the Lord of Majesty is said to have been crucified, so He who from all eternity is equal to the Father is said to have been exalted. For, since the unity of person remains inseparable, He is one and the same — wholly the Son of Man because of the flesh, and wholly the Son of God because of the divinity He has in common with the Father. Hence, whatever Christ received in time He received in His humanity, on which are bestowed the things it did not have. As regards the power of the Godhead, all that the Father has belongs also to the Son without distinction; He Himself, in His nature as God, was also the giver of those same things which He received from the Father, in His nature as a slave. According to His nature as God, He and the Father are one; in His servile nature He did not come to do His own will, but the will of Him who sent Him.[26] According to His divine nature, 'as the Father has life in himself, even so he has given to the Son also to have life in himself.'[27] But in His servile state, His soul is sad even unto death.[28] As the Apostle teaches, He is at once both poor and rich: 'rich' because, as the Evangelist says: 'In the beginning was the Word, and the Word was with God: and the Word was God. He was in the beginning with God. All things were made through him, and without him was made nothing.' But he was 'poor' because on our account 'the Word was made flesh, and dwelt among us.'[29] But what is His emptying of self, or what is His poverty, if not the taking on of a slave's nature, wherein the majesty of the Word was veiled and the design for human redemption was carried out?

The bonds of captivity with which we are born could not be loosed unless one of our species and our nature existed who was not bound by any previous conviction for sin and who by His stainless blood would blot out the decree of death against us.[30] On that account it so happened in the fullness of appointed time (as had been divinely ordained from the beginning) that the promise expressed in so many ways became the actuality so long awaited; and there could be no doubt about what had always been announced by continual testimony. But the impiety of heretics shows that they live in great sacrilege since they deny the reality of human flesh in Christ, under the guise of honoring His divinity; and they think they are religious in their belief in claiming that what brings salvation in our Saviour is not real. Yet, according to the promise repeated throughout all ages, the world was reconciled to God in Christ, but, if in so doing the Word did not deign to become flesh, no flesh could be saved. The whole mystery of the Christian faith, taken the way the heretics want it, is darkened with profound obscurity if the light of truth is thought to have hidden under the false guise of a phantasm. Let no Christians, therefore, feel that they should blush because of the reality of our body in Christ. For, all the Apostles and their disciples and all the illustrious Doctors of the Church who merited to gain the martyr's crown or the confessor's glory shone forth in the light of this belief. They everywhere in harmony proclaimed that we must profess but one Person in the Lord Jesus Christ, composed of divinity and flesh. By what species of reasoning, by what part of the divine books, do the impious heretics think they are supported, those who deny the reality of Christ's body? Yet the Law has not ceased to attest to this reality, the Prophets to herald it, the Gospel to teach it, Christ Himself to point it out. Let them search through all the books of Scripture for a means to escape from their darkness, not a way to obscure the true light, and they will find the truth so shining throughout all ages that they will see this great and wonderful mystery believed in from the beginning, one which finally came to pass. Although no part of holy Scripture is silent about it, it is enough to have set forth certain tokens of harmonious truth. By these, diligence may be directed into the most illustrious fullness of the faith and perceive by the pure light of reason that Christians ought not to blush for but ought constantly to glory in the Son of God, who professes without ceasing that He is the Son of Man and a man.

In order to let your Piety know that we are in harmony with the teachings of the venerable Fathers, I thought some of their views should be added to this letter.[31] If you deign to read these, you will find that we preach nothing different from what our holy Fathers everywhere taught, and that no one is at variance with these ideas, except only the impious heretics. Hence, venerable and most glorious Emperor, from these statements, which I have put together as briefly as possible, you realize that our teaching is also in line with the faith inspired in you by God and that we are in no way at odds with evangelical and apostolic doctrine or with the Catholic profession of faith in the Creed. As the blessed Apostle Paul teaches: 'Great is the mystery of godliness: which was manifested in the flesh, was justified in the spirit, appeared to angels, was preached to gentiles, believed in the world, taken up in glory.'[32] Hence, what is more useful for your salvation, what more in accord with your power, than for you to further the peace of the Lord's churches by your government, to defend the gifts of God for all those subject to you, and under no circumstances to allow the ministers of the Devil through his malice to vent their rage to the ruin of anyone. Thus you who are eminent for temporal rule in this generation will merit to reign forever with Christ. May the omnipotent God guard your realm and your welfare unto length of days, O most glorious and clement Emperor, Augustus.

Issued on the seventeenth of August in the consulship of Leo and Majorian, Augusti.

Notes

[1] The texts here are Silva-Tarouca, 9, pp. 44-58; Schwartz, II.4, pp.113-119; Greek version, *Abhandlung d. Bayer. Ges. d. Wiss.* 32 (1927), 52-62.

[2] Cf. Letter 156 n. 7.

3   Cf. Luke 12.49.

4   John 1.5.

5   Most of the rest of this letter was written about five years earlier, as Letter 124, paragraphs 2-7.

6   Luke 1.43.

7   Cf. Letter 21 n. 13, and Letters 26 and 109.

8   Cf. Letter 59, paragraphs 1 and 5.

9   For the version of the Nicene Creed used by St. Leo, cf. Turner, *Monumenta* I 306. In the *Tome*, Leo had relied upon the Apostles Creed. Since the heretics kept claiming to abide by Nicene definitions, Leo proved them wrong there, also. Cf. Letters 54 and 69.

10   John 1.14.

11   Cf. 2 Cor. 5.19.

12   From here to note 19 is taken largely from his *Sermo* 64.6 (*PL* 54.359-361).

13   Rom. 5.20.

14   Eph. 5.2.

15   Cf. Ps. 115.14.

16   John 12.32.

17   Matt. 3.17.

18   John 1.29.

19   Cf. Matt. 16.16.

20   John 1.14.

21   Luke 24.39.

22   Cf. John 20.27.

23   Acts 4.12.

24   1 Tim. 2.6.

25   Phil. 2.6-11.

26   Cf. John 10.30; 5.30.

27   John 5.26.

28   Cf. Matt. 26.38.

29   John 1.1-3, 14; cf. 2 Cor. 8.9.

30   Cf. Col. 2.14.

31   These views are translated at the end of this letter; cf. Letter 117 n. 8.

32   1 Tim. 3.16.

17 Antonius, *The Life and Daily Mode of Living of Blessed Simeon the Stylite* (465?, Syria)

Latin asceticism and Syrian asceticism moved in different directions. In the 420s, Paulinus was at his desk in Nola writing letters to his Christian friends, entertaining distinguished visitors with bottles of estate wine, and planning the celebrations for St. Felix' next feast day. At the same time, Simeon the Stylite was spending night and day in a position of prayer on a little platform twenty meters high off the ground, without protection from the noonday sun or the nighttime cold or the winter snow of the Syrian desert, and there he stayed put for another twenty or thirty years. Paulinus' Latin poetry and the classical architecture of the basilica he built at St. Felix' shrine express something of the continuity of Western Christianity with the classical tradition; Simeon, who did not know how to write, was a Syrian villager with no Greek urban culture to preserve, and subjected himself to appallingly brutal self-mortification. Each represents a larger pattern of spirituality, not simply an isolated figure. Simeon was venerated by generations of Syrian Christians and inspired generations of followers. Hippolyte Delehaye, in *Les saints stylites*, has identified by name dozens of prominent pillar-saints down through the centuries, with the last examples in 1833 and 1848. But Syrian asceticism put down no roots in the West. When, a few years after Simeon, a Western ascetic began standing on a pillar outside Cologne, the bishops told him to come down, and he did.

Three early biographers told Simeon's story, in different ways. One was Theodoret, bishop of Cyrrhus, who played a conspicuous role in the Christological controversies in the years leading up to Chalcedon. Simeon was still alive when Theodoret wrote about him. A second biographer was an anonymous admirer who wrote in Syriac; this work has come to us in three distinct and differing manuscript traditions. A third was the disciple of Simeon's who called himself Antonius; this is the one presented below. His work has been edited from nine manuscripts representing two distinct recensions; there is also an old Latin translation which represents a third recension. Antonius' work bears comparison in some of its historical detail with Theodoret's.

It is thought that Simeon may have been born in about 389, and that he may have arrived at Talanis in 412. (The name of the village is spelled variously in different documents: Thalanis, Thalanes, Telanissos, Telanessos, even Gelasois. It is the modern Zerzita, near Antioch.) Simeon died in 459. His pillar at Talanis was still standing in the seventeenth century; the ruins of the monastery can still be seen.

Questions on the reading

What can be known about the author? Why is he writing? Whom is he addressing? What does he say about his sources for his biography of Simeon? Can we distinguish whether a passage is invented, derived from oral tradition, or borrowed from the literary genre of saints' lives? What is the social situation in the background of the narrative? What is Simeon's role in asceticism, and what is noteworthy about it? What is the rationale for his self-mortification? Why does he keep his parentage a secret in the first monastery? Why does he climb the pillar at the second monastery? (To avoid crowds? to come closer to heaven? to draw attention?) What is Simeon's ministry? Why do crowds come to see him, and how do they benefit? What is Simeon's power, what is its social significance, and where does it come from? Why are Simeon's relics confined to his oratory? What is the relationship in this document between ordained and lay? male and female? village and town? nobility and commoner? health and sickness? Why does he receive such honour at his death? What is his contribution to Christian life in Syria?

The Life and Daily Mode of Living of the
Blessed Simeon the Stylite by Antonius

A strange and incredibly mysterious event took place in our time. I, Antonius, a sinner and least of all, thought to write it down insofar as I understand it, for the treatise is full of usefulness and contrition. So I beseech you: incline your ear and hear exactly what I understand.

2. When Simeon, among the saints and most blessed, was young in years, he cared for his father's sheep, just as the prophet David had done. On the Lord's day, he would enter the church at the time the oracles of God [are read] and joyfully listen to the holy scriptures, although he did not know what it was he heard. When he had come of age, impelled by the word of God he came one day into the holy church. On hearing the [words of the] apostle read aloud, he asked an old man, 'Tell me, father, what is being read?' The old man said to him, 'It is about control of the soul.' Holy Simeon said to him, 'What is control of the soul?' The old man said to him, 'Son, why do you ask me? I see that you are young in years, but possess the understanding of an old man.' Holy Simeon said to him, 'I am not testing you, father, but what was read sounds strange to me.' The old man said to him, 'Self-control is the soul's salvation, for it shows the way to enlightenment and leads to the kingdom of heaven.' Holy Simeon said to him, 'Teach me about these things that you mention, honored father, for I am uneducated.'

3. The old man said to him, 'Son, if one fasts unceasingly to God, he will rightfully grant all one's prayers — that is, one prayer at the third hour, likewise at the sixth, ninth, twelfth, and so on, just as it is done in the monasteries. So, my son, if you know what you have heard, reflect on these things in your heart, for you must hunger and thirst, you must be assaulted and buffeted and reproached, you must groan and weep and be oppressed and suffer ups and downs of fortune; you must renounce bodily health and desires, be humiliated and suffer much from men, for so you will be comforted by angels. Now that you have heard all these things, may the Lord of glory grant you good resolve according to his will.'

Source: "The Life and Daily Mode of Living of Blessed Simeon the Stylite by Antonius," in Robert Doran, trans., *The Lives of Simeon Stylites* (Cistercian Studies vol. 112), Kalamazoo: Cistercian Publications, 1992, 87-100.

4. When he heard this, holy Simeon went out of the church and came to a deserted area. He lay face down and, taking neither food nor drink, wept for seven days as he prayed to God. After the seven days, he got up and ran full-speed to a monastery. Falling at the feet of the abbot, he cried out and said, 'Have mercy on me, father, for I am a lowly and wretched man. Save a soul which is perishing and which yet desires to serve God.' The abbot said, 'Who are you, and what is your background? What is your name and from where did you come?' Blessed Simeon said, 'I am a free man named Simeon, but do not ask me, master, I pray, how I came here or who my parents are! Redeem a soul which perishes.' When he heard this, the abbot lifted him up from the ground and said, 'If you come from God, the Lord will protect you from every evil and deceitful deed; you will serve all, so that all may love you.'

5. Meanwhile, his parents, with tears, ceaselessly sought him. The saint, however, stayed in the monastery, serving all and loved by all and observing the rule of the monastery. One day he went out from the monastery and came across a bucket in front of the well from which the water was drawn. It had a rope attached, and he untied the rope, went to a secluded place and wrapped the rope around his whole body. Over the rope he put a tunic made of hair. Then he re-entered the monastery and said to the brethren, 'I went out to draw water and did not find the rope in the bucket.' The brethren said to him, 'Be quiet, lest someone tell this to the abbot.' No one perceived that underneath he was bound with the rope. So he remained a year or more with the rope wrapped around his flesh, and it ate into his flesh so that the rope was covered by the rotted flesh of the righteous man. Because of his stench no one could stand near him, but no one knew his secret. His bed was covered with worms, but no one knew what had taken place.

6. He would accept his food, but give it to the poor without anyone knowing. One day, however, one of the monks went out and found him giving the poor the bread and pulse he had received. Now everyone would fast till sun-down, but holy Simeon only ate on Sunday. One of the monks went in and reported Simeon to the abbot, saying, 'I beseech your holiness: this man wants to undo the monastery and certainly the rule which you handed down to us.' The abbot said to him, 'How does he want to undo the rule?' The monk said, 'We were taught to fast till sun-down, but he eats only on Sundays, and the bread and pulse he

receives he secretly gives to the poor every day. Not only this, but the stench from his body is so unbearable that no one can stand near him; his bed is full of worms, and we simply cannot bear it. You must choose: either keep him here and we will leave, or send him back where he came from.'

7. When he heard this, the abbot was astounded. He inspected his bed and found it full of worms, and because of the stench he could not stay there. The abbot said, 'Behold, the new Job!' Taking hold of [Simeon], he said, 'Man, why do you do these things? Where does this stench come from? Why do you deceive the brethren? Why do you undo the rule of the monastery? Are you some kind of spirit? Go somewhere else and die away from us. Wretch that I am, am I to be tempted by you? For if you are really a man from real parents, surely you would have told us who your father and mother and kinsfolk are and from whence you came?' When he heard these things, the saint, bowing to the ground, was absolutely silent, but the place where he was standing was filled with his tears. Quite beside himself, the abbot said to his monks, 'Strip him so we can see where this stench comes from.'

8. Then they wanted to strip him, but they could not do it, for his garment was stuck fast because of the putrefied flesh. So for three days they kept soaking him in warm water mixed with oil and in this way, after a great deal of trouble, they were able to strip him: but with the garment they also took off his putrefied flesh. They found the rope wrapped around his body so that nothing of him could be seen, only the ends of the rope. There was no guessing how many worms were on him. Then all the monks were astounded when they saw that terrible wound and they asked themselves how and by what means they could take the rope off him. But holy Simeon cried out, saying, 'Let me be, my masters and brethren. Let me die as a stinking dog, for so I ought to be judged because of what I have done. For all injustice and covetousness are in me, for I am an ocean of sins.'

The monks and the abbot wept when they saw that terrible wound, and the abbot said to him, 'You are not yet eighteen years old: what kind of sins do you have?' Holy Simeon said to him, 'The prophet David said: "Behold, I was brought forth in iniquities, and in sins did my mother conceive me."[1] I have been clothed the same as everyone else.' The abbot was astonished at his wise answer, that such an uneducated man had been spurred on to the fear of God. However, the abbot called two physicians, and, although the distress and the labor was so great that at one point they gave him up for dead, they finally separated from him the rope with flesh stuck on it. They tended him for fifty days and helped him somewhat, and the abbot said to him, 'Look, son, you are now healthy. Go where you wish.'

9. Then holy Simeon left the monastery. Now there was a well near the monastery which contained no water, but many unclean, evil spirits lived it: not only unclean spirits, but also unimaginable numbers of asps, vipers, serpents and scorpions so that everybody was afraid to pass by that place. Unknown to anyone, holy Simeon went there and, making the sign of the cross, threw himself into that well and hid himself in the side of the well.

10. Seven days after Simeon had left the monastery, the abbot saw in a dream an unimaginable number of men clad in white encircling the monastery. They held torches and said, 'We will burn you up this very moment, unless you hand over to us the servant of God, Simeon. Why did you persecute him? What did he do that you cast him forth from the monastery? What was his fault? Tell us before we burn you. Do you not know what you had in your monastery? For he will be found greater than you in that fearful, terrible day.' When the abbot awoke trembling from his sleep, he said to his monks, 'Truly I see that that man is a true servant of God! For I have suffered much evil this night in a dream because of him. I beseech you, brethren, spread out and find him for me, otherwise none of you can come back here.'

11. They went out and looked for him everywhere, and when they could not find him they went back to the abbot and said, 'Truly, master, there is no place left where we have not looked except that place where no one would dare to travel because of the hordes of wild beasts.' The abbot said to them, 'My sons, praying and bearing torches, go out and look for him there.' After praying above the well for three hours, they, with ropes, let down into the well five monks holding torches. At the sight, the reptiles fled into the corners, but on seeing them holy Simeon called out, saying, 'I beseech you, brothers and servants of God, grant me a little time to die. That I cannot fulfill what I set out to do is too much for me.' But the monks overpowered him with much force and pulled him out of the well, dragging him as if he were a criminal. They brought

him to the abbot who, when he saw him, fell at his feet, saying, 'Agree to my request, servant of God: become my teacher, and teach me what patient endurance is and what it offers.'

12. Holy Simeon wept unceasingly and prayed to God; he stayed in the monastery three years and then, without anyone knowing, left and went into a sparsely inhabited area where there were several villages, the nearest being called Talanis. He built for himself there a small place from unmortared stones and stood in the middle of it for four years through snow, rain and burning sun, and many came to him. He ate soaked lentils and drank water. After this he made a pillar four cubits high and stood on it for seven years, and his fame spread everywhere. After this the crowds built for him two enclosures from unmortared stone and they put up a door to the inner enclosure. They made for him a pillar thirty cubits high, and he stood on it for fifteen years during which time he performed many healings, for many who were possessed went there and were healed.

13. Holy Simeon imitated his teacher, Christ. Calling on him, he made the lame walk, cleansed lepers, made the dumb speak, made paralytics move about with ease, healed the chronically ill. Each one he warned and exhorted, 'If someone asks you who healed you, say, "God healed me". Do not even think of saying, "Simeon healed me", otherwise you will find yourself again in the very same difficulties. I say unto you: never lie or take an oath by God. If you are forced to take an oath, swear by me, your humble servant, either in truth or in deceit. For swearing by God is a great sin and a fearful thing to do.'

14. Hear this awesome and extraordinary wonder. After twenty years the mother of holy Simeon learnt where he was. She came in haste and wanted, after so many years, to see him. She wept much to see him, but she was not allowed to view him. Since she wanted so much to be blessed by his holy hands, she was obliged to climb the wall. While she was climbing the wall of the enclosure, she was thrown to the ground and could not see him. Holy Simeon sent a message to her, 'Leave me alone for now, mother. If we are worthy, we will see one another in the next life.' When she heard this, she only longed more to see him, but holy Simeon sent this message to her, 'Rest, my honored mother, since you have come a long way and grown weary on my humble account. Lie down at least a little while; rest and get your strength back. I will see you

soon.' When she heard this, she lay down before the entrance and immediately gave up her spirit to God. The door-keepers came to wake her up, but discovered that she was dead and told the saint what had happened to her. On hearing this, he commanded that she be brought inside and placed before his pillar. When he saw her, he wept and began to say, 'Lord, God of powers, guide of the light and charioteer of the cherubim, who guided Joseph, who made your prophet David prevail over Goliath, who raised Lazarus from the dead after four days, lift up your right and receive in peace the soul of your handmaid.' While he was praying, her holy remains moved and she smiled. Everyone who saw it was astonished and praised God. Having performed her funeral, they buried her in front of his pillar so that he kept her in mind as he prayed.

15. Hear another strange and extraordinary mystery. Some people were coming from far away to have him pray [for them] when they came across a pregnant hind grazing. One of them said to the hind, 'I adjure you by the power of the devout Simeon, stand still so that I can catch you.' Immediately the hind stood still; he caught it and slaughtered it and they ate its flesh. The skin was left over. Immediately they could not speak to one another, but began to bleat like dumb animals. They ran and fell down in front of [the saint's] pillar, praying to be healed. The skin of the hind was filled with chaff, and placed on display long enough for many men to know about it. The men spent sufficient time in penance and, when they were healed, returned home.

16. Hear another strange and wonderful event. A woman became thirsty during the night and wanted to drink some water. She took hold of the pitcher of water but along with the water drank a small serpent. Nourished in her womb it became large, and her face became like green grass in appearance. Many physicians came to heal her but were unable to. Her kinsmen learnt about the marvels and the healings which the saint of God Simeon was performing, so they took her to the saint and told him everything about her. He commanded them, saying, 'Put in her mouth some of this water and soil'. When they did as he had commanded, the beast stirred in the presence of all; it threw her on the ground, came out, put its head in the middle of the barrier, and perished. Everyone glorified God.

17. They changed his pillar into one forty cubits high, and fame of it spread throughout the whole world. Thus there came to him many Arabs burning with faith, and he spurred them to the fear of God. Then the devil, that hater of people, who habitually tempts the saints and is trampled under foot by them, smote him on his thigh with a pain called a tumour, just as happened to the blessed Job. His thigh grew putrid and accordingly he stood on one foot for two years. Such huge numbers of worms fell from his thigh to the earth that those near him had no other job but to collect them and take them back from where they had fallen, while the saint kept saying, 'Eat from what the Lord has given you.'

18. By God's will the king of the Arabs came to him to have the saint pray for him. As soon as he came near the pillar to be blessed by holy Simeon, the saint of God, when he saw him, began to admonish him. While they were talking together, a worm fell from [Simeon's] thigh; it caught the king's attention and, since he did not yet know what it was, he ran and picked it up. He placed it on his eyes and onto his heart and went outside holding it in his hand. The saint sent a message to him, saying, 'Come inside and put away what you have taken up, for you are bringing misery upon me, a sinner. It is a stinking worm from stinking flesh. Why soil your hand, you, a man held in honor?' When the righteous man had said this, the Arab came inside and said to him, 'This will bring blessing and forgiveness of sins to me.' When he opened his hand, a precious pearl was in his hand. When he saw it, he began to glorify God and said to the righteous man, 'Look! What you said was a worm is a pearl — in fact, a priceless one — by means of which the Lord has enlightened me.' On hearing this, the saint said to him, 'As you have believed, so may it be to you all the days of your life — not only to you, but to your children also.' So blessed, the king of the Arabs returned home safe and sound, rejoicing.

19. Hear another mystery. Eastward on the mountain on which he stood, there dwelt a huge dragon, and for this reason no pasture grew in that spot. Now when that dragon went out to cool himself, a piece of wood lodged in his eye and for a long time no one could bear his hissing in pain. Then one day the dragon came, dragging himself out of his cave, and came in open view and lay down at the entrance to [Simeon's] enclosure. All of a sudden his eye opened and the piece of wood came out of his eye. He stayed there three days until he returned to health. So,

in open view and without having harmed anybody, he returned to his spot. He had lain before the entrance of the righteous man just like a sheep: everyone was going in and out, and nobody was hurt by him.

20. Hear another extraordinary wonder. There was a robber-chief in Syria named Antiochus, also called Gonatas, whose deeds were recounted throughout the whole world. Soldiers were frequently sent to catch him and lead him to Antioch, but no one could catch him because of his mighty strength. Bears and other beasts were kept ready in Antioch because he would have to fight the beasts, and the whole city of Antioch was in a commotion because of him. Now when they went out to catch him they found him drinking in an inn in some village and the soldiers surrounded the inn. When he learnt of this, [the robber] began to stage a scene. There was a river in the village and that robber-chief had a mare he used to order about as if it were human. Rising up, he threw his clothes onto the mare and said to it, 'Go to the river and wait for me there'. The mare left the inn biting and kicking, and when it got to the river it waited for him. Then the robber-chief also came out of the inn unsheathing his sword, crying out and saying to the crowd of soldiers, 'Flee lest someone be killed', and none of the soldiers could overpower him. Escaping all those surrounding him, he crossed the river with his mare and, mounting her, reached the enclosure of holy Simeon. He entered and threw himself down in front of his pillar, and the soldiers then gathered together in the saint's enclosure. The saint said to them, 'With our master Jesus Christ were crucified two thieves, one of whom received according to his deeds while the other inherited the kingdom of heaven. If someone can stand against the one who sent him here, let him come and drag him away himself, since I, for my part, neither led him here nor can I send him away. The one who sent him here claims him for himself. So let no one rail at me, your humble servant, one who has suffered much because of my many sins.' When he had said this, he sent them away. After they had gone, the robber-chief said, 'My lord, I too am going away.' The saint said to him, 'Do you return again to your evil ways?' The robber-chief said, 'No, master, the Lord calls me,' and, stretching out his hands towards heaven, he said nothing more except, 'Son of God, receive my spirit in peace'. For two hours he wept so that he made even the righteous [Simeon] and the bystanders shed tears. Then, placing himself in front of the pillar of the righteous one, he

immediately gave up his spirit. The crowds wrapped his body and buried him near the enclosure of the righteous one. The next day more than a hundred men came from Antioch with swords to seize [the robber], and they began to cry out to the righteous one, 'Release to us the one you have.' The holy man said to them, 'Brethren, he who sent him here is stronger than you and, since he was useful, he had need of him. He sent to him two terrible soldiers armed to the teeth who could strike your city and its inhabitants with thunderbolts. They took him away and when I, a sinner, saw their terrifying appearance, I was terrified and did not dare stand against them lest they kill me too, your humble servant, as one who resisted God.' When the men heard these things from the saint and learnt how gloriously the robber-chief had died, they glorified God and, trembling, went back again to Antioch.

21. Hear another awesome and glorious miracle. There was no water to be found where the saint lived, and the crowd of animals and people coming to the place of the holy Simeon was on the point of perishing. The saint prayed and did not speak to anyone for seven days, but was praying on bended knee so that everyone thought that he had died. About the fifth hour of the seventh day, water suddenly gushed forth from the eastern side of the enclosure. They dug down and found a sort of cave full of water, and they constructed seven outlets for it. All glorified the God of heaven and earth.

28. So the blessed one stood on different pillars for forty-seven years, and after all these things [the Lord] sought him. It was Friday, and he was confined in prayer and, as was his custom, he spent the whole Friday [this way]; but on the sabbath and on the Lord's day he did not lift up his head, as was his custom, to bless those who knelt. When I saw this, I went up to him and I saw his face and it shone like the sun. Although his custom was to speak to me, he said nothing to me. I said to myself, 'He is dead', but then I was not sure; I feared to approach him, so, taking courage, I said to him, 'My lord, why do you not speak to me and end your prayer? The world has been waiting to be blessed for three whole days.' After standing for an hour, I said to him, 'You have not answered me, my lord.' Stretching out my hand, I touched his beard, and, when I saw that his body was very soft, I knew that he had died. Putting my face in my hands, I wept bitterly. I bent down, kissed his mouth, his eyes and his beard, lifted up his tunic and kissed his feet;

taking hold of his hand, I placed it on my eyes. Throughout his body and his garments was a scented perfume which, from its sweet smell, made one's heart merry. I stood attentively for about half-an-hour by his venerable corpse, and behold! his body and the pillar shook and I heard a voice saying, 'Amen! Amen! Amen!' Fearfully I said, 'Bless me, lord, and remember me in your beautiful place of rest.'

29. I came down and did not tell anyone the secret lest an uproar occur, but, through a trustworthy man, I informed the bishop of Antioch, Martyrius, and the military chief, Ardabur. The next day the bishop of Antioch set out with six other bishops. Ardabur also came with six hundred men so that the assembled villages should not seize the venerable corpse, as they were considering. They formed circles around his pillar, and three bishops went up and kissed his garments, saying three psalms. They brought up a leaden casket; they arranged his holy corpse, and brought it down by means of pullies. Then everyone knew that the holy Simeon was dead. All the Arabs had gathered armed and on camels, for they too wanted to seize the body. Such a crowd was gathering that the mountain could not be seen because of the numbers and the smoke from the incense, the wax tapers, and the innumerable burning lamps. The sound of the weeping men, women, and children could be heard at a great distance, and the whole mountain was shaking from the screeching of the birds which gathered and circled round the enclosure of the saint. So when they had brought him down, they placed him upon the marble altar before his pillar, and, although he was already dead for four days, his holy body looked as if he had died just an hour before. All the bishops gave him the kiss of peace. His face was bright, completely like light, and the hairs of his head and beard were like snow. The bishop of Antioch wished to take a hair from his beard as a relic, but his hand withered [at the attempt.] All the bishops prayed for him, weeping and saying to the holy corpse, 'Nothing is missing from your limbs or clothes, and no one will again take anything from your holy and venerable corpse.' As they spoke thus in tears, the hand of the bishop was restored to health. Then, with psalms and hymns, they placed him in the casket.

30. Eleven days before his death, I, a sinner, saw a man in frightening raiment which I cannot describe. He was as big as two men, and he spoke to him three times during the day and gave him the kiss of peace. I wanted to tell someone about him, but my mind was seized and I was

prevented from speaking until it was over. After the man whom I saw came to him, I saw them apparently eating, but what they ate I do not know. They sang, but what they sang I do not know save only the Amen. Fear gripped me at the sight of the man.

31. The coffin of the saint was placed on the carriage and in this way, with wax tapers and incense and the singing of psalms, he was brought to the city of Antioch. When they were about five miles from the city in a place called Merope, the mules stood still and would not budge. There, an extraordinary mystery happened, for on the right of the road stood a tomb and a certain man stayed in it. Now this is what the man had done: he had loved a married woman twenty years earlier, but could not possess her, and the woman died and was laid in that tomb. Then, so that the hater of good might gain the soul of that man, he went to the tomb, opened up the tombstone, and had intercourse with the dead body. He immediately became deaf and dumb, and was held fast to the tomb and could not leave that place. Travellers-by would notice him sitting on the steps of the tomb, and each, for God's sake, would offer something to him — some water or some food. When, by the will of God, the venerable corpse came by on that day and the carriage and the crowd stood still, the man who neither spoke nor heard came out of the tomb crying out and saying, 'Have pity on me, holy one of God, Simeon!' When he reached the carriage, what had restrained him was immediately taken away and his mind was restored. All who saw what happened glorified God, and that place shook from the shouts of the people. The man cried out, 'Today I have been saved by you, servant of God, for I had perished in sin.'

32. The whole city, clad in white and carrying tapers and lamps, went out to meet the venerable corpse, and it was brought into the church called Cassianus. After thirty days, Ardabur, the military commander, gave a command and had it placed in the great church. There, following a revelation by God, was built an oratory of the holy and revered Simeon, and there, in that oratory, with much glory and hymn singing, his holy body was laid.

33. Many people offered to give gold and silver to receive a relic from his holy limbs, but the bishop took no notice of anyone because of the oaths he had taken. In that place where his venerable remains are laid, many healings are performed through the grace given to him by our Master, Christ. [The saint of God Simeon died on the first of September in

the reign of our Lord Jesus Christ,] to whom is the glory and the power for ever and ever. Amen.

[34. I, Antonius, least of all and a watchman, have narrated part of his story. For who can worthily describe his wonders and healings, save only partially to represent his undefiled deeds to the praise and glory of God for ever. Amen.]

Notes

1   Ps 50:7. Note how in the next sentence birth is described in the familiar image of putting on a garment.

18 *The Penitential of Columbanus* **(590? Burgundy?)**

Irish Christianity in the fifth and sixth centuries developed distinctive practices and values, including a love of nature, especially as found in wilderness and rugged landscapes; a system of church governance based on the monastery rather than the diocese, a peculiar way of determining the date of Easter, a style of tonsure for monks and clergy related to fashions in the Christian East, and, perhaps most notably of all, the tradition of "pilgrimage for the sake of Christ." Irish Christian pilgrims were always on the move, taking their witness to Christ from place to place. One of the most significant of these pilgrims was Columbanus (not to be confused with Columba of Iona), and his ministry of pilgrimage and evangelism in Europe had far-reaching results.

Columbanus was born in northern Ireland in about 550, and he learned the life of a monk at a monastery at Bangor, County Down. Around 585 or 590 he sailed with a dozen other pilgrims to Gaul (France), and he began teaching the faith and castigating local Christian leaders for what he regarded as their spiritual laxity. He founded monasteries at three wilderness sites in Burgundy, and each of these monasteries became a mission centre for the founding of still other monasteries. Columbanus required of his monks a severe rule of life characterized by self-deprivation, hard work, and obedience to the monastic authorities, and for their shortcomings the monks were to receive corporal punishment. He also directed his monasteries to observe

Celtic rites and traditions, including the Celtic date of Easter. About 610 he embarked on a new pilgrimage; in part he was forced out because his ways were not popular with the local clergy or with the queen. During this new mission journey he founded a monastery in Switzerland. Shortly thereafter he was on the move again, and he founded a last monastery at Bobbio in the Apennines of northern Italy. He died in 615. For many years in Europe Columbanus' form of monasticism competed with the more humane approach of Benedict of Nursia (480?-550); Benedictine monasticism eventually prevailed.

Another distinctive of Irish Christianity was private confession. The Church in earlier centuries had provided that those separated from the Christian community because of grievous sin might be re-admitted, once in a lifetime, after public confession, a lengthy period of what was called 'penance' (the Latin *poena* means "penalty"), and a public ceremony of reconciliation administered by the bishop. (Cyprian was influential in this development.) The Irish system was different from this older arrangement in several respects, as the following reading will make clear. The first surviving Irish penitential book was authored by a St. Finnian, the abbot of an Irish monastery, in the years around the middle of the sixth century. The penitential of Columbanus reproduced below drew from it freely. Celtic and Anglo-Saxon pilgrims spread the Irish system of private confession and repeatable penance throughout Europe. At first the new system was resisted, but by the twelfth century, with some modifications, it had become a universal feature of Christian life in the Western world. Medieval priests came to rely on penitential manuals to help them classify sins and assign appropriate penances.

The Penitential of Columbanus is known from two manuscript copies of the ninth or tenth centuries, at Bobbio. A third manuscript was used for an edition of the seventeenth century, but has since been lost. It is generally agreed that Columbanus was the author, although parts of the text as we have it may have been added by later hands.

Questions on the reading

For whom is the penitential intended? How is it structured? How are "A" and "B" related to each other? (Might they have been originally independent documents? or are they addressed to different audiences?

or might they be two versions of the same document?) How is the penitential intended to function? (For instance, is it an instrument for assisting people in their growth in holiness; for civilizing a barbarian people; for establishing ecclesiastical authority; for curing sickness; for checking temptation?) What kinds of sins are identified? What is the author's understanding of sin? (Error; guilt; sickness; sacrilege; obstacle to holiness?) What is penance? What kinds of penances are assigned? Why does the author think that they might be helpful? Is his attitude legalistic, flexible, pastoral, or otherwise? What authority might the document have had in its original setting? From both the character and severity of the various punishments, what might you infer about the moral values of the author and of the author's society?

Penitential of St. Columbanus

[A:]

On penance here begins

1. True penance is not to commit things deserving penance but to lament such things as have been committed. But since this is broken by the weakness of many, not to say of all, the measures of penance must be known. A scheme of these has been handed down by the holy fathers, so that in accordance with the greatness of the offences the length also of the penances should be ordained.

2. Therefore, if anyone has sinned in thought, that is, has desired to kill a man, or to commit fornication, or to steal, or to feast in secret and be drunken, or indeed to strike someone, or to desert, or to do anything else like this, and has been ready in his heart to carry out these sins: let

Source: "The Penitential of Columbanus," in Ludwig Bieler, ed., *The Irish Penitentials*, Dublin, 1963, 97-107, alternate pages (i.e., omitting parallel text in Latin).

him do penance for the greater ones half a year, for the lesser ones forty days on bread and water.

3. But if any one has sinned in act with the common sins, if he has committed the sin of murder or sodomy, let him do penance for ten years; if he has committed fornication once only, let him do penance three years, if oftener, seven years. If a monk has deserted and broken his vows, if he repents and returns at once, let him do penance three forty-day periods, but if after a period of years, three years.

4. If anyone has stolen, let him do penance for a year.

4a. If anyone has perjured himself, let him do penance for seven years.

5. If anyone has struck his brother in a quarrel and spilt blood, let him do penance for three years.

6. But if anyone has got drunk and has vomited, or, being overfed, for this reason has vomited the sacrifice, let him do penance forty days. However, if he is forced by ill health to vomit the sacrifice, let him do penance seven days. If anyone has lost the sacrifice itself, let him do penance for a year.

7. If anyone has defiled himself, let him do penance for a year, if he is a junior.

8. If anyone has borne false witness knowingly, let him do penance for two years, together with the loss or restitution of the object in dispute.

So much about matters of importance; now about small matters of disorderly behaviour.

9. He who does something by himself without asking, or who contradicts and says: 'I am not doing it', or who murmurs, if the matter is serious, let him do penance with three special fasts, if slight, with one. Simple contradiction of another's word is to be punished with fifty strokes; if out of contention, with an imposition of silence. If it is made in a quarrel, the penance should be for a week.

10. He who slanders or willingly hears a slanderer, let him do penance with three special fasts; if it concerns the superior, let him do penance for a week.

11. He who has despised his superior in pride, or has spoken evil of the rule, is to be cast out, unless he has said immediately: 'I am sorry for what I said'; but if he has not truly humbled himself, let him do penance for forty days, because he is infected with the disease of pride.

12. The talkative is to be punished with silence, the restless with the practice of gentleness, the gluttonous with fasting, the sleepy with watching, the proud with imprisonment, the deserter with expulsion; let each suffer exactly in accordance with his deserts, that the just may live justly. AMEN.

[B:]

Diversity of offences causes diversity of penances. For doctors of the body also compound their medicines in diverse kinds; thus they heal wounds in one manner, sicknesses in another, boils in another, bruises in another, festering sores in another, eye diseases in another, fractures in another, burns in another. So also should spiritual doctors treat with diverse kinds of cures the wounds of souls, their sicknesses, [offences], pains, ailments, and infirmities. But since this gift belongs to few, namely to know to a nicety all these things, to treat them, to restore what is weak to a complete state of health, let us set out even a few prescriptions according to the traditions of our elders, and according to our own partial understanding, for we prophesy in part and we know in part.

First we must enact concerning capital sins, which are punished even by the sanction of the law.

1. If any cleric has committed murder and killed his neighbour, let him do penance for ten years in exile; after these, let him be restored to his native land, if he has performed his penance well on bread and water, being approved by the testimonial of the bishop or priest with whom he did penance and to whose care he was entrusted, on condition that he make satisfaction to the relatives of the slain, taking the place of a son, and saying: 'Whatever you wish I will do for you.' But if he does not make satisfaction to his relatives, let him never be restored to his native land, but like Cain let him be a wanderer and fugitive upon the earth.

2. If anyone has fallen to the depth of ruin and begotten a child, let him do penance as an exile for seven years on bread and water; then only, at the discretion of the priest, let him be restored to the altar.

3. But if anyone has committed fornication as the Sodomites did, let him do penance for ten years, for the three first on bread and water, but for the seven others let him refrain from wine and meat, and let him never again live with the other man.

4. However, if anyone has committed fornication with women, but has not begotten a child, and it has not become known among people: if he is a cleric, three years, if a monk or deacon, five years, if a priest, seven, if a bishop, twelve years.

5. If anyone has perjured himself, let him do penance seven years, and never take an oath again.

6. If anyone has destroyed someone by his magic art, let him do penance three years on an allowance of bread and water, and for three other years let him refrain from wine and meat, and then finally in the seventh year let him be restored to communion. But if anyone has used magic to excite love, and has destroyed no one, let him do penance on bread and water for a whole year, if a cleric, for half a year, if a layman, if a deacon for two, if a priest for three; especially if anyone has thus produced abortion, on that account let each add on six extra forty-day periods, lest he be guilty of murder.

7. If any cleric has committed theft, that is, has stolen an ox or a horse, a sheep or any beast of his neighbour's, if he has done it once or twice, let him first make restitution to his neighbour, and do penance for a whole year on bread and water; if he has made a practice of this, and cannot make restitution, let him do penance three years on bread and water.

8. But if any cleric or deacon, or a man in any orders, who in the world was a layman with sons and daughters, after his profession has again known his mate, and again begotten a child of her, let him know that he has committed adultery, and has sinned no less than if he had been a cleric from his youth, and had sinned with a strange girl, since be sinned after his vow, after he consecrated himself to the Lord, and made his vow void; therefore let him likewise do penance seven years on bread and water.

9. If any cleric has struck his neighbour in a quarrel and spilt blood, let him do penance for a whole year; if a layman, for forty days.

10. If anyone has defiled himself or sinned with a beast, let him do penance two years, if he is not in orders; but if he is in orders or under a vow, let him do penance three years, if his age does not forbid.

11. If anyone desires a woman and cannot commit the act, that is, if the woman does not admit him, let him do penance half a year on bread and water, and for a whole year let him refrain from wine and meat and the communion of the altar.

12. If anyone has lost the sacrifice, let him do penance for a year. If through drunkenness or greed he has vomited it up and cast it carelessly aside, let him do penance three forty-day periods on bread and water; but if through ill health, let him do penance seven days. But these provisions are made for clerics and monks collectively; now for laymen.

13. Whoever has committed murder, that is, has killed his neighbour, let him do penance three years on bread and water as an unarmed exile, and after three years let him return to his own, rendering the compensation of filial piety and duty to the relatives of the slain, and thus after making satisfaction let him be restored to the altar at the discretion of the priest.

14. If any layman has begotten a child by another's wife, that is, has committed adultery in violating his neighbour's bed, let him do penance for three years, refraining from the more appetizing foods and from his own wife, giving in addition the price of chastity to the husband of the violated wife, and thus let his guilt be wiped off by the priest.

15. But if any layman has committed fornication in sodomite fashion, that is, has sinned by effeminate intercourse with a male, let him do penance for seven years, for the three first on bread and water and salt and dry produce of the garden, for the remaining four let him refrain from wine and meat, and thus let his guilt be remitted to him, and let the priest pray for him, and so let him be restored to the altar.

16. But if any of the laity has committed fornication with women who are free from wedlock, that is, with widows or virgins, if with a widow, let him do penance for one year, if with a virgin, for two years, provided that he pays her relatives the price[1] of her disgrace; yet if he has no wife, but has lain as a virgin with the virgin, if her relatives agree, let her be his wife, but on condition that both first do penance for a year, and so let them be wedded.

17. But if any layman has committed fornication with a beast, let him do penance for a year, if he has a wife; yet if he has not, for half a year; likewise also let him do penance who, having a wife, has defiled himself with his own hands.

18. If any layman or lay woman has misused their child, let them do penance for a whole year on bread and water, and for two others let them refrain from wine and meats, and so first let them be restored to the altar at the discretion of the priest, and then let such a husband use his bed lawfully. For the laity must know, that in the period of penance assigned to them by the priests it is not lawful for them to know their wives, except after the conclusion of the penance; for penance ought not to be halved.

19. If any layman has committed theft, that is, has stolen an ox or a horse or a sheep or any beast of his neighbour's, if he has done it once or twice, let him first restore to his neighbour the loss which he has caused, and let him do penance for three forty-day period on bread and water; but if he has made a practice of stealing often, and cannot make restitution, let him do penance for a year and three forty-day periods, and further undertake not to repeat it, and thus let him communicate at Easter of the second year, that is, after two years, on condition that, out of his own labour, he first gives alms to the poor and a meal to the priest who adjudged his penance, and so let the guilt of his evil habit be forgiven.

20. If any layman has perjured himself, if he did it out of greed, let him sell all his property and give it to the poor, and devote himself wholly to the Lord, and receive the tonsure, bidding farewell to the entire world, and until death let him serve God in a monastery; yet if he did it, not out of greed, but in fear of death, let him do penance for three years on bread and water as an unarmed exile, and for two more let him refrain from wine and meat, and thus by offering a life for himself, that is, by freeing a slave or maidservant from the yoke of bondage, and by doing many alms throughout two years, in which he may quite lawfully use all foods except meat, let him communicate after the seventh year.

21. If any of the laity has shed blood in a brawl, or wounded or maimed his neighbour, let him be compelled to restore all the damage he has done; but if has nothing to pay with, let him first attend to his neighbour's work, while he is sick, and call in a doctor, and after his recovery, let him do penance for forty days on bread and water.

22. If any layman has become intoxicated, or eaten or drunk to the extent of vomiting, let him do penance for a week on bread and water.

23. If any layman has desired to commit adultery or fornication with a married woman, and has lusted after his neighbour's wife, and not committed the act, that is, has not been able to, because the woman did not admit him, yet he was ready to fornicate, let him confess his guilt to the priest, and so let him do penance for forty days on bread and water.

24. But if any layman has eaten or drunk beside temples, if he did it through ignorance, let him undertake forthwith never to do it again, and let him do penance forty days on bread and water; but if he did it in derision, that is, after the priest has declared to him that this was sacrilege, and if then he communicated at the table of demons, if it was only through the vice of greed that he did or repeated it, let him do penance for three forty-day periods on bread and water; but if he did it in worship of the demons or in honour of idols, let him do penance for three years.

. 25. If any layman in ignorance has communicated with followers of Bonosus[2] or other heretics, let him rank among the catechumens, that is, separated from other Christians, for forty days, and for two other forty-day periods in the lowest rank of Christians, that is, among the penitents, let him wash away the guilt of his unsound communion; but if he did this in derision, that is, after he was warned and forbidden by the priest not to pollute himself with the communion of an evil faction, let him do penance for a whole year and three forty-day periods, and for two other years let him refrain from wine and meat, and thus after imposition of hands by a Catholic bishop let him be restored to the altar.

Finally we must deal with the minor sanctions for monks.

26. If anyone has left the enclosure open during the night, let him do penance with a special fast; but if during the day, with twenty-four blows, if others were not following behind when he left it open. If someone has gone immediately in front of himself, let him do penance with a special fast.

27. If anyone, desiring a bath, has washed alone naked, let him do penance with a special fast. But if anyone, while washing lawfully in presence of his brethren, has done this standing, unless through the need for cleansing dirt more fully, let him be corrected with twenty-four strokes.

28. But if anyone, even while sitting in the bath, has uncovered his knees or arms, without the need for washing dirt, let him not wash for six days, that is, let that immodest bather not wash his feet until the following Lord's Day. Yet a monk, when standing privately alone, is permitted to wash his feet; while a senior even publicly, but with another washing his feet, is permitted to be washed standing.

29. But before sermon on the Lord's Day let all, except for fixed requirements, be gathered together, so that none is lacking to the number of those who hear the exhortation, except to the cook and porter, who themselves also, if they can, are to try hard to be present, when the gospel bell[3] is heard.

30. It is ordained that confessions be made carefully, especially of mental disturbances, before going to Mass, lest perhaps any should approach the altar unworthily, that is, is he does not have a clean heart. For it is better to wait until the heart is healed, and becomes a stranger to offence and envy, than rashly to approach the judgement of the throne. For Christ's throne is the altar, and His Body there with His Blood judges those who approach unworthily. Therefore, just as we must beware of mortal and fleshly sins before we may communicate so we must refrain and cleanse ourselves from interior vices and the sicknesses of the ailing soul before the covenant of true peace and the bond of eternal salvation. THE END.

Notes

[1]   See Deut. 22:28–29.

[2]   The followers of Bonosus, bishop of Naïssus.

[3]   *Tonitruum evangelii* might also be translated "the thunder of the Gospel" (the mighty word of God).